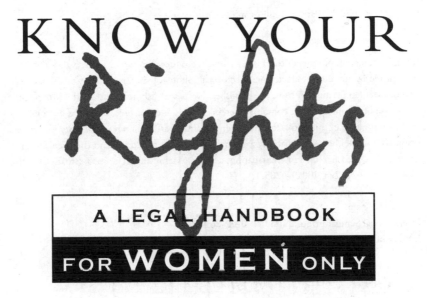

KNOW YOUR
Rights

A LEGAL HANDBOOK

FOR WOMEN ONLY

International Standard Book Number: 0-02-861696-0
Library of Congress Catalog Card Number: 96-079996

99 98 97   8 7 6 5 4 3 2 1

Interpretation of the printing code: the rightmost number of the first series of numbers is the year of the book's printing; the rightmost number of the second series of numbers is the number of the book's printing. For example, a printing code of 97-1 shows that the first printing occurred in 1997.

Printed in the United States of America

CONTENTS

PART FIVE–DON'T BE A BUG ON THE WINDSHIELD OF LIFE

APPENDICES

A NOTE TO THE READER

This publication contains the opinions and ideas of its authors and is designed to provide useful advice in regard to the subject matter covered. It is published with the understanding that the authors and the publisher are not engaged in rendering legal or other professional services to the reader in the publication. Laws vary from state to state, and if the reader requires expert assistance or legal advice, a competent professional should be consulted.

The authors and the publisher specifically disclaim any responsibility for any liability, loss, or risk, personal or otherwise, which is incurred as a consequence, directly or indirectly, of the use and application of any of the contents of this book.

WHAT THIS BOOK WILL DO FOR YOU

WHY AND WHEN YOU NEED THIS BOOK

There are, of course, a limitless number of subjects involving your life as a woman, but we have focused on the main areas of importance legally: Relationships, Work, Financial Security, and Personal Protection. This book contains guides to probate, criminal law, taxes, bankruptcy, changing your name, and being your own lawyer. It advises you on what to do if you're accused of a crime. It is a homeowner's legal guide that gives alternatives to the law and discusses the use of the small claims court.

In the 37 years from 1960 to now, the legal status of women has changed dramatically. Government policies have done a remarkable turnaround from reinforcing social and economic discrimination against women to recognizing gender discrimination and passing and implementing laws against it. However, what has been created are laws that most women do not fully understand. Lack of understanding results in ineffective use of the available protections now provided to women under the law.

Every woman needs to know how to protect herself legally because gender discrimination laws are not applied automatically. Often, even those in the legal system, police, lawyers, and even some judges, do not understand or apply the available statutes. Every woman needs to know how to protect herself against outrages and injustices on the job, in her personal life, and social relationships through the changing phases of her life. In short, women cannot rely on others for protection; each must have an understanding about the recently enacted laws which serve to protect women in the marketplace and in the work environment. Without pressure from knowledgeable women, these laws will not be enforced by those who are in positions to do so. The purpose of this book is to assist you in becoming one of the knowledgeable women.

For example, there have been many significant protections assuring fair treatment of women in a divorce; e.g., equitable distribution laws and recognition of the realities of what it costs to raise a child by increasing levels of child and spousal support. But many ex-husbands and their lawyers and even some judges ignore the law. *Know Your Rights* spells out how women can get the law working for them.

Another example: Many states make domestic violence and stalking specific crimes, but the justice system provides little help or protection. The newspapers are full of stories of women stalked AND murdered by their stalkers, even though those women have stay-away court orders in their purses. *Know Your Rights* gives legal and practical tips on dealing with stalkers and how to make the law more responsive.

Know Your Rights covers a wide range of situations the average woman will face in her life and gives solid, proven guidance for dealing with them. For example, this book deals with how a women can protect herself when she:

- Is unjustifiably fired from a job.
- Is one of several heirs fighting over an inheritance.
- Contemplates a major purchase such as a car or home.
- Is injured by an unsafe product.
- Is pregnant and working.
- Goes into her own business (1 out of 9 do).
- Is faced with credit discrimination.
- Is accused of a crime.
- Adopts a child.
- Breaks up a long-term relationship.
- Is confronted with the loss of custody of her children.
- Is stalked by an ex-lover.

Know Your Rights is more than an ordinary women's guide to the law. It not only concerns itself with showing women how to protect themselves through the legal system, but also offers a number of practical tips on how women can protect themselves even when the legal system cannot or will not. It is a realistic work that understands the difference between elegant theory and gritty reality.

Know Your Rights is a self-help book providing vital survival information for the millions of American women who must function in a new and evolving society. Laws are changing, and this book will give you a practical guide to dealing with them.

Fifty-four percent of American women now work outside the home full-time; even those with children usually return to work. Most of these women soon realize that they can depend only upon themselves—even if married or in a long-term relationship—to look out for their interests.

The U.S. Census Bureau estimates that there are currently 27 million women in the 25 to 45 year age bracket—single, divorced, and widowed. If you are one of these, you will benefit from *Know Your Rights*.

Part One

DON'T WORK IN THE DARK

CHAPTER 1

FINDING AND WORKING
WITH AN ATTORNEY

In many circumstances in your life you will need the help of an attorney. In some cases, you may need help from someone other than an attorney, depending on the kind of problem you have and your alternatives for resolving it.

For example, attorneys commonly handle problems relating to the acquisition and rental of real estate, estate planning, divorce, and automobile accidents. Many other life problems can be resolved with the assistance of other kinds of professionals in their respective fields, in the small claims courts or through arbitration, professional groups, or government agencies. For example, injury because of the use of a defective product might be handled by a local, state, or federal consumer agency; by an industry group or by the business itself; or even by a consumer reporter of a newspaper or broadcasting station. There is also a growing movement toward dispute resolution centers and alternative arbitration designed to ease the load on the courts and to provide the speedy resolution of legal problems. Even television has suggested alternative solutions. Remember the TV show starring retired Los Angeles Superior Court judge Joseph Wapner who tries actual, minor cases on camera, the participants having agreed beforehand to abide by the ruling of this judge-turned-actor.

When a legal problem arises, your best advice is to get an attorney—a good attorney. Your first and most significant decision is the selection of a competent lawyer to assist you in handling any legal issue. **The most expensive attorney you can ever hire is an incompetent lawyer**. What you are looking for is a lawyer who combines firmness, experience, and knowledge of the law—a skilled negotiator and confessional priest. You need a combination of Clint Eastwood, Henry Kissinger, and Mother Theresa.

The legal profession is just like baseball or lion taming. There are good players and tamers and there are poor players and tamers. Poor baseball players tend to lose, and poor lion tamers tend to be eaten alive.

FINDING A GOOD ATTORNEY FOR YOU

Finding a good attorney is not as complicated as it may seem, but it takes time. You should shop for a lawyer in the same way you shop for a dentist or doctor.

REFERRAL BY FRIENDS OR RELATIVES

One of the most common ways of finding any professional is by references from others. Ask friends or relatives who have engaged the services of an attorney. No matter who is recommended, it is mandatory that you interview these lawyers yourself.

LEGAL REFERRAL SERVICES

The local bar association in the community where you live usually has a referral service listed in the telephone book. Also, you may contact the American Academy of Matrimonial Lawyers, 20 North Michigan Avenue, Chicago, Illinois 60602 (312) 263-6477 (family law issues only) or the American Bar Association 750 N. Lakeshore Drive, Chicago, Illinois, 60611 (312) 988-5520. Your best bet is the local bar association.

LEGAL CLINICS AND LIMITED COST ALTERNATIVES

There are low cost law firms that work with your credit union, labor union, religious group, or even credit card companies. American Express, for example, now offers a legal services plan. There are also government funded legal services such as city, county, and state legal clinics in some areas as well as the Legal Aid Society. The problem with such low-cost alternatives is the attorneys are often overworked and most are not specialists. Complex issues may be involved in your case that will require experience and knowledge to work through.

DIRECTORIES OF ATTORNEYS

At the public library, you may consult several excellent directories of attorneys that will tell you about their practices, their specialties, their education and background. These include:

- *Martindale-Hubbell,* a giant reference work found in most major libraries. The entries in *Martindale* are paid for by the lawyers, but the information given will be helpful in learning the kinds of law each lawyer practices and his/her background.

- There is another directory that is worthwhile although it does not list as broad a range of attorneys and is focused on the states of Florida, New Jersey, New York, Massachusetts, New Hampshire, and Virginia. This publication, a separate book for each of those six states, is called the *Lawyers Diary and*

Manual and is available directly from the publisher, Skinder-Strauss Associates, New Jersey at prices ranging from $35 to $55 as of mid-1996. Call the publisher at (800) 444-4041 or fax (201) 642-4280 or write to P.O. Box 50, Newark, New Jersey 07101.

SPECIALTY

Many attorneys specialize in a particular area of the law, and it may be to your advantage to consult one in the field of law, that concerns you. Some 17 states now certify attorneys in various specialties (Alabama, Arizona, California, Connecticut, Florida, Georgia, Idaho, Louisiana, Minnesota, New Jersey, New Mexico, North Carolina, Ohio, Pennsylvania, South Carolina, Tennessee, and Texas.) Check with the State Bar for listings of certified specialists. Beyond that, there are several organizations of attorneys who specialize in certain aspects of the legal profession, for example, the American Academy of Matrimonial Lawyers. This Academy and the others that group together legal specialists publishes a directory of its members which may be available to the public. These are national organizations, and their members are generally tops in their respective fields. Specialization carries with it responsibilities for the lawyers, and generally a specialist's rates are higher.

INDIVIDUAL ATTORNEY OR FULL SERVICE LAW FIRM?

Part of your hiring decision will include deciding whether you should be represented by an attorney working alone in his or her own practice or working with a full service law firm. Today, around the country approximately 46% of attorneys practice alone. Consequently, the split between individual attorneys and multiple attorney firms is almost 50-50. This, of course, does not include those who work for governmental agencies and corporations.

INDIVIDUAL ATTORNEY

The advantage of hiring a sole practitioner is that he/she will be the only lawyer handling your case; you will know your lawyer well, and he/she will know you. The disadvantage is that the individual attorney may be overworked and may be taking on too many projects at once. Sometimes a solo practitioner, while well versed in the particular specialty, may lack access to or understanding of ancillary issues related to the substantive legal aspects of your case. Most well-known solo practitioners are more expensive, demanding between $10,000 to $25,000 up front to take the case. This is because a solo practitioner cannot afford to finance your litigation. However, unless your lawyer is on a contingency, the lawyer should not be expected to finance your litigation, and you should be prepared to pay as you go.

FULL SERVICE LAW FIRM

Even in a full service law firm, you must be sure that your case is handled by a specialist. A full service law firm will provide you, the client, with other specialists if needed. Usually the lawyer specializing in the area of your case has the advantage of having tax or other specialists working with him/her.

The fee that you pay for services of lawyers in the larger law firms will vary according to the age and experience of the lawyer involved in your case. Thus, some hourly rates will be less than that of the sole practitioner, and some may be more. In large metropolitan areas, it's not unheard of for sole practitioners to charge $450 an hour or more. Sometimes arrangements for payments can be more flexible in a larger law firm because it may be able to accommodate different payment plans. However, pressures to bill and collect are high in all law firms.

NO MATTER WHAT LAWYER IS RECOMMENDED TO YOU, MAKE THE CHOICE PERSONALLY, YOURSELF. There are incompetent lawyers. There are incompatible lawyers. There are inexperienced lawyers. You should not be timid in asking a prospective lawyer for names of former clients to call for a reference. It is critically important that you are compatible with your attorney. Thus, your own personal interview with the lawyer is essential, notwithstanding the recommendations of friends.

WHAT SHOULD A GOOD LAWYER BE?

There are many qualities you need to look for in a lawyer. Don't rush and pick the first lawyer you contact without checking his or her background thoroughly; make careful and wise decisions.

LEGALLY COMPETENT

Your attorney will be handling three types of work for you during your case, and he/she must have the professional competence to handle all three. These three types of work are legal research and writing connected with the issues, negotiations with the opposing side—which is how most cases are resolved even before going to court, and trying the case in court if it becomes impossible to settle through negotiation.

COMPATIBILITY

Your attorney is neither your therapist nor your best friend, yet he/she will be assisting you through a difficult time. Your attorney must, therefore, be someone with whom you are comfortable in a crisis situation; he/she will know your most intimate and embarrassing secrets and at the same time must have the capacity to be discreet and sensitive to your particular situation.

FINANCIALLY COMPETENT

Most cases are about money, and your attorney must be knowledgeable about finances. While he/she needn't be an accountant or banker, your attorney must understand real estate, financial accounts, stocks and bonds, options, pensions, and, generally, the financial world. The ability to read and understand a balance sheet is essential in most cases involving contractual disputes, family law, and tax issues.

CANDID

Your lawyer must tell you what he/she thinks the case will cost, what the problems are, and what are your advantages and disadvantages. Many of the decisions with which you will be confronted during the course of the case cannot — nor should they — be made by your attorney. Beware the lawyer who paints nothing but a rosy picture of your matter. There are two sides to every story.

WHAT TO EXPECT FROM YOUR LAWYER

Understand at the beginning that your attorney is your attorney—not your psychotherapist or doctor. You are entitled to expect that your attorney will represent you exclusively in your case, will have no conflicts of interest adverse to you and your legal position, and will be your advocate both in the negotiations and in the courtroom.

You are entitled to be treated fairly and with respect by your attorney; you should not feel intimidated, confused, or manipulated. Your attorney should treat you as an adult with a problem that he/she, as a specialist, will assist you in resolving. He/she should not embarrass you, ridicule your lack of technical legal knowledge and legal jargon, or make fun of you or the situation that has caused you to seek his/her advice. Be wary of the attorney who treats you like a helpless child. This may happen in a situation where a devastated client in a divorce turns the decision-making process over to the lawyer.

Your attorney must be honest with you, telling you the truth about the facts in connection with your case. There will be some unpleasant aspects of your case, and he/she should be candid about the downside of your case and advise you about the positive aspects of your situation. Your attorney will counsel you on what is important to the judge, which often has little to do with what annoyed you enough to sue or be sued.

Your lawyer must acknowledge that the final word on every important decision about your case is yours and only yours. Your attorney's job is to advise you about potential alternative outcomes of various decisions and help you weigh your choices with the knowledge that, in the end, you must make the decisions.

Finally, you have the right to be treated with respect, candor, and courtesy by your attorney's colleagues and staff.

WHAT YOUR ATTORNEY EXPECTS FROM YOU

Your attorney is going to be your colleague during one of the most stressful times of your life, and if that relationship is going to work, you must both trust and be completely honest with him/her. If, for any reason, you don't feel you can trust and be honest with your attorney, you have the wrong attorney.

Just as you are entitled to respect from your attorney, he/she is entitled to your respect. An honest attorney will tell you things you may not want to hear and may advise you to do things or NOT to do things that are contrary to your feelings at the moment. It is helpful to remember that this may be one of the few lawsuits in your life, but it's probably the 100th or 1,000th lawsuit for your attorney.

So, your attorney is like your doctor who may tell you that you have an unpleasant illness requiring surgery or that you must adhere to a specific diet and regimen in order to be healthy. You don't have to like what your doctor or your attorney is telling you, but you should respect his/her professional judgment.

It is also important that you be realistic about the legal process. You need to understand the objective of the legal process is to solve a problem and not to gain private vengeance for either party. That's why your attorney must clearly understand what your REAL goals are. Your real goal may be to play a high stakes game of chicken to force the other party to do something out of fear of litigation. Whatever your real objective is, that must be made known to your attorney early on in the relationship so that he/she can negotiate the settlement for you with that goal in mind.

HOW MUCH MONEY IT WILL COST YOU

Naturally, the cost of the case is very important to you, and each attorney you interview should spell out the fees and expenses in as much detail as is possible. There are usually three different ways attorneys charge for the work they do (expenses and court costs are additional):

- *Time.* Most often an attorney will simply charge you for the amount of time spent on your case. While this may be likened to a taxi meter that keeps running every time you attorney works on your case, it is the most accurate way your lawyer has of informing you what is being done for you and the time expended.

■ *Trouble.* Attorneys sometimes charge on the basis of the amount of difficulty and complexity involved. A simple, straightforward case may be less expensive, obviously, than a complicated one.

■ *Final Result.* In some kinds of cases, an attorney will base his/her fee on the final outcome of the case. This is called a contingency fee arrangement. Here the attorney is paid a percentage of the recovery, usually ranging from one-third to one-half of the money awarded if he/she wins or settles the case in your favor. The lawyer gets nothing if the case is lost.

In divorce cases, the usual fee arrangement is either of the first two we mentioned: time spent on the case or the trouble involved in resolving it, with the hourly arrangement by far the most prevalent.

THE INITIAL INTERVIEW

You may be charged for the initial interview. Be sure to check with the attorney or his/her secretary when you make your appointment so you won't be surprised when you are billed for an initial consultation. It could well be worth the cost even though you will want to interview two or three lawyers before you make your decisions as to whom to hire.

During the initial interview, you should discuss the charges and fees you will be expected to pay as well as anticipated expenses. Surprisingly, some attorneys are reluctant to talk about money, but it is important that the financial arrangements be in the open and agreed upon before the legal work begins. Otherwise serious conflict may be created between you and your attorney. Indeed, in most states, ethical rules are breached when an attorney attempts to negotiate fees after he/she has taken on your case. Simply ask the attorney you are interviewing candidly what the case will cost and what the different payment options are.

Do not expect that he/she will be able to predict the amount of time the case will require. The attorney can give you his/her hourly rates and tell you what will be done in his/her representation; however, the amount of time the attorney must expend on your case is often a function of how reasonable the other side wants to be.

Most lawyers will ask for a retainer fee as a type of down payment on the work to be done on your matter. It is a fee paid up front before the attorney begins the legal process for you. This ought to be a refundable retainer and, if it is not, you should carefully consider whether you need this attorney. By refundable, we mean that, if you change attorneys before your retainer is used or there is a quick settlement so that the cost is minimal, the attorney will refund whatever part of the fee is not used.

Of course, a critical question for you in beginning litigation is the anticipated cost. We cannot answer that question for you, and an honest lawyer will have difficulty in accurately answering that question. There is no "typical" case. Each has different complexities inviting any number of possibilities, which means the cost will differ for nearly every case. However, your attorney should be prepared to discuss the estimated costs of various activities that will occur such as, for example, taking a deposition or sending interrogatories and preparing for a mandatory settlement conference with the attendant briefing.

Having alerted you to those two problems, it is our current experience that attorney fees now run between $150 and $325 an hour. In metropolitan areas rates could run, as we noted earlier, as high as $400 to $450 or more an hour. Even the simplest matter with no court appearances and no major depositions probably will require 20 to 40 hours time to settle. That can give you some sense of what is involved in your case.

On occasion, you may find an attorney who will undertake your case for a flat fee ranging between $2,500 and $25,000. In order to make that type of offer the attorney must be reasonably assured that the case will be easily and simply resolved and no court battles are anticipated. This assumes a fairly simple case that can be settled through negotiation because, the minute you get into a courtroom, your costs begin to skyrocket.

THE INFORMATION YOU NEED TO GIVE YOUR LAWYER

Your attorney will need complete and detailed information from you in order to do his/her job properly. This may include personal, financial, or, even, medical information relevant to the case. Some clients abhor the thought of making lists of assets and obligations, of giving details of personal information, and other confidential data. However, the lawyer for the other side will probably subpoena such information and bring it out in court. If you don't provide the needed information to your attorney, it means he/she has to fly blind until the information is obtained by subpoena. You can lessen the amount of time your attorney has to spend on your case by gathering the basic information yourself at the beginning. So, take the time; make the effort; get the information needed so your attorney can do the job representing you that you expect him/her to do. And be sure to give full and accurate information. Don't let your lawyer be surprised by facts that the adversary counsel brings out for the first time in a court hearing.

CHAPTER 2

YOUR RIGHTS AS
AN EMPLOYEE

Let's start with a general overview of some important legal protections you have on the job and, then, we will get into details about some of the more significant work-related issues.

Your rights as an employee are protected by a Federal law, meaning a law which is enforced in all the states of the union, called Title VII of Civil Rights Act of 1964. This comprehensive law prohibits job discrimination in hiring, firing, setting of wages, promotion, transfer, benefits, or retirement on basis of race, color, religion, sex, or national origin. It applies to state and federal employers, private employers, unions with 15 or more employees, and educational institutions. Your employer is liable for actions of co-workers and, in some instances, customers, even if the employer is unaware of the discrimination. The law makes exception for jobs that are clearly gender specific such as an attendant in a rest room or a counselor in a single gender camp. If you are discriminated against, you have 180 days from the date of the discriminatory act to file a complaint with the Equal Employment Opportunity Commission (EEOC) or comparable local or state agency.

Congress has also passed the Equal Pay Act of 1963, which is a federal law that has application throughout all the states. It applies to companies doing business across state lines that have at least two employees or do $250,000 worth of business each year. It also applies to all government employees including federal, state, and local agencies, but it excludes those who work in schools, hospitals, nursing homes, laundries, and construction.

Despite the fact that the Equal Pay Act of 1963 was passed by Congress nearly a third of a century ago, it is often not obeyed or enforced. In one classic example, Marianne Stanley, the head woman's basketball coach at the University of Southern California has sued the school for $8 million charging that she was paid less that her male counterpart. Many men think this is a ridiculous lawsuit and, in fact, the first Los Angeles judge to hear the case turned Ms. Stanley's claim down, and the case is now on appeal. But query: Should a man and a woman doing the same job be paid equally? Under the Equal Pay Act they should.

No matter the outcome of this well-publicized case, the less publicized truth taken from the United States Census Bureau reports is that the average woman employee in America in 1997 earns $22,205 a year contrasted with the average male employee who earns $30,854.

The basic idea of the Equal Pay Act is simple, women should be paid at the same rate as men if each is doing the same job. Of course, this simple principle has created questions and interpretive ambiguities. In summary, equal work means work that requires essentially the same skill, effort, responsibility, working conditions, location, and hazards. This definition applies regardless of job title, shift, or any union contract.

Yes, there are exceptions. Differential pay is permissible if the pay scale is based on something other than gender differences such as seniority, a merit system, or production output (in either amount or quality).

If you believe you have been discriminated against in pay, you have to prove that you are doing essentially the same work with the same skills, effort, working conditions, and responsibilities as someone else—not necessarily male—who is being paid significantly more. For more information about equality of pay issues, but not legal advice, you may call The National Committee on Pay Equity at this Washington, D.C. number: (202) 331-7343.

If you are discriminated against under the terms of the Equal Pay Act, you can complain to the Equal Employment Opportunity Commission (EEOC), or you can simply sue your employer in court. You have two years to file a complaint with the EEOC from the date of the incident (see Appendix for locations of EEOC offices) and, if you win, you may be awarded two years pay at the rate you should have earned or even more if you can prove that the employer was intentionally discriminating against you.

As the national population gets older, age discrimination is becoming a more significant problem. The Age Discrimination Employment Act of 1967 generally applies to employers who have 20 employees or more. There are three situations where the law does not apply. (1) An employer can discriminate where age alone is not the factor (the job may require physical strength), (2) where the employee is terminated as part of a generally applied retirement plan, and (3) when the employee is fired for good cause.

RIGHTS OF HANDICAPPED PERSONS

In July, 1990, Congress passed the Americans With Disabilities Act (ADA), which applies to most employers in the country with over 25 employees. It does not apply to Indian tribes, private clubs, the federal government, or churches. ADA forbids discriminatory hiring practices based on physical or health disabilities. For example, it makes it illegal to refuse to hire somebody solely because they have AIDS or a history of drug use or epilepsy or a congenital disability.

The Rehabilitation Act of 1973 forbids discrimination against the handicapped; it applies only to the federal government or to companies that work for the federal government or that are the recipients of federal funds. Obviously, this covers an important exception to ADA.

ON-THE-JOB PREGNANCY DISCRIMINATION

Women often are discriminated against because they are pregnant. However, federal law makes it illegal for a prospective employer to ask you any specific intimate questions when interviewing you for a job. A question regarding your gestation status is permitted if the employer can show that being pregnant may adversely affect your ability to do the job. For example, if the job is such that it might be physically impossible to do the work while pregnant or the work might involve handling hazardous material that would be dangerous for you or your unborn child, then questions regarding your gestation status are permissible.

If you become pregnant after you are employed and you are doing your job, your boss cannot make you take pregnancy leave before you want to take it; he/she can't unreasonably limit your leave time nor refuse to let you come back to work to the same or a comparable position. Finally, your employer cannot cut off benefits to you that are normally given to other temporarily disabled employees.

PAY EQUITY

Women are still paid less than men in careers with the same or less responsibility, danger, and effort. Women are now entering fields formerly dominated by men and are getting paid 35 to 40% less than men doing essentially the same work. This discrepancy in pay may be due to the social attitudes of our culture ingrained for over a century that women work for pin money and the serious wage earners in the family are the men. In many families, the reality today is that the *only* wage earner is the working woman. Naturally, employers prefer to defer to a cultural attitude that allows them to pay less money for the same work, but that isn't fair or legal; this unfairness is recognized by the law and some union contracts as an unjust hardship on women and is called "invidious discrimination" resulting in "pay inequity." It's important to note that most efforts to end pay inequities are *not* attempts to freeze the wages of men while those of women are raised. Such a plan would pit men and women employees against each other and breed resentment. Pay equity can be achieved through a system that adjusts wage increases over a time period so that both men and women are given increases, with women temporarily given bigger increases until they are paid at the same level.

Some employers may try to subvert the concept of pay equity by labeling the jobs with different titles. This gimmick involves calling the same job by different titles and using that as an excuse for paying different wages. You can defeat this trick through use of the job evaluation system in your company that standardizes the job description by assigning points for the requirements needed to do the job. Points are noted for education, training, experience, hazards, different working hours, and so on. Jobs with comparable point scores are to be paid similar wages regardless of what their titles are.

MINIMUM WAGE AND TIP CREDIT

The minimum wage that must be paid to workers is usually set by Federal and, sometimes, state law. It is controversial; some employers claim that the minimum wage requirement eliminates jobs (employers simply won't hire these low-paid workers at all), and others say it is a guarantee against slavery. In 1996, the minimum wage issue became a hot topic again with the Republicans in Congress generally opposed to it and the Democrats generally in favor of it. One comedian observed that Republicans would be in favor of the minimum wage if it covered everybody— not just the poor. As we go to press, the minimum wage has increased to $5.15 an hour.

Be aware of laws connected to tips and overtime wages. Some workers, for example waiters, rely heavily on tips as a part of their income. In some states, if you earn at least a certain amount in tips every week, you are called a "tipped employee," and the minimum wage for "tipped employees" is lower than the minimum wage for other employees.

Overtime pay and your entitlement to it varies with states and with union contracts. Traditionally, the concept of overtime is that the employee should be paid 1½ times regular pay if required to work more than eight hours in a single day or 40 hours in a single week. Overtime pay for working on special days—often including Sundays, national holidays, or religious holidays—is traditionally two times regular pay.

Unfortunately, these traditional concepts may be manipulated and exploited in cases that sometimes make circumstances worse for other employees. For example, in some entertainment industry contracts, if a worker has less than an eight-hour break between working sessions, she is paid at the rate of the earlier scale. What's that we said? Let's try again, using another example. A group of movie industry workers are working on a Sunday drawing double-time pay. If they leave work on Sunday and come back on the job on Monday before eight hours has elapsed since the last work on Sunday, all their hours on Monday are paid at the Sunday, double-time rate. Obviously, this can lead to excesses and is something that the studios and producers work hard to avoid.

WRONGFUL TERMINATION

The concept of wrongful termination—which is legal jargon for being unjustly fired—came as a surprising change for workers. Prior to the institution of the legal concept of wrongful termination about 50 years ago, bosses generally were free to hire and fire people at whim and for any reason. If the boss didn't like the shirt you had on one morning or thought you weren't smiling enough or if he got up on the wrong side of the bed, he could fire you and that was it, finished, kaput, ended, zap! The courts changed that; one reason was because workers were fired for their involvement in unions. In those laissez-faire days for employers, a union organizer was a troublemaker and ripe for firing. After some businesses and factories became unionized, the union contracts began to contain provisions prohibiting termination without a fair and justified reason. Thus, the concept of wrongful termination grew out of the union activities and was made stronger with the passage of the Civil Rights Act of 1964.

This federal law specifically says that the boss can't sack an employee because of race, color, religion, the country of origin, or gender. Some states also passed laws dealing with wrongful termination and this principle is now firmly fixed in the law. You cannot be fired from your job without a just cause. Well, of course, this struggle between the boss and the worker didn't stop there and it would be unnatural if it did. Now, people are fussing in the courts over what "just cause" means. Most would agree if you stop showing up for work or you don't do the work you're hired to do, the boss should be able to fire you. But, there are nuances to being fired for just cause. For example, what if the boss doesn't fire you, but fires the whole job, that is, eliminates a division or factory? Or, suppose the company goes broke and closes down the business or the factory? Or, suppose the factory burns down and there isn't any place to work? Or, suppose the boss decides labor costs are lower in Paraguay or Haiti and moves the operation where you work to a foreign country? Or, suppose the boss doesn't like the fact that you're a whistle-blower who has tipped off the authorities that the boss is doing naughty things. Or, suppose the boss says he wants to be sure your personal habits or lifestyle don't affect your job, and he wants you to submit to drug tests, or he wants to know about your political or sexual preferences?

Some of these situations are new and as yet untested in the courts. Some do not have cultural support; there are gray areas. Many government employees and some private employees now are required to undergo urine tests to make sure they are not on drugs; if they are, they are reprimanded, suspended, or fired. This occurs in jobs where employees are required to operate vehicles transporting the public (trains or buses). In professional sports we often hear of players who are suspended or even fired when they have tested positive for drugs. Obviously, it is in the best interests of all that people who are responsible for the lives of others such as pilots, train and bus drivers, and missile silo commanders not be on the job under the influence of drugs.

CHAPTER 3

DEALING WITH SEXUAL HARASSMENT

The popular tort of the day is sexual harassment on the job; the cases are many and because of their titillation value, are well known: the U.S. Army Training Centers, Anita Hill/Clarence Thomas, U.S. Senator Bob Packwood, and Los Angeles City Councilman Nate Holden. With the focus on these types of cases, one would think that employers would be more sensitive to the problem, and it would diminish. To the contrary, the number of sexual harassment cases has skyrocketed in recent years. The number of harassment charges filed with the Equal Employment Opportunity Commission (EEOC) has more than doubled since 1990. Of course, that may be due in part to the fact that women are now aware of the law that provides protection from sexual harassment that gives them a reasonable remedy for job harassment. Another possibility, women are invading job areas that have traditionally been dominated by men. For example, in mining and construction there is a ratio respectively of 90 and 52 sexual harassment complaints for every 100,000 women workers as contrasted with 17 in the fields of real estate, insurance, and service industries.

A lawyer with the EEOC sees it this way, "Obviously, we are going through a major social change, and women are moving into industries where they've historically not been present. Unfortunately, we see resistance (by men) and we don't expect that to go away soon." Lawyer Jane Lang of Duluth, Minnesota, reportedly is handling 15 sexual harassment cases, sees job uncertainty as a major cause of sexual harassment: "The idea that a woman is taking something that belongs to a man is increased when there are fewer good jobs to go around. Our clients have been told they are taking bread out of the mouths of men. You hear a lot more about economics than you do about politics." There were 15,691 sexual harassment cases filed with the EEOC in 1995 alone.[1]

---

[1] Ellen Neuborne, Cover Story, *USA TODAY*, May 3–5, 1996.

To resurrect a tired old cliché, this is only the tip of the iceberg. Experts say that despite increasing litigation, most sexual harassment is not reported because women are fearful of the consequences including being fired from the best-paying job they have ever had. In addition, what many men refuse to grasp is that most women who work NEED THE JOB because THEY are supporting their families. Shivawn Newsome, a D.C. prison guard says, "I have a mortgage and a car note and child care costs, and I really can't afford to make a change." In a 1995 study of harassment on FEDERAL jobs, where one would expect enforcement of the federal law to be most strict, it was reported that only 6% of the workers filed harassment complaints and that was half of the number that actually took place.[2] At the prison system of Washington, D.C., Newsome endured sexual harassment from fellow workers for years because she needed the work, but she finally got fed up and joined with five other women and, significantly, one man, in a harassment suit against the D.C. Department of Corrections. They won a $1.4 million judgment in April of 1995.

A case that received significant news coverage in early 1996 was the complaint by 300 women at the Illinois plant of car manufacturer Mitsubishi Motor Manufacturing of America. The case triggered an aggressive public relations reaction by the company supported by many of the male employees. At about the same time the women at the Fenton, Missouri, Chrysler minivan plant complained about male co-workers groping them from behind, and at the Oxnard, California, RJR Nabisco chili processing plant women workers complained that the chilies weren't the only hot things on the assembly line. These women were upset because in spite of the heat, the bosses refused to give them bathroom breaks and made them wear diapers. Jennie Vargas, who filed a harassment complaint, described what it was like, "It was like a prison. It was hot and sweaty, but we didn't want to drink water because we were afraid we'd have to go to the bathroom." Women who managed to sneak out to take a bathroom break were suspended for three days without pay. Vargas' lawsuit was settled April 14, 1996. A United Parcel women worker in Kansas City, Serita Wright, was harassed, threatened, and had her tires slashed by a male co-worker stalking her on the job. At a warehouse in Independence, Missouri, forklift operator Donna Terrill was routinely chased around the lunch table, was confronted with signs announcing her availability for oral sex, and was subject to sexually harassing jibes from co-workers.

Susan Webb, a consultant and publisher of the *Webb Report* that deals with sexual harassment on the job, states her view: "When we get a Mitsubishi or a Tailhook everyone gasps in surprise, but the fact is, this happens every day." Symbolic of some of the deeper issues is the fact that busloads of Mitsubishi workers picketed the EEOC office in Chicago in support of their employer and against their co-workers

---

2 Federal report, "Sexual Harassment in the Federal Workplace," *USA TODAY*, May 3–5, 1996.

who complained of sexual harassment. The attorney for those six women who had filed complaints, Mary Ann Sedey, said, "It is so painful to see the busloads of Mitsubishi workers lining up to call their co-workers liars."

Q. What is sexual harassment?

A. It is deliberate or repeated unwelcome and unsolicited sexual verbal comments, gestures, or physical contact. The U.S. Supreme Court held this was illegal in 1986 in the case of *Meritor Savings Bank, FSB v. Vinson* (477 U.S. 57, 106 S. Ct. 2399, 91 L. Ed. 2nd 49 [1986]). That case held that there was illegal sexual harassment whenever the actions were severe or pervasive enough to create a hostile or abusive work environment. It is not always necessary to prove that the harassment actually affected your job, but it's helpful if you can prove it. Sometimes, it's only necessary to prove that there was a hostile environment.

Q. What if the victim gives in to the harasser?

A. An important point to understand is that the victim giving in to sexual harassment does not obviate the harassment nor the charge. In the Supreme Court case mentioned, *Meritor v. Vinson,* Michelle Vinson was subject to harassment for four years by her boss, Taylor; she finally gave in to his demands because she was afraid of losing her job. During the time that followed, he fondled her in front of other employees, went into the women's rest room when she was there alone and exposed himself, had intercourse with her approximately 50 times, and raped her several times. She consented because she felt that she was forced to do so to retain her job. When Vinson filed a complaint against Taylor and their employer Meritor, she won.

Q. What if the victim had an earlier, voluntary love affair with the harasser?

A. This is a bit dicier. Under the circumstances, the victim must have strong proof that she (or, surprisingly sometimes, he) terminated the voluntary love relationship and made that very clear to the other person.

Q. Just how bad does the harassment have to be?

A. You want to carefully document what went on so that it meets all the tests of unwelcome, repeated conduct that unreasonably interferes with your job by creating a hostile work situation.

THE CONDUCT YOU WANT TO DOCUMENT INCLUDES:

- Whether the abuse was physical or verbal or both.

- The specifics of what was done or said (exact language or acts, date, time, place, others present, etc.)

- How often the incidents of harassment occurred.

- Who was involved? Was the harasser a boss?

- Who was the target? You alone? Others? Gender of other victims?

An accidental or an isolated flirtation probably doesn't qualify, but in one situation where the woman was in a vehicle from which she could not exit and the male talked about sexual acts and fondled her, that was deemed to be harassment (*Barrett v. Omaha National Bank,* 584 F. Supp. 22, 35 [D. Neb. 1983] aff'd, 726 F. 2nd 424 [8th Cir. 1984]). Generally, isolated crude jokes or a single incident, an obscene message, or one incident of sexual solicitation probably don't qualify as harassment(*Scott v. Sears, Roebuck & Co.*, 798 F. 2d 210, 214 [7th Cir. 1986] et al..

STUDIES OF SEXUAL HARASSMENT [3]

To better understand some of the nuances of sexual harassment, we have included a summary of some significant studies of sexual harassment. For example, recent studies of sexual harassment, most often on the job, concern the following issues:

1. **Is sexual harassment invited?** Do women knowingly or unknowingly send out cues that invite sexual advances by their male co-workers?

2. **Is sexual harassment in the eye of the beholder?** Women and men are raised differently, ingrained with different cultural expectations; each sex has a different way of looking at the world and so does each individual. What is sexual harassment to one woman may be warm and friendly horseplay to a man or even to another woman. Remember, the Supreme Court has now set the standard: that of the REASONABLE WOMAN.

3. **The role of power in the relationship.** Seventy-five percent of women work for male bosses who control their success or failure on the job. Do male bosses use that power to gain sexual favors that would otherwise not be available to them?

---

[3] Bette Ann Stead, Women in Management, Prentice-Hall, Englewood Cliffs, New Jersey, 1985, PP 173–226.

4. **What are the solutions to sexual harassment?** There are laws that provide remedies, but the cost of exercising rights under these laws is sometimes higher than the aggrieved woman is willing to pay.

These four studies looked at each of four issues:

NON-VERBAL GENDER COMMUNICATION[4]

Men often are unable to accept women as equals; some men spend much of their time looking at their female co-workers fantasizing about possible sexual activities with them. A *Harvard Business Review* and *Redbook* joint study, concluded in the spring of 1980, concerning on-the-job sexual harassment, revealed some interesting defenses. One 56-year old woman who had been working for 40 years advised her younger counterparts to develop "The Look." This is a devastating look of disapproval that she turns on any male who crosses the harassment line.

This study underscores the prolific use of nonverbal communication in our daily lives and our need to understand the effect of such communication on the job. For example, men and women long have communicated nonverbally with what the social scientists call courting or quasi-courting cues. Quasi-courting means making a statement of one's gender; courting cues are statements of one's gender, the other person's gender, or suggestions for further contact. Such cues may relate to dress, gestures, or body language. As this study noted, interpersonal relations are not neutered when people arrive at the workplace. Indeed, traditionally, many personal relationships begin with friendships made at work. Flirting always has existed in the workplace, and it probably always will even in the face of strict laws and under the scrutiny of the human resource police. The issue, then, is not flirting or nonverbal sexual communication, but UNWANTED flirting or nonverbal sexual communication. One problem noted in this study is that "nonverbal communication is not usually under conscious control." In other words, he didn't even know he was doing it!

The *Harvard-Redbook* study cites Al Scheflin, one of the earliest behavioral scientists to study courtship cues [5] for signs of such cues which may occur in settings when men and women are together including:

- **Grooming Cues.** Men and women alike may adjust clothing, hair or may even engage in mutual grooming.

---

[4] Lynn Renne Cohen, "Nonverbal (Mis)Communication between Managerial Men and Women," *Business Horizons*, Jan-Feb, 1983, pp. 13–17.

[5] Albert E. Scheflin, *Body Language and the Social Order*, Prentice-Hall, Englewood Cliffs, New Jersey, 1972.

- **Prolonged Eye Contact.** One of the first connections between men and women is eye contact; we all learn to break eye contact quickly with people who do not interest us.

- **Chest Presentation.** Women stand straight and thrust out their breasts, and men may take a similar stance to appear big and broad shouldered.

- **Pelvic Motion.** Both genders roll their pelvis slightly—backward by men and forward by women.

- **Touching.** Mutual, apparently friendly and innocent, touching of another's arm, shoulder, or upper body.

Later studies connect these cues to power positions in the workplace. Erving Goffman[6] suggests that when women give off flirting cues or are receptive to male flirting cues, the on-the-job power status of the women is lowered; men become the aggressors and, thus, the more powerful. As a result, men often believe that women don't take work seriously. Part of this superior attitude may stem from the different traditional roles of men and women in society. Work is a very serious part of a man's life and, in fact, a man's occupation most often defines who and what he is whereas women are frequently defined by other aspects of life such as family and children. Often women in the workplace, confronted with courting cues, see co-worker males as overbearing and threatening or sometimes just a little bit silly.

The point is that courtship cues are present in work situations—however unintentional—and must be guarded against if potential harassment situations are to be avoided.

In her study of sexual attraction and harassment, Jeanne Bosson Driscol makes a sound point: "Sexual attraction is a fact; sexual harassment does not have to be." [7] A difficult situation is created when there is legitimate sexual attraction between a man and woman on the job that blossoms into a romance which later fizzles. At that juncture, either or both parties may be uncomfortable working with the other. Such discomfort worsens if either or both begin dating other people in the same company. This could lead to subsequent charges, legitimate or not, of sexual harassment.

Companies do not handle romances, affairs, living together, and other female-male relationship arrangements uniformly. The issue of privacy comes into play. What policies, if any, are fair and sensible about fraternization and nepotism? Generally, as set forth in the Driscoll article, whatever policy is adopted, it should be:

[6] Erving Goffman, *Gender Advertisements*, Harvard University Press, Cambridge, Mass., 1979.

[7] Jeanne Bosson Driscoll, "Sexual Attraction and Harassment: Management's New Problems," *Personnel Journal*, Costa Mesa, California, January, 1981.

1. Consistent and apply to everybody.

2. Be clearly and concisely stated.

Former Postmaster General William F. Bolger issued the Postal Service's policy statement:

> "Sexual harassment is unacceptable conduct which takes various forms. It is deliberate or repeated unsolicited verbal comments, questions, representations, or physical contacts of an intimate sexual nature which are unwelcome to the recipient. Sexual harassment can also take the form of making or threatening to make decisions affecting an employee's job on the basis of an acceptance or refusal of a request for sexual intimacy.

> "Sexual harassment is a form of employee misconduct which undermines the integrity of the employment relationship. It undermines morals and interferes with the productivity of its victims and their co-workers. While it is not the Postal Service's intent to regulate employees' social interactions or relationships freely entered into, conduct constituting sexual harassment will not be tolerated." [8]

Driscoll suggests that employers not only implement clear harassment policies, but also provide counseling for people experiencing feelings of attraction for another employee that might lead to harassment. Also, counseling guidance for harassment victims and for those accused of harassment is urged.

The employer may also be held liable for sexual harassment that occurs at the hands of customers, suppliers, and others who are not company employees but who have necessary contact with employees of the company.

SEXUAL HARASSMENT

Sexual harassment is a common and complicated issue, and there are many different ways to deal with it, beginning with being able to correctly identify it.

IDENTIFYING SEXUAL HARASSMENT

Sexual harassment is broadly defined and is not limited to a situation where a male supervisor forces a female subordinate to have sexual relations with him. Women may be guilty of sexual harassment toward men or it may be found in a same sex situation. Sexual harassment may be identified as:

---

[8] U.S. Postal Service, Postal Bulletin 21240, April 10, 1980, p. 1.

Sexual advances ranging from rape, sexual battery, or molestation to pinching, touching, grabbing, or brushing against all fall into this category.

Requests for sexual favors in return for promotions, salary increases, or better working conditions.

Maintenance of sexual materials in the workplace.

Use of sexually explicitly language or sexually patronizing terms such as "babe," "honey," or "doll."

YOUR FIRST STEP TO DEALING WITH SEXUAL HARASSMENT

After you have determined that you are the victim of sexual harassment, you need to review your position and the possible courses of action you can take. Here are some of the questions you need to answer as you go ahead. As an employee—to whom do you report? What if there is no reaction? When do you hire a lawyer? Your employer should give each employee instructions, preferably in writing, designating those to whom a complaint should be directed. Each employer must provide an effective means of redress of complaints even if the employee does not request that any action be taken. The complaint procedures should be set out by the employer including information as to the investigative officers. Your complaint should be protected from disclosure by confidentiality provisions. Since the law provides that the employer is strictly liable if he/she knows or should have known about the sexually harassing conduct, the investigative officer should immediately report your complaint to the President of the company and the company's Chief Executive Officer.

Retaliation—Be aware of the possibility of subtle retaliation if you complain. Such retaliation can take various forms such as giving you inaccurate work information or refusing to cooperate or discuss work related matters with you. Of course, the ultimate retaliation is termination.

Hearing (administrative or court)—The question to be answered in a sexual harassment case is whether the conduct or environment complained of would be deemed by a "reasonable woman" to fall within the purview of sexual harassment. That means that the standard of measurement is not that of a reasonable man, but rather that of a reasonable woman and that standard may be different for each woman. Conduct that may constitute harassment in one context will not be such in another context. But the important point is that the issue of the presence of sexual harassment is to be decided by looking at the events from the eyes of the woman and not the man.

CHAPTER 4

HANDLING PREGNANCY AND SEX DISCRIMINATION

FACTORS AFFECTING PREGNANCY DISCRIMINATION ON THE JOB

When you are working and become pregnant, there are several things to consider that can affect your relationship with your employer.

WHEN YOU ARE PREGNANT AND EMPLOYED[1]

When you become pregnant and you are working, there are several things to be concerned with besides the coming child.

One of the first considerations is when to tell your co-workers. Obviously, at some point, your pregnancy will become obvious, but you may not wish to defer your news until then. The timing of telling your employer and co-workers is important to consider even though you are personally excited and have already shared the news with friends and family. The minute you announce to the boss that you are pregnant, you officially pass from being an employee to being a PREGNANT employee enroute to becoming a working mother, which changes your status officially and unofficially with your employer in many ways.

---

[1] Anne E. Weisberg and Carol A. Buckler, *Everything a Working Mother Needs to Know*, Doubleday, New York, 1994, pp. 16+.

As a general rule, those who have lived through pregnancy and continued working generally agree that it is best to say nothing during the first three months of your pregnancy. Your devotion to your job will be underscored by the fact that you have worked through the first trimester and adds credibility to your intention to return to work after the child is born.

Obviously, there are exceptions to the idea of not disclosing your pregnancy for the first three months. If there are medical complications and you need a doctor's attention frequently or if you are hospitalized, you need to disclose your pregnancy immediately, and your employer should treat it as he or she would any other illness insofar as sick leave and benefits are concerned.

You may tire quickly or be nauseated in those early months. It may be important to have the cooperation of co-workers whom you trust to help you keep your secret for a time.

The timing of the announcement—probably in the fourth month—should take into account the corporate culture of your workplace, your boss's attitude toward women and particularly pregnant women, the support system offered by your co-workers, unions, and so on. It can't hurt to announce your happy news after you have closed an important deal or finished an important project.

Your boss should hear the news first from you and not from others. If he/she gets the word from the rumor mill, it may suggest that you don't trust him or her. Pick a time convenient for your boss, and then carefully and proudly announce the news along with a statement of your plans after the baby is born. If you plan to return to work, be sure your boss knows that, and both of you are agreed on your status upon return. After telling your boss the news, you may want to send a note thanking him or her for the warm wishes and letting your employer know that you are looking forward to returning to work after the baby is born.

Some points to remember: Female supervisors are not always as sympathetic to your new condition as male supervisors who are married with children. Also, the supervisor with whom you came to the original understanding about your returning to work may be replaced while you're on maternity leave, and the new one may not honor the deal. While it may be advisable to leave some details of your post-birth plans a little vague because you may have an entirely different outlook once you're a mother, do, however, make it clear that you plan to return to work. You should obtain a general agreement about how your work will be handled in your absence. Your employer is obligated to offer you your job or a substantially similar one upon your return. Discuss coverage of your job with co-workers who may be covering your workload for you during your absence. One very important thing to understand—particularly with your first child: Having a new baby is not like buying a puppy.

Your attitude toward work and motherhood will, predictably, be very different after your child is born. You will worry about the infant's colic, crying, you and the child not sleeping at night, the two of you bonding, and the altered relationship with the father of your child. You will be elated, frustrated, tired, ecstatic, resentful, angry, adoring, and out of tempo, and you will exhibit a new you that you didn't imagine existed.

Planning the length of your leave of absence is difficult to do in advance, but you can get a sense of what is possible with your particular employer (they are all different in real life) from your own assessment of attitude and philosophy where you work. Beyond that, it is a good idea to talk with other women at your work or who previously worked there and had babies about their experiences. Of course, ask for a copy of the company's pregnancy policy.

Some employers believe that the fact you would allow yourself to become pregnant is a sign that your job is less important to you than your family. Yet, surveys and studies show that women who work at jobs where the employer is sympathetic and helpful in handling the pregnancy are many times more likely to like their jobs and return to the employer.[2] Planning the transition back to the job is just as important as planning for the birth.

PREGNANCY, MOTHERHOOD, AND THE LAW

Regardless of the attitude and mood of your employer when you are pregnant and having a baby, the law assures that you have certain rights. Some states have their own laws. You need to know them as well as two applicable Federal laws. They are 1) the Family and Medical Leave Act that applies to employers with more than 50 workers, and 2) the Pregnancy Discrimination Act that applies to employers with more than 15 workers.

The Family and Medical Leave Act gives mothers AND fathers up to 12 weeks unpaid leave when they are

SPECIAL TIP

The Federal Family and Medical Leave Act specifies that, if there is a state law on family leave, too, the law giving you the maximum benefits will apply.

[2] Ibid., p. 44.

adding a new child to the family. This applies whether they are giving birth to the child or adopting a child. There are some limitations, but you do not jeopardize your seniority or other benefits. You need to give your employer 30 days notice of when you are going to take leave except in unusual situations such as complications of pregnancy or a premature birth.

The Pregnancy Discrimination Act prevents employers from firing you for being pregnant and requires that the employer give you the same benefits for pregnancy as you would be entitled to if you were ill. At this point some 23 states have their own laws protecting pregnant workers and working parents. A number of other states are in the process of evaluating the enactment of similar laws covering pregnancy and working parents.

CHILD CARE

For working parents, child care is vital. Your ability to assure that the person in whose care you leave your child is qualified, competent, and loving is critical to your continued success as a productive employee. Some mothers have tried to solve the problem by bringing the child to work. Most experts agree that this is impossible or difficult in many work situations and undesirable in most.

Things to remember about getting day care for your child:

1. **Take plenty of time.** You need time to check out references, make comparisons, and consult other parents. Start early. Don't wait until your child is born or until you are ready to return to work. Start looking as soon as you know you are pregnant and can do so without prematurely tipping off your employer.

2. **Admit your mistakes quickly.** Often you may make a decision that turns out to be wrong. Admit you've made the wrong choice, do it quickly, and move on to the next choice.

You have essentially four kinds of day-care options:

1. **Family.** You may have a mother, mother-in-law, sisters, or aunts who are willing to care for your child. This family solution may be significantly cheaper than, say, professional day-care providers, but might not be the best choice. Subject this alternative to all the tests you use in evaluating other alternatives. For example, you wouldn't leave your child with an deranged or incompetent person in unsafe physical facilities, and these standards should apply universally whether it's within the family or day-care centers.

2. **Family Day Care.** This is a variant of having a family member care for your child. It is a small group of children under the care of one of your relatives, a

friend, a retired person, or a stay-at-home mother. Care is provided in the home of the person giving the care. The laws regulating such informal centers are less stringent and less frequently enforced and followed up than those with a commercial day-care center. Since the whole arrangement depends on the adult who provides the care, problems arise when that person goes on vacation, gets sick, or is unavailable for some other reason. However, with the right care giver, these situations can be very satisfying for you, your child, and the care giver.

3. **Live-In Care.** Another more personalized kind of care involves hiring a nanny or live-in baby sitter or mother's helper. Princess Diana had a job for a time in her teens, as a live-in mother's helper for an American family living in England. This is usually the most expensive option and has the downside of encroaching upon your privacy at home.

4. **Day-Care Facilities.** These are larger, organizationally run operations often connected with some institution such as a church or, perhaps, your employer's company. Some of the good features include stability of care because there is a staff instead of just one or two people. Facilities are usually more child oriented, more regulated, and frequently inspected. The cost is probably less than live-in care, but more than family-care options. The downside is that it exposes your child to many other children and possible sources of disease and that you and each child, including yours, receive less individual attention.

CHILD-CARE CHECKLISTS[3]

There are two checklists you need to have when picking a care facility for your child. And, remember, the main consideration at all times is your child's health and safety.

FIRST CHECKLIST—YOU AND YOUR SPOUSE'S CONSIDERATIONS

Make a REALISTIC evaluation of what you need and can afford in child care. For example, be honest with yourself about your time commitments to the job. If the child care facility closes at 6 p.m., for example, can you or your husband realistically ALWAYS be there by that time? Financially, can you and your spouse realistically afford the child care you want? Remember, to the astonishment of most couples, child-care expenses become one of the three biggest costs of your family! However,

[3] Ibid., pp. 88+.

don't fall into the mommy-money, daddy-money trap by comparing what you earn against child-care costs with the idea that it may be sensible for you to quit your job and take care of your child. The cost of rearing a child is a joint cost of both parents, and many of the expenses will continue no matter who cares for the child during the day. Beyond that, women who quit work for a few years and then return find it difficult to and may never catch up on the career ladder. Like it or not, employers want to be your first—if not, only—love, and they erroneously consider women who put family first as unreliable employees. Finally, remember not all will be well with your child in day care all the time. There will be times—more than you think—when you need to get to where your child is in a hurry. If the child's day care is at some distance from both parents' work or you have to go through a traffic bottleneck such as a tunnel, bridge, or congested area, that could create serious problems. Once you take into consideration time, money, and location, you will have narrowed down the list of available child care possibilities significantly.

SECOND CHECKLIST—ALTERNATIVE CARE PLACES AVAILABLE

You must interview the people who are going to care for your child and listen very carefully to what they say—not what you would like to hear. Have them tell you what your child's daily routine will be, observe the physical environment, the feeding arrangements, sanitary care, and how they handle discipline. A delicate but critical area, if you are dealing with a child-care facility that employs others to care for your child, is whether or not all employees are screened for criminal records. Too often, pedophiles seek out work where little children are available to them. In 1994, Oprah Winfrey fulfilled a promise she made in memory of Angelica Mena by hiring ex-governor of Illinois Jim Thompson to shepherd through Congress and onto President Clinton's desk the National Child Protection Act, which is known as "Oprah's Law." It provides a national computer database where anyone contemplating hiring a person working in a child-care center can check on a job applicant's previous criminal record. Angelica Mena lived in Chicago, as does Oprah, and Angelica was sexually abused, murdered, and her body thrown into Lake Michigan by a man who would have been identified by the National Child Protection Act screening.

You must visit the care center yourself and make your own inspection of the physical facilities where you child is going to spend most of his or her waking hours. Make surprise visits more than once.

TAX CREDITS

You are allowed to take advantage of the child care tax credit by a deduction on your income tax form 1040. Review the Internal Revenue Service instructions to assure that you are getting the full credit.

FACTORS AFFECTING SEX DISCRIMINATION ON THE JOB

Here are summaries of some significant studies about why there is sex discrimination on the job. We think these are helpful because most material on sex discrimination on the job tells only "what" it is. Rarely is any attention given to "why" there is sex discrimination on the job and understanding the causes of discrimination can help you deal with such discrimination constructively.

HOW COMPANIES AND OTHER ORGANIZATIONS FUNCTION[4]

Generally, companies and organizations organize their power and decision making in a pyramid or hierarchical pattern. The key to this arrangement working is INFORMATION. Information gathering and processing systems, formal and informal, develop as people compete for the inside information they need to progress upward in the organization. Interestingly, most of the jobs in these systems, even today, are occupied by men.

To position yourself to have access to information systems that affect your promotion, you need to cross what the author, Asplund, calls the "Promotion Bar." On-the-job mentors often help younger people pass the promotion bar. However, most people will seek out those they are most comfortable being with, and often male companionship is preferable to the male bosses. Thus, men beyond the promotion bar tend to help other men cross the bar. When a man chooses to mentor a woman, problems may be created. Other males may feel betrayed; a personal relationship is suggested. However, both men and women can benefit from having a mentor, a person with a history at the job who knows the ins and outs and is willing to share that knowledge and experience with the younger employer. Some firms make it a policy to establish a mentoring system in which men may mentor younger employees of either sex, making it acceptable in that workplace to do so.

An understanding of gender differences in how work is viewed and how women executives are perceived can be helpful in understanding some of the problems women encounter in the workplace. So, we include some points in four relevant studies for you to review.

MALE AND FEMALE JOB DIFFERENCES[5]

1. **Women's job choices are less conscious than those of men.** Women often don't plan ahead nor are women as single minded as men.

---

[4] Gisele Asplund, *Women Managers*, John Wiley & Sons, New York, 1988, p. 7.

[5] Ibid., pp. 19.

2. **Women's climb up the ladder is slower than that of men.** Women have to try harder and wait longer.

3. **Women get less support from the boss.** Often women may lack the informal and sometimes confidential communication with the boss that male counterparts receive.

4. **Women's incentives differ from those of men.** Men look to careers for status and power. Women look to careers for self-realization and self-actualization.

SOURCES OF RESISTANCE TO WOMEN EXECUTIVES[6]

Three variations of sexual stereotypes have formed barriers to women's advancement in work:

1. Sex characteristic stereotypes that characterize women as irrational, ambitious, independent, and emotional.

2. Sex role stereotypes that put women in the home caring for husband, children, and aged parents, too timid for the rough and tumble of the marketplace.

3. Sex labeling of occupations that say certain jobs are not "appropriate" for women.

SEX VARIATIONS ON JOB EVALUATION OF WOMEN [7]

Barriers that keep women from advancing on the job might be internal—lack of motivation, non-work objectives, personality—or external depending on the way the job functions. One of the critical parts of advancement is how the worker is evaluated from time to time. The Nieva-Gutek study looks at prejudices in evaluating women workers; their theory is that men normally get better evaluations than women. Some of the reasons for this are that people who are in positions that deviate from the traditional gender roles society has assigned are regarded in a negative way. Men in a role that is traditionally thought of as feminine or women in a role that is traditionally thought of as masculine, therefore, get lower job evaluations.

[6] Dafna N. Izraeli, et al, "Women Executives in Multi-National Corporations," *California Management Review*, vol. 23, no. 1, 1980, pp. 53–63.

[7] Veronica Nieva and Barbara Gutek, "Sex Effects on Evaluation," *Academy of Management Science*, vol. 5, no. 2, 1980, pp. 267–276.

Ironically, too, there is often a bias against women who are highly qualified and perform well, so that they are sometimes ranked below less effective men. In short, sex-related evaluations are more biased against successful or competent women. [8]

HIDDEN BARRIERS TO PROMOTION OF WOMEN IN BUSINESS [9]

A 1982 study of women in management by Dr. Anne Harlan and Dr. Carol L. Weiss reported in the *New York Times* suggests that while senior male managers are most likely to promote women to middle management those women are not likely to go on into top management. Beyond that, male managers seem unable to give women who work with them an honest assessment of their work performance.

On the first finding, Dr. Harlan said, "Middle management supervisors gave the highest ratings to older, less aggressive women. These were women who didn't rock the boat, who were less threatening, less dynamic. At the same time, senior management was looking for different kinds of people to fill high-level spots. They wanted young, aggressive dynamos and the women who might have fit that picture weren't being promoted."

On the matter of work evaluation, Dr. Harlan said that male supervisors chew out other men who screw up, but ignore poor performance in women. Harlan reported that supervisors confided to her, "When a guy comes in your office, you can chew him out and then go out and have a few beers with him. But the managers believed they had to be careful in what they said to women because they thought they'd break down in the office and cry."

And while women are attempting to conquer their work world, the males in the organization are struggling to get to the top as well. Few do. Men have many—albeit different—problems confronting them as they attempt to advance in their jobs. Most feel extremely threatened by any woman, particularly the talented woman with her eye on their jobs.

There is resistance, the study said, to the first woman hired into a company, but that resistance drops as more women are hired until the critical level of about 15% women is reached. That's when men begin to see women as a threat to the males' advancement.

---

[8] Bette Ann Stead, *Women in Management*, Prentice-Hall, Englewood Cliffs, New Jersey, 1985, pp. 111–127.

[9] Ibid., pp. 161–175.

CHAPTER 5

ALTERNATIVE WORK PATTERNS: MOMMY TRACK AND GLASS CEILING

THE MOMMY TRACK

This term comes from a *Harvard Business Review* article arguing that employers should identify career primary women versus those who are career-and-family oriented. The article contended that the career-oriented women should be encouraged by employers and promoted to zoom to the top along with men. The premise of the article is that the company should accommodate a different pace for women on the mommy track because they were more interested in family than in the company (considered a cardinal sin by some employers).

The truth is that many women who have children are also dedicated to their careers. Indeed, even if the law allowed such discrimination—which it does not—employers are ill-served by this advice. However, your employer may adopt this career track vs. mommy track philosophy. You need to be alert to that possibility and raise your objection to this double tracking if it does occur to you.

Of course, if you desire a more flexible work schedule generally such arrangements can be worked out, again to the advantage of the company who will have a dedicated part-time employee who will utilize every working moment for the benefit of the employer.

For example, you can choose to work part time, although this may mean working as "an independent contractor" with few, if any, fringe benefits such as a health plan or workers' compensation. When you are calculating the costs of working rather than staying home with a new child, you need to factor into this calculation the cost of providing your own health care versus working a few hours more each week and being entitled to full-time benefits. You may have the advantage of coverage under your spouse's coverage, and for same gender couples employers such as the City of San Francisco, Disney Studios, and IBM provide benefits for the companions of their employees.

Other approaches to alternative work styles to accommodate your particular situation include such arrangements as a 4-day week, job sharing, and telecommuting. A 4-day week plan usually has you working 10 hours or more a day for each of four days so that you put in a full 40-hour week, but you do it in four days instead of five. This permits you three days off each week to tend to your family responsibilities. Job sharing is where two workers split one job and one salary. The advantages of this are obvious, but finding the right person to share with may be difficult. Finally, there is telecommuting; you remain at home, connecting with your employer by telephone, fax, e-mail, and other instant electronic modes. You might be many miles away from your employer's place of business and never visit there while still doing all the work required of you. In a dramatic example of telecommuting, many large operations are transmitting data to foreign countries where the labor is much cheaper. For example, the preparation of tickets for airlines in the United States is often done by banks of telecommuting computer operators in Haiti. In another example, some hospitals electronically transmit the audio tape of a doctor's notes about his/her patients dictated that morning to transcribers in India. In India, the transcriber transforms the notes into typed pages that are transmitted electronically back to the United States and are on the doctor's desk before he or she goes to lunch that very afternoon.

If you are fortunate enough to be able to work out such flexible working arrangements, be sure you and your employer understand—preferably in writing—what your official working relationship is, including pay, benefits, hours, and potential to become full time.

CHAPTER 6

WORKING FOR YOURSELF

Many more women start businesses of their own than do men—one out of every nine women working are in a business established on their own. Most new jobs in America are created by such women who start their own business.

There is a library full of books on starting and running your own business, and we won't try to duplicate that here. We will give you a basic overview of some of the important legal concerns and other aspects of going into business, on your own. For example, before you jump into starting a business, you should think it through, analyzing the advantages and disadvantages from every possible scenario.

First, is your idea for a business a sound business idea? The famous financial wizard of Wall Street, Bernard Barauch, said the secret to business success was to find a need and fill it. That is still true today. Ask yourself and other knowledgeable people, what do people need and how can I fill that need? Of course, you will properly tend to focus on the kind of business in which you already have experience because if there is a need and you DON'T know how to fill it, that could be a costly business disaster. A method of determining whether a need exists is through market research that can help answer the question of what the community needs are, how to fill them, and where you and your ideas fit in. Location is key, and many experts say you should put yourself in the shoes (or the car) of the customers you are trying to serve. If your location is remote, hard to find, impossible to get to, or without parking (if that is needed), you will never get a chance to fulfill people's needs.

Second, you must develop a financial plan. There are many guides for developing a financial plan including books and computer programs; there are also bankers who will help and extension courses at your local city college. Even the Small Business Administration may help. Check your local phone book under United States Government/Small Business Administration for the office most convenient for you, or write the main office at the Small Business Administration, Washington Office Center, 409 Third Street S.W., Washington, D.C. 20416, or telephone their toll free number (800) 827-5722. Ask for publications about going into business and about your particular field of business. Some of the SBA's publications include: *Incorporating a Small Business, Checklist for Going Into Business, The ABC's of Borrowing, Planning and Goal Setting for Small Business,* and, most important, *Woman's Handbook.*

You will probably need financing. Most new, small businesses do. If you do not already have an established credit line, you may find yourself in the unenviable position of borrowing from friends and family. Banks and other financial organizations (credit unions, venture capitalists) are usually not willing to loan money to a new, unproven business. This means that regardless of the legal organization of your business, the lender will require personal guarantees from you, your partners, and, perhaps, financially solid friends or relatives. There are also some state and federal government sources for loans to help businesses get started. Start by checking with the SBA and appropriate state economic development agency.

Getting started in business is complex and requires a knowledge of the corporation code and real estate matters. It is wise to have a lawyer advising you to clarify the consequences of what you are committing to when you are asked to sign loan documents and leases. Hiring a lawyer at this early stage of your venture will pay off in the long run. It is a much less expensive and painful to do it right in the beginning by obtaining the assistance of a lawyer who is qualified to assist you at the start of your venture.

PITFALLS OR NOT? SOME THINGS TO THINK ABOUT

There are so many things to be aware of when you are thinking of purchasing an existing business or starting your own business. It is crucial to take these factors into consideration, because they potentially can make or break your business.

FRIENDS AND FAMILY AS PARTNERS

Quite often, people go into business with friends and family. This has many advantages in that you know each other, are mutually supportive, and can trust one another. At least, those are the assumptions. However, where money is involved, things can sometimes turn sour whether the business does well or not. In fact, sometimes the partnership relationship is hurt by the success of the business. Jealousy, fears, and different agendas can all disrupt partnerships, notwithstanding the close personal relationships of the participants or perhaps because of that close personal relationship.

Be sure that all your understandings and arrangements in the partnership or business relationship are committed to writing. This is not unlike having a prenuptial agreement because, in a business sense, you are getting married. A good business lawyer can draw up a partnership agreement that will meet the needs of the business and the partnership. A lawyer experienced in this area of the law will have standard agreements containing all the provisions (some of which you have not even thought about) to allow your partnership to be run smoothly and to provide for contingencies such as the death of a partner or the termination of the partnership.

Such provisions may include what might happen when two people are not only married to each other in a business sense but are married to each other in their personal lives. Special care has to be taken to protect yourself in the event you and your partner spouse are divorced in your personal life. This is particularly important because the business may be a valuable asset for both of you and the major asset of the marriage. So, you don't want your personal conflict to destroy the business and leave both of you with a substantial business loss.

BUYING AN EXISTING BUSINESS

Buying a franchise or an existing business may be appealing if you want to go into business for yourself but you don't have a lot of money or experience. However, your best advice is to thoroughly investigate the prospective business or franchise before you buy. This is called "due diligence." Let's review some of the general rules of buying any going business.

Not every business is financially or personally right for everyone and the Federal Trade Commission, which oversees commercial matters, attempts to protect you when you are thinking of buying a franchise by requiring that franchise seller and/or other sellers of existing businesses to provide certain information. Under FTC rules, a franchise or business opportunity seller must give you a detailed disclosure document at least 10 business days before you pay any money or legally commit yourself to buying that business or franchise. This disclosure document requires that the seller disclose 20 important items of information about the business including:

- **Other Buyers.** The names, addresses, and phone numbers of others who have bought this franchise or business (if it has more than one operation).
- **Audited Statement.** A fully audited financial statement of the seller.
- **Seller's Background.** The background and experience of the business's key executives.
- **Operation Costs.** The cost required to start and keep the business going.
- **Mutual Responsibilities.** The responsibilities that you and the seller will have to each other after you have bought the business or franchise.

The disclosure document is a valuable tool that not only helps you obtain information about a proposed business, but also assists you in comparing it with other business opportunities and franchises available to you. Even if the law in your state does not require a disclosure statement such as the one contemplated by the FTC, insist that the prospective seller provide you with such disclosure. If he/she is slow to do so, think again about buying this particular business. In addition, your own due diligence consists of contacting customers and creditors to assure that the business is a viable one. Ask for financial statements and tax returns and be sure to review these documents and understand them.

The FTC guide for buying a franchise or business lists several areas in which you should do your due diligence. These include:

1. **Study.** Carefully read the disclosure documents and all proposed contracts. Definitely hire a lawyer with expertise in the area of buying and establishing businesses. It may be necessary to find a lawyer who is familiar with the particular kind of business you are buying.

2. **Talk.** Talk with the current owners of other franchises or businesses to whom the seller has sold. These individuals can be important sources of candid and trustworthy information. Discuss with these contacts what is set forth in the seller's disclosure statement as compared to their own experiences. Don't rely only on the seller's list of "references"—insist on the names, addresses, and phone numbers of actual franchise and other business operators. This is required by federal law.

3. **Check Earnings.** Projected earnings listed in promotional material are often based on estimates that may or may not be based on facts. The FTC requires that companies put in writing the facts on which they base their earnings claims; have your accountant review this information with you to assure that you understand the basis of the seller's earnings claims. Not only does the price you may pay for this business depend on the accuracy of the stated earnings, but your future success in the business does, too. Watch for footnotes or endnotes in the printed material; these notes may reveal important information about the earnings reports and projections.

4. **Other Successful Ventures.** Sellers must disclose in writing the number and percentage of other owners who have done as well as they claim you will do. Remember, broad-based sales claims about a successful area of business such as, "Be a part of our four billion dollar industry," may have no bearing on the likelihood of your own success. Keep in mind, too, that once you buy the business, you may be competing with other franchisees or business owners who have greater capitalization and more experience.

5. **Shop Around.** Compare the franchiser of the business you are interested in with other businesses that you may also be qualified to run. You may discover a better deal in another business opportunity or franchise. You should order a copy of the U.S. Department of Commerce's book, *The Franchise*

Opportunities Handbook. This informational booklet describes more than 1,400 companies that offer franchises. Contact a few of these and request their disclosure documents for comparison. *The Franchise Opportunities Handbook* is published every year and you can get it by contacting the Superintendent of Documents, U.S. Government Printing Office, Washington, D.C. 20402, (202) 512-1800.

6. **Listen.** Pay close attention to the sales presentation that the seller gives you. Certain sales tactics should alert you to exercise caution in proceeding. For example, if you are pressured to sign immediately "because prices will go up tomorrow" or "another buyer wants this deal," you should instead, slow down, take two steps backward and reevaluate your decision to purchase. A seller who is offering a fair sale does not have to use this sort of pressure. Remember, under the FTC rules, the seller must wait at least 10 business days after giving you the required disclosure documents before you pay any money or sign any agreement. Be on guard too for the "easy money" ploy. The thought is appealing, but, success usually requires hard work.

7. **Everything in Writing.** Any promises that you are relying on should be written into the contract you sign. If the seller says one thing but the contract says something different or says nothing about the subject , your written contract is what counts—not any oral representation upon which you may have relied. If a seller balks at putting verbal promises into writing, this may not be the deal you want to consummate.

8. **Professional Advice.** When you buy a business, it is more than likely that you will be committing substantial funds, effort, and time. Make sure that your own level of experience is sufficient to take over the business and surround yourself with the appropriate advisors to assist you in getting your new business off the ground.

FRANCHISE BLUES

As we said, franchising is an increasingly popular way to get into some businesses; there are some half-million franchise operations in the country today. Some are very well known, such as those in the fast food business including McDonald's, Burger King, and Wendy's. To get an idea of the scope of franchising, just flip through the classified section of your daily newspaper or that of the *Wall Street Journal* or *USA TODAY.* You can also contact the National Franchise Association, 1350 New York Ave, N.W. Suite 900, Washington, D.C. 20005, (202) 628-8000, for books and brochures on franchising.

Franchising is basically a marketing system through which a business person with a unique product or service licenses another to sell that product or service in a specific territory. Typically, the franchiser grants this "franchise" in the specified geographic territory and agrees to train and assist the franchisee in setting up and operating the business. In return, the franchisee typically pays a fee for the exclusive right to operate the franchise in the specified territory and agrees to operate the business according to the rules the franchiser establishes. The franchisee usually also agrees to buy all her materials from the franchiser and to pay the franchiser a percentage of the sales.

The positive side for the franchiser is that it allows him/her to expand his/her operation without investing more money and, in fact, earns him/her a franchise sales fee. In addition, the franchiser may earn a percentage of the sales of the expanded business and make a profit from the merchandise he/she may sell to his/her franchisees. The positive side for the franchisee is he/she gets a business with an established reputation, expertise that might have taken years to learn and, in theory, the advantages of mass advertising and purchases of supplies and merchandise.

The downside occurs when the representation made in granting the franchise are exaggerated or when the competition is so tough as to make the franchise unprofitable. Franchise agreements are usually legally complex. You and your lawyer must fully understand exactly what you are committing to in the deal and the basis for your expectations of success. Again, a good lawyer is essential to this process.

The financial projections and earnings claims made by the franchiser must be carefully examined by a professional certified public accountant. Your decision to enter into the franchise agreement is probably based on dreams of making large sums of money just as the master franchiser has done. However, check those books and records that the franchiser provides to sell you on the deal and assure yourself that the franchiser's biggest profits come from the product and not from selling franchises. Remember, get it in writing.

Another important business tactic is to talk informally with others who are franchisees in other areas including those who have franchises in areas close to your location and find out their experience with the franchiser. We mentioned that the franchiser is required by the FTC to give you names of other franchisers to contact, but it is frequently a good idea to seek out your own references.

Many people have done well operating franchises, but many have also had trouble, lost money, and soured on their franchises. If there was ever an instance to live by the advice of the Better Business Bureau—namely, investigate before you invest— this is it.

As the FTC says, "Many people dream of being an entrepreneur. By purchasing a franchise, you often can sell goods and services that have instant name recognition and can obtain training and ongoing support to help you succeed. But be cautious. Like any investment, purchasing a franchise is not a guarantee of success."

A franchise typically enables you, the investor or "franchisee," to operate a business. By paying a franchise fee, which may cost several thousand dollars, you are given a format or system developed by the company of the franchiser, the right to use the franchiser's name for a limited time, and assistance. The franchiser may help you find a location for your outlet, provide initial training and an operating manual, and advise you on management, marketing, or personnel. Some franchisers offer ongoing support such as monthly newsletters, a toll free 800 telephone number for technical assistance, and periodic workshops or seminars. However, you may be required to relinquish significant control over your business and take on serious contractual obligations with the franchiser. Here are the major components of a typical franchise that you and your attorney and accountant should clearly understand and carefully review.

THE COST

In exchange for using the franchiser's name and business system, you often are required to pay a variety of fees that may include:

- **Initial Franchise Fee and Expenses.** This is usually nonrefundable and often runs to several thousand dollars. You may also have to put up the money to rent or build and equip the business facility. Some franchisers also assess an extra "grand opening" fee to initially promote your outlet.

- **Continuing Royalties.** You typically will have to pay the franchiser a percentage of your gross income. Sometimes you have to pay such royalties even if you are not making a profit; you may technically be obligated to pay the royalty just for the use of the franchiser's name even if he does not perform under the contract as required. Avoid these pitfalls by hiring a knowledgeable lawyer at the outset of negotiation. Your royalty obligation should be tied to the franchiser doing what he promised and not limited just to the use of his name.

- **Joint Advertising.** You often have to pay into a joint advertising fund that is supposed to be used for national advertising as well as regional advertising. Some of this advertising may be to attract new franchisees and have nothing to do with promoting your business. This is something you should anticipate and try to avoid since it is advertising that doesn't directly benefit you.

CONTROLS

The franchiser normally will insist on a variety of controls over how you and the other franchisees conduct your business. This can be helpful because it ensures the integrity of the brand name, but it also can put a straight jacket on how your particular business outlet operates; you need to consider the implications of these restrictions. The franchiser will normally try to control:

- **The Location of Your Business.** This can be good and bad. It keeps other franchisees from overlapping and competing with you, provided they are operating under all the same controls as you, something which you and your lawyer have checked out prior to your purchasing the franchise. Of course, control of location may also deny you the site you think is best for your outlet.

- **Design and Standards.** Franchisers normally demand that you adhere to the design of the store, signs, and equipment that is their trademark. This is usually good for you. Some franchisers provide that their contractor will construct the facilities to the franchisers' standards and then turn the premises over to you. However, you are normally responsible for paying for the construction work.

- **Goods and Services.** The franchiser will almost always restrict what you are allowed to sell from your outlet, as well as dictate employee rules of conduct, uniforms, hours of operation, advertising, bookkeeping system, and much of how you run the place. In fact, many franchisers will insist on doing the bookkeeping using computer connections between your outlet and the franchiser's headquarters so that often the franchiser knows more about what's going on in "your" business than you do. This can be very sticky, and many accountants and attorneys urge against it. It is certainly something you want to review with your attorney and accountant because it puts you, in essence, in the role of having paid money to be an employee of the franchiser. Another sticky point that franchisers are often not quick to mention is that your contract may require you to buy all your equipment, uniforms, supplies, and merchandise from the franchiser at a price he sets. This is often a price higher than you can buy some of these things on your own. This is another point to review and negotiate with your advisors.

- **Sales Territory Limits.** Most franchisers will limit the territory in which its franchisees can operate so as to avoid competition among franchisees. This is beneficial to you when you are starting out and struggling to succeed, but bad when you are doing well and want to expand because the franchiser may demand a new franchise deal and further fees for expansion. If you think your venture will be a successful operation, you may want to attempt obtaining an option for expansion at the beginning of your negotiations when the franchiser is possibly more open to dealing. Of course, you must be careful to assure that your franchise contract doesn't allow the franchiser to reduce your initial territory.

LEASING BUSINESS PROPERTY

The lease you sign for your business locations is one of the most important early decisions you will make, and it will have an impact on your operations for as long as you are there. It can, if not analyzed carefully, cut deeply into your profits and cause you all kinds of trouble, so it needs to be considered very carefully.

FIGURING THE RENT

Usually rent for commercial property is quoted as so many dollars per square foot per year. However, this can be misleading and you need to analyze it very carefully. For example, how is the square footage of your space measured? You may measure it from the inside of the walls, but the landlord may measure it from the center of the walls or even the center of the public corridors on the other side of the walls. Also, what do you get for your rent? Is it only the right to occupy the space? Who pays utilities, janitorial services, taxes, cleaning of public areas and the outside of glass windows, insurance and security services? Is the rent level for the term of the lease? What circumstances can cause an automatic increase in your rent? What do you get for your rent in addition to the obvious, bare-walled space you will occupy? Do you get a number of exclusive parking spaces? Do you get space on outside walls or signs? Knowing what to ask for in a lease and knowing what to insist upon is essential for business success.

In addition to a flat rent per square foot per year, there are many other ways of charging rent. There might be a sliding scale with the rent moving up or down with changing circumstances or the passage of time. Also, the level of the rent might be tied to some index such as the consumer price index or the prime interest rate or your sales. Tying it to the tenant's sales is popular with retail stores, but it raises additional problems. Typically such a rental agreement might call for either a guaranteed minimum rent or a percentage of your sales, whichever is larger (landlord's advantage) or smaller (tenant's advantage), or it might call for a combination of the two. The key issue of such a percentage lease is defining what are your "sales." The landlord will want the rent based on your gross sales, before any of your costs are deducted; that is not in your best interests because it could mean higher rent when you may be selling your goods below cost. You will want a formula based on your net sales; again, definition becomes an issue. What is "net?" You will want net to be defined as the gross sales price minus all of your expenses except rent.

The advantage of a good net percentage lease is that it puts the landlord into business partnership with you because if you don't make money, he/she doesn't make money. This should encourage him/her to make it easier for you to make money by keeping the premises inviting, secure, clean, and accessible.

OPTIONS

Do you have important options that may be critical to your business in the future? For example, suppose your business thrives: Your ability to stay at that location could be critical for continued success. So, you'll want an option to renew the lease on the same or similar terms that binds the landlord, but doesn't bind you. That means you can renew the lease, but you are not obligated to do so.

You will also want options to terminate the lease ahead of schedule if something happens that jeopardizes your business, for example, if the landlord does something that hurts your business such as leasing to a competitor, ripping up the parking lot, not providing adequate security or sanitation, or not maintaining the attractiveness of the premises. Also, ideally, you should be able to terminate the lease ahead of schedule if one of your key partners dies or you were disabled or sued and a judgment was entered against you. Your supplier may go out of business or no longer be able to supply you with merchandise to sell. State or local governments may make your business illegal or hurt it by public works projects that make it impossible for customers to get to your business. Your lease agreement should protect you against these contingencies.

PROTECTION FROM COMPETITORS

Do you get exclusive rights to operate your business on the property and any other property the landlord owns within a certain radius of your business? For example, you don't want to open an ice-cream store and then find out that the landlord has also rented to a competing ice-cream store nearby, or to a store that is technically not an ice-cream store, but that sells ice cream anyhow.

AT HOME

Many women start businesses in their homes to save on rent and make it easier to care for dependent family members. If your business is clean, quiet, and non-disruptive to the neighbors, you will probably have few problems. However, most local government requires all businesses to have a license, and your community may not sanction home businesses. Thus, you will have additional expenses of renting a commercial space and getting a license. If you do operate out of your home be sure you have proper insurance for your employees and to cover accidents that may happen to customers who call on you. This, of course, raises another possible serious problem: If you have a personal injury or liability or other claim against you while you are operating your business out of your home, the insurance company may not pay the claim if it can show your business required a license from local or state government and you didn't have one. In other words, the insurance company may not have to pay a claim if it arises from the operation of an illegal business. If that situation should arise, you might be hit with a personal financial loss that breaks you. So, here again, it is wise to consult a good business attorney who can foresee and advise you on all the possibilities.

EMPLOYER TAX IDENTIFICATION NUMBER (EIN)

You will need an employer tax I.D. number before you open for business. This allows the federal government and most state governments to identify you for regulation and tax purposes and for record keeping of Social Security and Medicare payments, your income taxes, and your employees' income tax withholding. Obtain the form for application for your EIN (SS4) from any government office that has Internal Revenue Service forms. Mail it to the appropriate address shown on the form or fax it to (816) 926-7988. If you mail it, you may have to wait a month or two before receiving your EIN. Faxing it normally will get you a response within a day or two. Alternatively, you can get the number issued by phone by calling (816) 926-5999. Enter the number you are given over the phone on the SS4 form, mail it in, and you're ready to go.

INSURANCE

Here is a checklist of some of the kinds of insurance you may need. You don't necessarily need all of the types we have listed, and you should discuss your business plans with your insurance agent so he/she can advise you on what insurance is needed. In any event, coverages that you may want to have include:

- **Liability.** Protection against damages claimed by anyone, including employees, who have sustained injury on the premises or as a result of using a product or service provided by you.

- **Fire.** This is basic and under the "fire insurance" umbrella. Insurance companies often group a variety of risks under such an umbrella policy.

- **Medical.** This is a critical perquisite for most employees. It is costly and you must be familiar with the various options available to the employer, especially one with very few employees.

- **Business Interruption.** Business interruption insurance pays you a portion of the profits you lose during a time when your business is interrupted by fires, natural disasters, and so on.

- **Malpractice and Errors and Omissions.** This type of insurance covers you and your employees when someone else is harmed because of mistakes or omissions you have made.

- **Key or Partners Life Insurance.** If you are in a partnership and the success of the business is dependent on all the partners contributing their individual money, ideas, and effort, the partnership may purchase a life insurance policy on each of the partners so the death of one will not mean the death of your entire business.

- **Unemployment Insurance.** This is a mandatory payroll tax collected by the state and payed out to your employees who lose their jobs through no direct fault of their own. Each state has it's own rules for paying such out-of-work employees. As an employer, you need to know these laws; the amount you are required to pay into the unemployment insurance fund in many states is determined by your record of claims against you for unemployment benefits.

- **Disability Insurance.** Disability insurance is mandatory in most states: It provides a fund to pay employees, and, often employers, who are unable to work because of an on-the-job injury. Again, the percentage you have to pay, in many states, is determined by the number of claims against you and is, therefore, intended to encourage on-the-job safety.

TYPES OF BUSINESS ORGANIZATIONS

A key issue before you start your business is what legal form your operation will take. Traditionally, there are three forms: sole proprietor, partnership, and corporation. Over time, variations and permutations of these have been created, but the root structures are still these three. Permutations include the sole proprietorship, the general partnership, the limited partnership, the regular corporation, the Sub-Chapter S corporation, the close corporation, the professional corporation, and the limited liability company.

In determining which of these is most suitable for you and your business you may consider the following questions: First, what are your personal desires; second, what are the legal considerations; and, finally, what are the tax considerations. You will have to decide for yourself what your own personal considerations are. You may not be comfortable in a rigid corporation organization, or you may have a fear of the unlimited liabilities of a sole proprietorship. However, we suggest that you consult your attorney and accountant to understand what the legal and tax consequences are of each of the business forms.

Part Two

RELATIONSHIPS, COMMITMENT, AND OTHER MYTHS

CHAPTER 7

RELATIONSHIPS WITH YOUR SPOUSE

GETTING MARRIED

Your relationship with the person who will be your spouse generally begins with the typical meeting-dating-engagement scenario. However, marriage itself is becoming more complicated given our highly mobile population, the high divorce rate, and the growing interest by people of the same gender in some form of legally recognized "marriage."

Even the concept of a legal and traditional marriage can be different in different states and countries. The idea of two people joined in holy matrimony is, of course, a very private matter, but it is also something that the state takes an interest in and therefore, throughout the states there are laws governing the existence and validity of marriages. These laws are concerned with obligations of support between the spouses, property ownership, and protection and care of children of the union.

Still, getting married is easy and relatively inexpensive, indeed probably the least expensive legal exercise in which you will be involved. The law takes an interest in issues relating to the age of parties to be married, the health, and the mental capabilities of the parties who contemplate marriage. Therefore, most states require that each party be a minimum age, not married to someone else, not be closely related, and be mentally competent to enter into marriage. For protection, a blood test and sometimes a physical exam is required in some states, but no test for HIV is required. Some states won't issue a wedding license if either party has a venereal disease, but some will if both parties know about the disease.

As you can see, different states have different requirements for marriage, but remember, laws change all the time and requirements may already be different in your state, so check the specific requirements to obtain a marriage license with the governmental agency issuing the license in your community.

Most states require the bride and groom to be at least 18 if they are marrying without the approval of their parents or 16 or 17 if they have the okay of their parents. In most states, blood relatives closer than first or second cousins are not allowed to marry.

For many years in the United State, often in the part of the country known as frontier territory, common-law marriages were not unusual. This type of marriage occurred when a man and woman lived together as man-and-wife and acted as if they were husband and wife. Nowadays, this is much less common, and only a few states recognize it.

In addition to obtaining a license, generally couples recognize their marriage by a ceremony in which they pledge themselves to each other and announce the fact of their marital status to the world. The ceremony can be religious or civil (performed by a government official).

IMPORTANT LITTLE-KNOWN FACT

In some states, you are technically married when the wedding ceremony is completed. In other states, you are not technically married until you have had sexual intercourse after the ceremony.

Usually the law requires that a certificate be issued and *recorded* with the proper government bureau with the signature of at least one witness to make it official. In California, a couple may marry without a license if they have been living together. The event of their marriage is recorded in the public record after the event.

SAME SEX MARRIAGES

There has been some agitation in gay circles about recognizing same-sex marriages, but no state has done so as of 1997, and the Congress passed and the President signed specific laws prohibiting legalizing such marriages. Hawaii has come the closest in its consideration of legalizing same-sex marriages. However, there have been some communities that have recognized a domestic partnership, which applies to both same-sex couples living together and couples of different gender living together. The couple is required to register with a city office and declare that they are in a committed relationship. As such, the city permits them to share benefits of health plans, family leave programs, and other advantages that normally are shared by a married, heterosexual couple.

NAMES

Traditionally, women adopted the last name of their husband, but that is changing. A woman can retain her maiden name, adopt her husband's name, or use both names. The only legal requirement is that the name change is not done in a effort to deceive or defraud others.

PREMARITAL AND MARTIAL AGREEMENTS

In most other countries of the world, marriage is regarded in a more pragmatic way as a relationship between two people designed to fulfill mutual needs. A marriage contract signed before the consummation of the marriage is common in Europe, Latin America, Asia, and Africa. Yet, the romantic ideal in America is that marriage is forever and to insist on a premarital agreement is bad luck or displays a lack of commitment, faith, or love.

The American public has regarded with distaste rich men who require their prospective brides to sign premarital agreements as did Ari Onassis of Jackie and Donald Trump of Ivana. In the past, premarital or prenuptial agreements were the province of the older, wealthy man marrying the sweet, young, penniless thing and his desire to protect his property from her demands in the event of divorce. Such agreements were not favored by the courts which often found that the less wealthy spouse (and usually less sophisticated) was induced to sign the agreement through various devices including undue influence, duress, or threats of refusal to go through with the wedding, which in most cases was scheduled for the day the agreement was presented to the bride for her signature.

Premarital agreements have come a long way since that time. Because couples are marrying later, each may have had an opportunity to accumulate property prior to marriage, which they each may want to retain separately after marriage. A premarital agreement can accomplish that.

The attitude of the courts with regard to the enforcement of such agreements has changed. What is called The Uniform Premarital Agreement Law has been adopted in all 50 states, indicating the acceptance of the concept. Judges now look at the circumstances of execution of the agreement (for example, was the bride forced to sign it on the day of the wedding with the guests waiting in the chapel or some two or more weeks before?; is the non-wealthy spouse represented by a lawyer?; does the agreement fairly state what property each has that they wish to maintain as separate as well as the value thereof?) Still, courts will look at whether the terms of the agreement appear to be unconscionable. As people become more sophisticated and knowledgeable, their own responsibilities increase, and agreements that meet the test of the Uniform Premarital Agreement Law are now being upheld with great regularity.

We have scattered some recent rulings on various related subjects throughout this chapter just to give you the flavor of how different states deal with different aspects of relationships.

FAMILY LAW IN THE 50 STATES—Prenuptial Agreements
View of Recent Cases In Various States

- **Alabama.** The Coggins entered into a prenuptial agreement saying that neither would ever file for a divorce and, if either of them did, that person would pay the other spouse from $1,000 to $5,000 a week in damages. The court threw out the agreement saying it was unreasonable.

- **Nevada.** The Ficks signed a premarital agreement under which the bride-to-be waived any future alimony. The court ruled on appeal that the alimony waiver was invalid because engaged couples have a confidential, fiduciary relationship and he should have told her about his financial condition before she signed the agreement.

- **Florida.** The Osbornes had a prenuptial agreement saying the wife waived all rights to any property owned by the husband. The court awarded the home to the wife, but the appellate court reversed that saying she was entitled to nothing just as she agreed in the prenuptial agreement.

Interpretations of the law vary from state to state and from time to time. These views are only illustrations, and you should check with current rulings in your own state.

A premarital agreement can be a means of protection for a nonwealthy and nonworking spouse, too. After all, you don't have to sign the agreement. If you do sign, you should not have to give up your rights to accumulate community or joint property. You should bargain for a clause that provides for the creation of community property, despite the fact that your spouse intends to work at his separate business and maintain it as separate during the marriage. If it is unrealistic to expect that there will ever be any community property, you should bargain for a lump sum payment for each of the years of the marriage in the event of divorce. You should include within your premarital agreement obligations to provide for you in the event of your wealthy husband's death during the marriage. You should certainly provide for revising the agreement in the event that children are born as a result of the marriage.

The Uniform Premarital Agreement Law as adopted by most states allows for an agreement prior to marriage on the amount and duration of support in the event of divorce. In some jurisdictions an agreement limiting support on divorce is considered against public policy because it is thought to promote divorce. Therefore, in such jurisdictions such a clause in the agreement is invalid. Usually, however, such an offensive clause can be severed from the balance of the agreement in the event of divorce. And a clever lawyer can draft an agreement that poses a certain term and amount of support as an attractive alternative to seeking support from a court on divorce.

Prior to your wedding, discuss with a family law attorney the meaning of the premarital agreement and fashion it to meet your needs. You should do this in private without your prospective spouse. Do not be surprised if your prospective mate asks you to sign a premarital agreement. Just be prepared.

There are other not so obvious advantages to a premarital agreement. It will force you and your fiancee to sit down together and discuss what your life and marriage goals are. The two of you will have an opportunity to develop a clear understanding of who the other is and what each of you expects from the marriage. You may find in these discussions that your expectations are so different that the marriage is doomed to fail. Pay heed to these warnings as they arise.

FAMILY LAW IN THE 50 STATES—More Prenuptial Agreements
View of Recent Cases In Various States

- **Nevada.** In the case of *Sogg v. Nevada State Bank,* the court disallowed the prenuptial agreement because the husband did not reveal his net worth to his wife.

- **Texas.** In *Winger v. Pianka* an engaged couple signed a prenuptial agreement providing that each spouse's income after marriage would be that spouse's sole and separate property. The court upheld the agreement on appeal.

- **Wisconsin.** The Court of Appeals underscored that prenuptial agreements must contain a full disclosure of both parties assets. It is not enough that reference be made to other documents or information—a financial statement of both parties must be part of the prenuptial agreement.

- **Washington State.** It is all right, said the court in the *Foran* case, for a person to sign a financially unfair and one-sided prenuptial agreement, but only if the person fully understood how unfair the contract was.

Interpretations of the law vary from state to state and from time to time. These views are only illustrations, and you should check with current rulings in your own state.

GETTING A DIVORCE

The last thing you want to think about when you're getting married is about getting a divorce. However, the smart woman DOES think about the possibility of a divorce before she gets married and how to protect against it or, if divorce happens, what to do. Divorce, when it comes, is an equal opportunity mauler of money and emotions, and it is best to be prepared in the chance that it should happen to you. It's a good idea to know how to swim even if you never expect to be in a situation where you might drown.

To emphasize the point, note that even though being rich and famous can protect you from many things, it can't always protect you from a bad divorce. Too often women with power, money, and stature still are devastated in the divorce process. The point is if women with resources can be victimized by a divorce, imagine what can happen to you. Admittedly, some wealthy women have done well financially in their divorces. Soraya Khashoggi received $800 million in her divorce from international arms dealer Adnan Khashoggi; Anne Bass was awarded $200 million in her divorce from Sid Bass. The late Frances Lear concluded life with Norman Lear with $112 million, which she used to start *Lear's* magazine. And the $100 million Amy Irving took from the divorce with Steven Spielberg was not peanuts.

However, even these settlements have to be placed in context of the collective wealth of the family. For example, take the divorce between Patricia and John Kluge in Virginia several years ago; Kluge is one of the richest men in the world. The publicized story was that Pat Kluge got a settlement of a fine Virginia estate, Albemarle House, and $8 million. That is not much for a man worth over a billion dollars, but it is even less when you examine it closely. She did not get $8 million—only the annual interest on $8 million with the principle reverting to Kluge upon the occurrence of certain conditions. She also did not receive Albemarle House, but only the *use* of it if for some years. Both Albemarle House and the $8 million remain John's, and Pat only has the temporary use of them. Thus, for her lifetime, in a sense, she remains under the control of the man she has divorced.

How was this result possible? Apparently John Kluge is a decisive man who moved quickly to protect himself and his assets when his marriage was disintegrating. Mrs. Kluge should have done the same. While the Kluge divorce was front page material, both the press and most observers missed the key to the lopsided settlement: The minute John and Patricia separated, John jetted to Mexico and obtained a divorce, and the Virginia divorce, months later, was their *second* divorce. What is the point of that move by Kluge? While there is some question as to the legality of the Mexican divorce, it created an issue that would delay the inevitable. To settle the issue created by the potentially invalid Mexican divorce would have required court hearings and, after appeals, more court hearings to the point that the final divorce might be delayed several years. Long, drawn out court battles are something spouses generally want to avoid, either because the wealthy spouse can afford it and the other spouse cannot, or the stakes are too high, or perhaps the alternative offer is good enough to make the battle less appealing.

In giving advice to husbands involved in divorce the September 1991 issue of *M, Inc.* magazine noted, "While the wife may stand to get a sizable alimony and a healthy property settlement after the case is settled, for the time being she could very well be broke. A hardball approach to her desperate straits would be to threaten to hold out through a long divorce proceeding, even through appeals, without settling. Since the husband knows that he is unlikely to lose more than half of his holdings no matter how long the divorce takes and he will have use of his cash in the meantime, it is definitely to his advantage to hold out." Of course, the courts are there to protect against this unconscionable type of "stone-walling" and should be utilized immediately by a woman who finds herself in that position.

There are number of ways that the husband, particularly if he is the major income earner, can play hardball during a divorce. Most attorneys will advise husbands who believe their marriage is destined for divorce court, to file for the divorce as early as possible because each passing year may raise their earning potential and increase the value of the settlement he will have to pay. Generally, the key to a successful financial settlement is preparation. Some wage earners instruct their accountant to use a variety of innovative accounting devices to depress the value of the estate to be divided, create a new set of books, undervalue the property, or segregate the property to enable the husband to claim that the property was his before marriage. The wife can counter that tactic with experts of her own, but expert testimony is expensive and it adds to the cost of the divorce for both spouses and could price it out of her ability to pay. In that case, she may feel that she has to settle for less because she cannot afford to mount a sufficient counterattack. In most jurisdictions, however, the wealthy spouse will be ordered to advance funds to enable the wife to hire competent counsel and experts. Still, the spouse in control of the money can spend what he thinks is necessary. You will have to justify your need for funds to the court.

Levering a woman's emotions against her can also work to the husband's advantage. For example, threatening a knockdown, drag-out battle over custody of the children is draining emotionally and financially and a ploy that many husbands—even those who have no intention of taking the children—often use as a lever. Believe it or not, some husbands have introduced a younger girlfriend into the situation even when she is a ringer. Most wives regard this behavior with rage and act irrationally, which makes them appear foolish to the court and, sometimes, to their own attorney. Such behavior is not helpful to their case, in any event.

As women begin to earn better salaries, the tables may be turned. TV's Joan Lunden of *Good Morning, America,* certainly was not happy about being liberated when she was ordered to pay her estranged househusband, Michael Krauss, $18,000 a month in temporary alimony. Elizabeth Taylor had to pay her ex $5,000 a month maintenance while their divorce was pending.

The objective here is to level the playing field and to help you avoid the costly and painful pitfalls common in contemporary divorce. Older women who have invested much of their lives, energies, and souls in a long marriage too frequently are taken advantage of and destroyed emotionally and financially by a divorce. This devastation may be due to the enormous resistance of some women to approach their life situation realistically. Some are insecure and lack the determination and know-how to obtain a fair shake in the divorce. The selection of a good family law attorney is critical in all divorces.

When it becomes clear that divorce is unavoidable, you need to be prepared to play one of the most vicious, unfair, hardball games in our American culture. Your preparation and ultimate success is critical not only for yourself, but also for your children and will dictate the way the rest of your life will be lived.

To understand the problem of women who enter divorce unprepared and unprotected, you need only contemplate what has happened to women who are married to powerful and wealthy men and who are not prepared to face and

NOTE

Divorces often take longer than you anticipate, and sustaining yourself during the divorce proceedings may be difficult. However, take heart that your divorce will not take as long as that of C.B. and Marcella Schetter of Broward County Florida which was originally filed when Lyndon Johnson was President in December 1966 and was finally settled May 19, 1993—over 26 years later. The case lasted through two judges, several attorneys, and C.B. Schetter who died in 1986.

meet the realities of the dissolution of their marriage. Johnny Carson, one of the richest men in Hollywood, has had several wives. The last one he divorced received a generous settlement that will provide her with a lifetime of comfortable living while Johnny's first wife, according to press reports, today lives in poverty. Jack Kent Cooke divorced his first wife and gave her what was then the largest settlement in the history (it was even listed in the *Guinness Book of Records*.) The last woman Cooke divorced, Marlene Cooke, bore him a daughter but received virtually nothing in the divorce and had to sue Cooke to obtain support for their child. Why would one of the richest men in the world be unwilling to support his own child? Those who know Jack Kent Cooke will tell you the issue is not money but rather control. Many men continue to control their former wife's destiny long after divorce by controlling her purse strings and by limiting her right to relocate when their children are in her custody. Your best protection is to anticipate these issues and prepare for them.

THINK ABOUT DIVORCE BEFORE YOU MARRY

While this heading may sound somewhat cynical, prepare yourself for whatever eventuality may occur in your marriage and, indeed, in your life long before you marry and certainly long before you find yourself in the midst of a divorce or the dissolution of your marriage. Don't wait until the first signs of deterioration of your relationship to think about the possibility that you will be on your own without the comfort and security of a life long partner. It was just one generation back when women married young, raised families, provided a home for their working spouses, and did volunteer work. Times have changed, and whether it is for better or worse, the job market has opened to women. Over 50% of the work force now is composed of women.

With the opening of opportunities for women in the workplace have come responsibilities that are not always welcome. The stay-at-home wife and mother appears to be the exception now. With this change in our social and family structure, we have experienced a phenomenon: Women, including single parent women with small children, are expected to work and to support themselves. Financial independence is an important and worthwhile goal. Unfortunately, the pay scale for women continues to lag far behind that of men in the majority of middle income jobs.

Your challenge is to plan ahead for making your own way in the world. You may be a high school graduate, a college graduate, or neither. But you must look to yourself for your own support and satisfaction in life. Gone are the days when a young woman went from her father's home to her husband's home and there lived happily ever after. This fantasy dooms a young woman to victimization in love and in life.

The traditional view that marriage will provide economic security and support for life is unique to the American view of marriage. Our thesis is that security comes from the knowledge that, regardless of your marital status, you and you alone are capable of supporting yourself without reliance on the contributions of another or on an order of court that may be disobeyed before the ink is dry on the paper. We are not recommending that each bride delay her wedding until she has a Ph.D. in business. The development of your own self-confidence begins early in life; it should be nourished and cherished by you, and should be part of your preparation for your own daughter. Preparation begins in high school by setting academic goals and doing your best to achieve them, by taking classes that are less traditional for girls, and by never being afraid to follow the different path or create your own style!

Women and men are delaying their entry into marriage these days. Use that extra time between the end of your formal education and your marriage to establish yourself. While it is difficult to start out in the workplace at any time, it is easier to begin at age 20 or 21 than at age 45 or 50. Begin your career with a purpose, and do not allow yourself to make your career secondary to your search for a husband.

Those women in their 40s, 50s, and 60s who go through a divorce are shocked when they find how ill-prepared they are for life on their own. This is a situation which you must work to avoid. And avoidance will come naturally if you are prepared. That is not to say that you are not justified in looking forward to marriage, children, and life with a loving husband. Those goals have not changed despite the professional demands placed on women. But those goals can be met in a more leisurely manner with some attention paid to the ultimate goal—that of taking care of yourself and knowing that no matter what happens, you will always be able to take care of yourself.

After the wedding you must continue to remain independent and knowledgeable. You are the one who should be in charge of the family finances even though you are staying home with the children. Don't for a minute think you don't have time to do this. Do it. In most instances a hardworking spouse will be grateful for your interest and welcome your work on family finances. Be involved from the beginning. If you have not been involved, you will be at the mercy of others who may not know you or your husband or your financial picture.

If your husband will not allow your participation which, in itself, is a bad sign, do what you can with your own finances. Maintain accurate accounts so you can show what the lifestyle of the family is during the time of marriage in the event that you are confronted with divorce. Maintain your own financial independence. Keep your own assets separate. Do not put your husband's name on your separate real property just because some lending institution says you must. If you are compelled to do so, obtain a quitclaim deed concurrently with the execution of the grant deed. Always maintain your separate charge accounts so that you have credit in the event of divorce.

Avoid signing on to the myths of marriage like the Cinderella Myth; that being married will relieve the frustration, pain, and struggle in your life. The truth is that life is always full of problems, and marriage brings its own set of problems including those of your new spouse. The Cinderella Myth lulls a woman into thinking that love and marriage is forever (and we hope it is) and that she never need trouble herself about family finances, her husband's business, or keeping understandable financial records. This is a dangerous attitude, and if divorce occurs, as it does in almost 50% of marriages, the ignorant spouse is at a terrific disadvantage.

Knowledge is Power—this concept central to winning in war is a maxim equally applicable to the war of divorce. Know the financial facts of your marriage. Do not allow yourself to be the victim in divorce.

Your idyllic marriage will change from the day you say "I do." The relationship between spouses never remains the same as on the wedding day. Even if there is never a divorce, people change and grow. Be sure you are growing with the marriage.

FAMILY LAW IN THE 50 STATES—Cohabitation Agreements
View of Recent Cases In Various States

- **North Dakota.** In *Kohler v. Flynn,* the court ruled that live-ins are not required to share their property with each other unless they have an agreement in writing.

- **Nevada.** The Nevada courts in *Western States Construction v. Michoff* ruled that a couple living together for nine years established a contract for equal division of property.

- **Georgia.** Crooke and Gilden were lesbian lovers who had an agreement to live together, but when they had a fight and Crooke tried to sue Gilden under the contract, the trial court said the contract was illegal because the consideration for making the contract was an illegal and immoral relationship. The Supreme Court overturned that trial court ruling saying nothing in the co-habitation contract required either party to do anything illegal.

Interpretations of the law vary from state to state and from time to time. These views are only illustrations and you should check with current rulings in your own state.

HOW TO TELL IF YOUR MARRIAGE IS IN TROUBLE

If love is blind, that blindness sometimes carries over into your marriage. The curious thing about many divorces is that often the spouses miss or ignore the telltale signs. To the unwary wife or husband, the divorce sometimes comes like a bolt of lightning out of the blue. Yet, to outsiders, the coming divorce is often very obvious.

It is interesting that most divorces occur for the same reason that most marriages occur. Most women, according to contemporary studies, marry for the emotional connection between themselves and the man in their life. When they think they have made an emotional connection with an acceptable man, women tend to marry. When they find that the emotional connection is broken, most women divorce. Obviously, each person marries for various and different reasons including security, desire for children, pressures from their peers or family. Still, most surveys confirm women are more likely to marry for love and emotional stability, and when they are in a marriage that doesn't provide those or when marriage becomes a lonely life of isolation and abuse from the partner or a combination of both, divorce becomes a serious option.

TWO MYTHS ABOUT MARRIAGE AND DIVORCE

There are two great myths about marriage and divorce that, unfortunately, load us with shame and guilt when we fail.

The first myth is that it wasn't like this in the "olden days." Our grandparents married for life; divorce was unthinkable. While it is true that earlier generations stigmatized divorce, sociologist William J. Goode, formerly on the faculty of Stanford and Harvard universities, says the perception of grandparents' marriages being better than our own is classic nostalgia for the perceived easier and simpler times of the past. In our view, that notion happens to be quite wrong or, at least, inconclusive. Marriages were just as unhappy in those "olden days" as they are now, but people could not divorce easily and remained trapped in their misery. There is no more sense in doing that today than there is in refusing modern medical treatment that was not available to our grandparents.

We also need to remember that life expectancy was significantly shorter in days gone by and, astonishingly, has almost doubled in this century. In previous centuries most people didn't live beyond what we now consider to be middle age. This was so true that, for example, menopause was not a major event in most women's lives because they never became old enough to reach that stage. In days gone by, people married, had children, and, by the time the children were grown and off to school, the husband and wife had but a few years left to live; divorce, therefore, was impractical.

The second myth is that the high divorce rate—roughly one out of two marriages ends in divorce—is something peculiar to the United States. Dr. Goode makes the point that there is a high divorce rate in almost all industrialized countries. This may be because women are less dependent on men for financial security in such countries and economically more able to support themselves outside of marriage. Modern times have brought a liberalization of sexual mores and greater opportunities for women to live on their own without suffering the label of "old maid."

In Dr. Goode's study of more than 30 countries he notes a significant rise in divorce among all industrialized countries including those with strong Catholic traditions such as Italy, France, and Spain. Goode believes we need to recognize that divorce is a natural part of our culture and social life and adjust to it to make it less painful. As a mark of our changing social culture, comedian Rita Rudner says that the first question she asks when she starts dating a man is whether he is the kind of person she wants her children to visit on weekends.

The causes of severance of the loving link between husband and wife run the gamut. Modern times have brought new sources of friction and distress among spouses, including a husband's resentment of his wife's successful career coupled with her freedom to do nontraditional things with her life. Economic recession exacerbates the pressures on marriages; many companies are "downsizing" and laying off longtime workers, middle-aged and middle-class men who have always had a job and supported themselves and their families. These men are not just being temporarily laid off by IBM, AT&T, Xerox, and Bank of America; their jobs are permanently gone. If the husband has had a long career providing financial security and stature and, suddenly, all that disappears, so does his self-esteem. Often the male responds to such a situation by withdrawing into drug or alcohol abuse, distancing himself from his wife through emotional and physical abuse, absenting himself from the home, or remaining in the house engrossed in himself, with the silences between him and other family members becoming long and frequent. Substance abuse is a major contributor to divorce, but it is only the symptom of the deeper alienation, resentment, and fear the spouses have developed and which they cannot or will not work through together.

A keen barometer of a marriage in trouble is sex or lack thereof. In one survey 72% of the women reported that sexual incompatibility was an important cause of their divorce. Among younger women, there was a tendency to lose interest sexually in the husband first, and, among older women, the reverse tended to be true. The loss of sexual compatibility ranges from mismatched desires on frequency to type of sex. The loss of this emotional connection often leads to alienation and withdrawal, to loss of passion, and possibly to infidelity. A note on the modern marriage is that, among the higher income brackets, more wives seek refuge in extra-martial affairs than do women in lower income brackets.

Another fascinating aspect about divorce (and marriage) is that many women know they are in the wrong marriage very early in the game. In one survey, 54% of divorced women said they knew it wasn't going to work from the first year. However—and this is a critical point for us to understand—although the wives knew the marriages were in trouble, most women move slowly to do something about it. The average woman in this circumstance does not act until the marriage is four years old. And, the average separation lasts up to two years before divorce is finally initiated.

TWO MORE PRE-WEDDING MYTHS ABOUT MARRIAGE

There are other well-known myths that serve to undermine the marriage even before the wedding. According to Jacqueline Cook, University of Oklahoma, marriage and family therapist, other great myths about marriage exist BEFORE the wedding that often lead to divorce after marriage:

The first is that the other person can be changed or molded significantly to make them into the perfect spouse. "Men and woman are constantly surprised," says Cook, "that they are unable to change their spouse's 'undesirable' habits after marriage. People still enter marriage believing that any annoying habits or patterns their partner has will disappear after the marriage, or that they can mold their partner to fit their own design." A variation of this is that you will become accustomed to those habits of your partner that you don't like, and there will no longer be an issue about his annoying habits. Just the opposite is true. Those little annoying traits become major irritants.

The second myth, according to Cook, is that the birth of a child will bring the parents together and rescue a floundering marriage. This also is rarely accurate, and when the unreality of these two myths comes home to the married couple, divorce looks like the only option.

WHAT ARE YOUR ALTERNATIVES?

When you finally decide that your marriage is dead, you have two basic alternatives: stay or leave.

STAY

There are many reasons you may decide to stay in the marriage; the most common reasons are:

- **Money.** You are afraid that you will be forced into a less secure and less comfortable life style. In fact, that is more often true than not. The standard of living for women tends to drop after a divorce. The reasons: There is not enough money to go around upon divorce to support two homes, and the newly divorced woman has not prepared herself for the reality of life, which is that she must rely on herself to provide her own lifestyle. She may not have received a fair settlement with which she can be comfortable.

- **Loneliness.** It isn't pleasant for people to be alone, and they would rather have some company than no company at all. Some of us are unable to be content alone with ourselves. In fact, the problem may be that you are not comfortable with yourself, and you require the validation of a man to prove that you are worthy. How many women do you know who need to validate themselves through a man? Who need to prove they are attractive enough to snag and keep a husband? With these women, their problem is their image of themselves. Neither marriage nor divorce will resolve this lack of confidence.

- **Children.** Worrying about how the divorce will affect the children is a major reason that women stay in a marriage; often women are willing to endure severe hardship to hold the household together for the sake of the children.

- **Hope.** Some women cling to the hope that the marriage will ultimately work out because they still love their husbands (or think they do) and hope he will change into a different man who will make their marriage work. Too often this is more hope than reality. It is truly a source of bewilderment as to why women marry and stay with men who are different than the men they wanted to marry (although usually not different than the man they did marry).

- **Pregnancy.** If you have become pregnant, of course, you feel more vulnerable. The problems of financial security and loneliness are even more difficult to face. That does not mean that divorce is not an alternative.

- **Outside Pressure.** Sometimes there is no internal glue holding the marriage together, but only pressure from outside from family, friends, or church to hold the marriage together.

- **Fear.** Another reason women stay in an unhappy marriage is that they fear starting over again with the dating game with a different man. Or, they may enjoy some aspects of marriage (sex or stature in the community or lifestyle) and are reluctant to give up these goodies.

Given all these reasons for staying in an unhappy marriage, it is interesting to note that the greatest single regret harbored by most divorced women is that they didn't divorce sooner. Divorce opened a door to new freedom and confidence and, usually, new and better relationships.

If you do stay in your dormant marriage, you are certain to have to cope with emotional problems. How you personally cope with the situation depends on your own emotional stability and will vary with everyone's personality. Whether you live separate lives and endure the time you are together, or you live in an armed camp with constant conflict is primarily an emotional choice. However, there may be economic consequences of your decision to lead separate lives. If you continue to be legally married, but emotionally divorced, both of you are entitled to share the combined income and assets of the marriage. You should act to protect yourself legally to make sure your husband isn't hiding income or assets from you, for he may be preparing for what he sees as the ultimate eventuality: divorce. If you are actually separated, in some jurisdictions, the wage earner's salary is separate property. You should check with an attorney familiar with the law in your area to protect your rights.

LEAVE

If you decide to leave the relationship, there are several alternatives including simply walking out, annulment, a legal separation, and divorce. Most of our attention will be on obtaining a divorce because that is the most common choice. However, there are legal consequences arising from each of the other alternatives.

Walking Out

Sometimes just walking out the door and not turning back seems appealing. It is neat. It is clean. It is quick. It is also stupid and may carry adverse consequences to you. Even so, enough people do it to mention it here.

In some jurisdictions you will be viewed as deserting the marriage, which puts you in a weak position under the law. You are viewed as having abandoned the marriage and, in the process, abandoned all legal claims to your property and other legal rights. The law varies from state to state, but to prove abandonment, a period of time is required before the law considers the marriage dissolved. This can vary from a few months to a number of years. The legal effect of your walking out of a marriage should be understood and carefully considered before you take that route.

Annulment

Annulment means that the marriage never legally existed, and in some states there may be nothing to settle. Most states have a set of circumstances under which an annulment will be granted. The usual causes are:

- Marriage of blood relatives of close degree
- Bigamy
- Insanity
- Legal incapacity (usually, too young)
- Duress
- Fraud
- Concealed felony conviction, addiction, or pregnancy
- Impotency

Annulment is unlike a divorce in that you petition the court to set aside the marriage as if it never happened. However, assets acquired during a marriage that is annulled will be equitably divided.

Separation

Legal separation is a divorce from the bed and board of your spouse and involves separate households and separate maintenance. If done properly with a written agreement, the court divides property and orders support, but the couple legally remains married. Spouses opt for a legal separation instead of divorce for a variety of reasons including religious affiliation or tax advantages. Senior citizens sometimes do so for financial security to take advantage of social security or a pension. Sometimes it is done as a prelude to divorce or to make the steps toward the ultimate divorce easier. We're told that television talk show host, Tom Snyder and his wife were legally separated for years to protect financial interests they owned jointly.

Legal separation is common when you and your husband want to maintain some of the advantages of the marriage without having to share the same bed. There are other reasons for a legal separation such as social stature or money, but the separation contract must clearly spell out the rights and obligations between the two of you to assure your protection and fair treatment. Legal separation also carries hazards you must be aware of to protect yourself from the irresponsible behavior of your husband. For example, you want agreements restraining his squandering the marital property half of which, under most circumstances is yours. For instance, his using your half of the property of the marriage to entertain and support an extramarital affair is not a recommended method of protecting your property.

Some advantages of legal separation are:

- It provides a cooling off period during which both parties have a chance to think over what they are doing and, possibly, to reconcile.

- It helps husband and wife to move into the mental and emotional mind-set of being apart and, possibly, divorced. It may ease the parties into the final resolution of their relationship.

- The legal and economic benefits of being married continue such as health insurance, pensions, inheritance, and a stronger credit rating.

- It is usually quicker and easier to obtain an order for a legal separation than a divorce. The benefits of a divorce such as separate homes and freedom from the strain of an unhappy relationship are realized much more quickly. If both parties want a legal separation, it is easier to obtain in some jurisdictions where it is necessary to meet residence requirements in order to file for divorce.

Some disadvantages of separation are:

- If the marriage is doomed, it is possible that the separation will simply prolong the process, which, in turn, may make it that much more painful. Depending on the law in your state, it could also be financially more expensive if you go on to obtain a divorce later because there may be some duplication of attorney fees and court costs.

- It sometimes gives the edge to the husband with the job because the non-working wife will not have the economic benefits of living together.

- Because you are still technically married, you might be held responsible for the debts or actions of your husband. The separation agreement can protect against that, but a third-party creditor may sue you claiming you are responsible for your husband's credit card debts. You will have the expense of defending yourself. Also, you and your husband may still be treated as a married couple for purposes of pensions, life insurance, and other contractual obligations. In order to avoid much of this hassle, you need a carefully drawn separation agreement that is approved by the court. If you reach this point, it is a simple matter to change the legal separation to a divorce when the time comes, as it almost always does.

Divorce

This is, unfortunately, the most frequently chosen alternative. It is complicated; complicated because people are complicated. Usually, divorcing couples are as consumed by the emotions of the divorce as they were consumed by the emotions of the marriage when they were married. What's missing in most divorces is the love and mutual respect once cherished by the parties. Somebody once correctly said that marriage is about love and divorce is about money; quite an accurate statement.

When you decide to move ahead with a divorce, you should be as confident as you can that you understand what is ahead for you. In fact, you probably should give your divorce more thought then you gave your wedding. For a fast reality check, understand that divorce is:

- A *Big* Decision

- An *Expensive* Process

- An *Emotional* Roller Coaster

Also bear in mind that you will have fewer assets than you share with your husband, and your standard of living will probably be lower.

Given that divorce is often better than living in the marriage, if you go ahead, your objectives should be to obtain the best property settlement possible in an expeditious and amicable manner so you can begin your new life as soon as reasonably possible.

Once you have decided your marriage is over, the business of protecting yourself is just beginning. (Let's hope you have begun the job of protecting yourself before that.) Here we discuss how you can protect yourself mentally and emotionally, as well as legally, so that you come out a winner and not a basket case.

Your single most important goal is protection for yourself. You may have to protect yourself physically from an abusive husband, you will have to protect yourself emotionally because uncoupling the relationship will be traumatic, and, you definitely will have to protect yourself financially to ensure that what you take away from the marriage is your fair share.

Earlier, we talked about how to find and engage a good attorney. Everything we said earlier about finding and hiring a good attorney applies, but this section deals with some of the particulars you should understand about that painful process known as divorce and how you can be sure you get a fair deal. Your choice of a divorce lawyer could mean the difference between winning and being eaten alive.

Understand clearly at the beginning that the wife is very often at a disadvantage in a divorce proceeding. She is generally at a disadvantage financially, emotionally, mentally, and socially. Of course, you may think about not getting a lawyer at all. This is invariably a bad decision.

Here are some pointers about what your divorce lawyer should and should not be. *Your Divorce Lawyer Should Not Be:*

1. **In Conflict with Your Interests.** You and your husband MUST NOT share one lawyer. A friend or family business lawyer may offer to represent both you and your husband in a "friendly" divorce. First, God has not yet created a "friendly" divorce. Second, one of you may become the lawyer's enemy before the divorce is over. Third, a husband and a wife with the same lawyer are a husband and a wife with no lawyer.

2. **Paternalistic or Sexist.** It is important that you know your attorney's personal view toward divorce. A good divorce lawyer should be gender neutral and regard divorce as an unpleasant but necessary part of many people's lives.

3. **A Dazzler.** A good divorce attorney won't try to dazzle you with legal jargon, fancy footwork, and unrealistic promises leaving you confused as to what has to be done, what it will cost, or what's involved for you. You are interested in competence, not show-boating or publicity hype.

4. **An Avenger.** The avenger is passionate and dedicated to destroying the opposing party no matter what it costs you both financially and emotionally. This may appeal to you emotionally because you are in pain, but revenge in litigation is an expensive luxury.

Handling the preliminary interview. Take the time and effort and invest the money to interview several prospective attorneys before you decide who can best represent you. Some attorneys will provide an initial consultation without charge and others will charge at a reduced rate. In either case, it is well worth it. You would do the same in selecting a housekeeper or day care for your children or choosing a doctor. Your interview with each attorney is protected by the attorney-client confidentiality safeguards. There are some important things you need to ask a lawyer before you hire him or her. Some of the quesions include:

1. How much of the lawyer's practice is in family law?

2. Who will be handling your case?

3. While it is extremely difficult for a family law lawyer to estimate fees at the outset of a case, you should know in detail how you will be billed. Besides the cost of your attorney ask the lawyer what she estimates the total charges will be and what is included.

4. What is his/her judgment of the outcome of your case?

5. Will she go to court if it can't be settled?

6. What are alternative arrangements for payment?

7. What does the lawyer expect from you?

8. What kind of interim arrangements can be expected for that period between filing for divorce or separation and the final decree?

There are some certain things a lawyer will be looking for during the initial interview. Some of those things are:

1. **Signs You Will Be a Difficult Client.** Do you appear to be an argumentative, complaining, self-pitying client who will require a lot of hand-holding?

2. **Signs You Want Vengeance Most of All.** Most smart divorce lawyers don't want a client whose main goal is vengeance. Remember: Marriage is about love. Divorce is about money. Period.

3. **Perennial Divorce Lawyer Shopper.** We urge you to shop around for a good attorney and pick one that fits you. The extreme of this is the woman who has been shopping around for months and is simply going from attorney to attorney to pour out her grieving heart over the cretin to whom she is married.

There are certain things a lawyer needs to know about your case in the interview. Some of those things include:

1. Why you want a divorce and can the marriage be saved

2. Personal data of the parties

3. Marriage statistics: date, place, prenuptial agreements, post-nuptial agreements

4. Financial details

5. Other parties involved: children, relatives, pets

6. Cause of breakup: personal, emotional, financial, mental, physical, third parties

7. Outcome sought—what are your goals?

8. Is there a chance for reconciliation?

You need to be careful to avoid common pitfall and mistakes when choosing a lawyer. Some things to look out for are:

1. **Referral by Interested Parties.** Do not use an attorney referred to you by your husband or his friends or associates. Get your own.

2. **Both Husband and Wife Using Same Attorney.** Don't do it.

3. **Enticement by Advertising, Not Ability.** You are hiring an attorney, not a party clown.

4. **The Do-It-Yourself Kit.** There are do-it-yourself divorce kits, and most just get you into trouble and run up your legal bills when you have to hire an attorney to unscramble the mess.

5. **Picking a Lawyer on the Basis of Price.** The best lawyer for you is not necessarily the most expensive, nor is the least expensive lawyer necessarily the biggest bargain. The most expensive professional you can hire—doctor, lawyer, dentist—is the one that doesn't do what she is hired to do.

6. **Do Not Hire on the Basis of His/Her Physical Attractiveness.** Remember your state of mind and heart when you set out to hire a lawyer. You may very well feel you are a scorned, abused, deserted woman. Choose based on ability, not physical attractiveness, because too often Mr. Stud turns out to be Mr. Dud in the courtroom.

Your lawyer will do many things for you, but there are things that he or she can't do for you. The following lists show some of the things a lawyer can and can't do.

He/She Will Usually:

1. Do the legal work including filing for divorce or dissolution of marriage, advising you on the legal aspect of the case, hiring experts as necessary, and providing you with information to assist you in making the relevant decisions

2. Help you keep on track emotionally

3. Help you find the assets of the marriage

4. Craft a settlement if that's possible

5. Try in court matters that can't be settled

He/She Won't Usually:

1. Arrange for the murder or maiming of your husband

2. Do all your work for you

3. Be able to obey court orders for you

4. Resolve irrational emotional problems

Your attorney is your champion, and both of you must trust each other. If a barracuda represents your husband, don't ask your attorney to behave in the same way. Keep everything open and clear between the two of you. If you don't like something, tell him/her about it right away.

It is unusual, but sometimes you have picked both the wrong husband and the wrong divorce attorney. If you decide on firing your attorney, do it quickly and decisively and move on with what you need to do. Key Point: Have the new lawyer lined up before you fire the old lawyer.

There is some special information needed in divorce cases, and some of the special information you will want to collect and preserve for your attorney includes:

1. **Personal Mail.** Your personal mail and the extent to which you have access to your husband's mail may be helpful to your attorney. For example, you may have letters available that demonstrate your husband's intentions regarding division of the family property or his suitability for custody. There are other forms of communication or indications of mind set and attitude such as photographs, video, or audio tapes that you should collect. Watch for financial information that comes in the mail. Make your own copies which you should give immediately to your attorney.

2. **Receipts.** Credit card slips and other receipts showing who spent what, where, and when can be helpful as evidence of misuse of community funds to maintain an extra-marital relationship and as evidence of a lifestyle unsuitable for caring for children. Such documents also will establish the family lifestyle, which will to show the level of spending for joint expenses. This can be extremely

TEN IMPORTANT POINTS TO REMEMBER

1. You will probably not get all you want and neither will he.

2. Again, marriage is about love. Divorce is about money.

3. She who seeks vengeance should dig two graves—one for her victim and one for herself.

4. Custody of the children is no longer a sure thing for mothers.

5. Do not have sex with your divorce lawyer. Don't pay couch fees.

6. Learn and understand the language of law and accounting.

7. Your lawyer is your lawyer, not your therapist, your plumber, your best friend, your doctor, or your car mechanic. He/she is a professional as a lawyer and an amateur at all those other things.

8. It is okay to follow your gut feeling about your lawyer. You must be comfortable with him/her.

9. Tell your lawyer you want the truth about your case at all times and not just the warm and fuzzy news.

10. In the final analysis, you are the person who must make the decisions.

useful information to your attorney as a tool in negotiations.

3. **Canceled Checks and Bank Statements.** Canceled checks are also a good barometer of community lifestyle and the spending habits of both parties. An inordinate number of cash withdrawals or cash checks deserves investigation. Secure the bank statements to establish cash flow and as a means of assuring that you have all the canceled checks.

4. **Telephone, Audio, or Video Recordings.** Telephone conversations, statements made and recorded on audio or video tape or telephone answering machines can be very valuable if in these conversations the other party agrees to terms of settlement or confesses guilt in a jurisdiction where that is necessary for a divorce. Sometimes spouses will agree in telephone calls to a

DIVORCE SECRETS THEY DON'T TELL YOU ABOUT IN SCHOOL

- The cost of the divorce comes out of the estate that you and your husband have. The more combative you both are, the less you'll get.

- In the real world, most cases are settled by negotiation—not Perry Mason–style trials. Between a good negotiator or a hot-shot trial lawyer, pick the good negotiator.

- Believe it or not, it is also in your best interest that your husband get a competent attorney.

- Have the details of your relationship with your lawyer in writing.

schedule for visitation or to allow the children to be taken out of the county or state in which they are living—an agreement that they later disavow. A recording can be invaluable in these situations.

In most states it is illegal to tape record a telephone conversation either without the express permission of the other party or without the recording party's ability to prove that she informed the other party of the tape recording, and they continued to talk. Thus, it is important that you state on the record that you are recording before beginning the taping.

You may wish to allow your answering machine to screen your calls. You will be surprised at the wealth of information that your spouse will leave on your answering machine. Do not make the same mistake yourself. Be wary of voice activated tape recorders anywhere near your telephone. Your husband can simply leave one of these in the room where you use the telephone. It is turned on and off simply by the sound of your voice. He can retrieve it later and hear what you said on the telephone to your friends, family, and your lawyer.

5. **Records of Medications.** Drug prescriptions or records of other medications or treatment could suggest that the other spouse is not in any condition to have custody of children. Be aware of what drugs your spouse is using and understand that he will be looking for the same information to use against you.

6. **Calendars and Daily Diaries.** These can reveal personal lifestyle patterns and possible unsuitability to have custody of the children. Such diaries may show that one spouse was the primary care provider for the children most of the time, information which can affect custody decisions.

7. **Telephone Records.** Records of telephone calls can also be important to your attorney to establish contacts, lifestyles, and interests that can be used to trace family assets and the use thereof or to establish an unstable child care situation.

Hot information is the information that either your husband or you or both of you don't want anybody to know about; information that can explode the divorce settlement sky high if it gets out. This is information that is severely damaging to either side in its claim for money or custody.

For example, records of wrongdoing or suspected wrongdoing such as arrest records, prison records, criminal or civil trials, commitments to mental institutions, or tax evasion may be quite damaging to one or both of you. These could all have a decisive impact on financial and custody questions.

In diaries, either you or your husband may have kept detailed accounts of very private activities or thoughts that, if discovered, could be damaging to either side. In addition, many couples take sexually intimate or incriminating photographs of each other singly or together.

KEY POINT: SECURE INFORMATION IN SAFE PLACE

All these documents and information are important to your case, and you should not only gather them, but you should immediately put them in a safe place beyond the reach of your husband. Get a safe-deposit box or some other safe depository. Don't leave important documents with relatives or friends who may turn against you. If you have the time, it is smart to make copies of everything and put the copies in a secure place. Excessive precautions? No. The outcome of your divorce depends on your having control of this information.

Threats to disclose these photographs could have a deleterious effect on the outcome of the divorce from the perspective of the compromised spouse.

In the tough contest of divorce it is to your advantage to secure this hot material from your husband safely in your possession and control. Likewise, any such material that compromises you such as diaries, tapes, photos—all copies—should be secured by you and either destroyed or safely hidden. In most cases, these materials will have little relevance, but they can be used to embarrass the other party and force settlement.

In any case, it is important that your attorney know about the existence of such material whether or not you allow him/her to read, see, or hear it. If it exists, tell your attorney; otherwise he/she may be blindsided in negotiations and be unprepared to protect you.

What You Need to Do Before Your Divorce Is Filed

The importance of planning ahead for a successful divorce is, in some peculiar ways, more important than all the advance planning that often goes into a wedding. However, the importance of planning a divorce is underscored by financial concerns, as we have said before.

Keep your actions secret. Keeping your actions secret may make or break your case, so follow your lawyer's advice; generally it is best to keep your meetings with your attorney confidential until you are ready to make a move. Don't tell him, the children, your mother, anybody, until you are ready. There are good reasons for this:

1. **You May Change Your Mind.** One obvious reason is that you may change your mind and decide that you don't want a divorce.

2. **Prevent Husband's Preemptive Counterstrikes.** Your husband may make a preemptive strike that harms your interests. For example, he might cancel charge accounts, strip all the money out of bank accounts, move to hide assets, seize and conceal important family assets, and even attempt to leave with the children.

3. **Prevent Physical or Sexual Abuse.** For some men, the threat of a divorce may trigger a violent reaction.

4. **Establish a Strong Position.** A divorce is the ultimate power struggle between you and your husband. You must put yourself in a strong bargaining position and this may take time.

5. **Premature Emotional Upset to Children and Others.** By letting the word out about the divorce too soon, you may upset your children, your family, your friends, and others before you've had time to lay the ground work.

What Not to Do Before Filing for Divorce

1. **Do Not Move Out of the House.** Moving out of the family residence can seriously affect your bargaining position and, perhaps, custody of the children.

2. **Do Not Communicate with Your Spouse's Lawyer.** Under no circumstances should you ever communicate directly with your spouse's attorney.

3. **Do Not Fight with Your Husband.** It is always unwise to lose your temper or quarrel with your husband. It is your attorney's job to work things out with your husband's lawyer.

4. **Do Not Have Sexual Intercourse with your Husband.** Certainly, after the divorce action is filed, you should not have sex with your husband or anyone else while the case is pending. Having sex with your husband may nullify the divorce action and can embarrass you in court and jeopardize your chances for custody of the children.

Preparing Yourself Mentally

1. **Your Lawyer Can't and Won't Do It All.** Don't be a passive spectator at your own divorce. You weren't a passive spectator at your own wedding, and your divorce is more important and more complicated.

2. **Don't Wallow in the Pain.** You have a life to live ahead of you. Meantime, it doesn't help to whine about the hurt, the sacrifice, and the injustice. Just do what you have to do and move on.

3. **Don't Play Lawyer.** Don't make any major moves without checking with your lawyer; moving out, custody of the children, or financial arrangements are critical decisions that you need to clear with your attorney first.

4. **He Is Not Your Husband—He's Your Adversary.** Don't assume your husband will take care of you. Don't, for example, rely on his voluntary generosity because that may set a precedent for the amount the final support or alimony. Remember, you are legally entitled to certain assets with or without his generosity.

5. **Be Prepared to Protect Yourself Physically.** If your husband becomes a physical threat or stalks you, immediately call the police; get "stay away" orders through the court, make him post a peace bond, and, take self protective measures. This is very serious business and you must treat it as such.

6. **Act Like a Savvy Adult with Your Husband.** While you need not be overly loving to your future ex, you should always be polite—not docile— and avoid arguing and fighting during separation. Rehearse saying, "Your lawyer should talk to my lawyer about that." That's what you should say to him most of the time.

CHAPTER 8

DEALING WITH LOVERS— LIVE-IN OR NOT

The thought of living in an unmarried state with a member of the opposite sex no longer elicits raised eyebrows. What causes eyebrows to raise in this permissive era is the failure of a live-in to protect herself in this situation.

Do not for a moment believe the laws that protect a married couple, defining their rights and responsibilities as to the property acquired during their marriage and the rights and obligations of support, are the laws that will protect you. They will not. In most states there are certain specific requirements that entitle you to the protections of those who are married. Usually this requires a ceremony, a license, or at least a colorable ceremony under the law or a holding out as husband and wife.

When you are simply living with a person or allowing that person to live with you, your rights and obligations are determined by the agreements that you and that person make with each other. This is the crux of the problem.

For cohabitants or live-ins, the issue revolves around the validity of the oral agreements (most do not have written agreements) that the parties may have made with each other. Generally, one of the parties will contend that the conduct of the other implies an agreement, for example, to pool earnings and share assets or to support the other forever.

The success of these claims will depend upon the credibility of each party. In California recently, a jury believed the female partner; the parties had lived together for 30 years without being married. (In California there is no common-law marriage.) The "wife" testified that they had built their multimillion dollar business together, side by side. She proved her case through their mutual conduct throughout the years, their joint life together, working together, and testimony from other witnesses. The jury believed her and did not believe her live-in. She proved the existence of a contract that entitled her to share in assets worth many millions of dollars. Of course, she worked for it.

In the *Marvin* case, the most famous of the live-in cases (also a California case), Michelle Triola Marvin thought she had proved her implied contract with Lee Marvin that he would support her for life. Unfortunately, the appellate court found the lower court had abused its discretion and reversed the judgment of the trial court, which had been in her favor. Still, the doctrine of the implied contract as between two persons living together was established.

Since *Marvin,* people are getting smarter. People are now entering into written agreements that define their rights and liabilities during the time they live together. Such contracts have a wide variety of provisions depending upon the goals of the parties. Often, the financially dominant spouse will require provisions that will preclude the accumulation of property together unless there is a written agreement specifically setting forth the property and the circumstances of acquisition—even if it is a gift of jewelry. In order to preclude a claim that the agreement is unconscionable and thus unenforceable, the wealthier party may provide for regular payments to be made to the other party.

Such a contract should include responsibilities for payment of living expenses and a provision that precludes the accumulation of an interest in the other's property because one person has devoted time or effort to its improvement such as, for example, decorating or remodeling a home that belongs to the other.

If there are children involved, whether those of either party or of the two parties, the rights and obligations of the parties with regard to the children should be set forth. While live-in relationships are not protected by the laws that protect those who are married, children born out of wedlock have the same rights of those born within a marriage.

The validity of cohabitation agreements depends upon the fairness of the agreement as well as proof that the agreement meets the requirements of the law with regard to contracts. To assist in establishing the fairness of an agreement, both parties should be represented by competent counsel who will attest that she has explained the legal effect of the agreement to the client and that the client has indicated that she understands the document.

Parties who marry after a period of living together are still entitled to enforcement of their rights accumulated during the live-in relationship prior to marriage. This situation may arise in the event of divorce of the parties. One party may assert the existence of an agreement prior to the marriage and seek to enforce it by order of court. In some jurisdictions, the rights of the spouses and the rights before marriage can be consolidated into one action, and the issues litigated in one action. However, in most states, an alleged breach of contract entitles a party to a jury trial while the family law case may only be tried by a judge. Thus, consolidation depends on the willingness of a party to give up the right to a jury trial.

Often, one might wonder when it is necessary to have a written agreement. How long or how intense must the relationship be to be concerned about protecting your rights? One man had agreements drafted for him to use for every occasion: a date, a sleep-over, and a live-in. He had a lot to protect. You may, too.

CHAPTER 9

WHOSE CHILDREN ARE THESE AND WHAT DO WE DO WITH THEM?

With the introduction of a family unit that no longer resembles that of the Cleavers, the question of "whose kids are these anyway" became a reality. There is the concept of blended families where the second wife and husband bring their children from their respective prior marriages together à la "The Brady Bunch." That bunch may be expanded to include stepchildren of either as part of the new family. It's not just the younger side of this group that has changed; mom and dad are now, on occasion, Dad and Pops or Mom and Mother. The traditional family may be some not-so-traditional families including gay and lesbian parents.

By far the most prevalent new family structure is the single parent family, most often a woman and her children who are on their own after a divorce. Fathers also fit the description of single parents, and more often families are headed by dad as the single parent.

There is now the surrogate parent family where the child may be the biological child of only one or neither of the two parents. This status, made possible by the wonders of genetic science, is mired in the swamplands of the law where the requirements with regard to a valid surrogacy contract are often ill-defined and difficult to enforce.

So long as these families remain intact, the lives of the children seem not to be impacted by the makeup of their parents or the sexual orientation of the parent. As with the children of the traditional couple, it is when the family separates that the children suffer.

The law is not helpful in these difficult situations. In a recent case, half of a lesbian couple lost not just custody but visitation of the child whom she had helped to raise for the first eight years of the child's life. The mother of the child had been impregnated through artificial insemination; the partner had not adopted the child. On their separation, the court found that she had no rights at all, not even to visit with the child. We have to wonder whether that abrupt loss in that child's life is in the best interests of the child?

Gay and lesbian adoptions are becoming more common in some states. Generally, most states allow an unmarried person to adopt a child if that person can meet the jurisdictional and legal requirements for adoption. The next step is to find a jurisdiction that will allow the second half of the homosexual couple to adopt the child. In California this can be accomplished depending on a demonstration to the Court that such an adoption would be in the child's best interest. Generally, the courts will approve such a petition; after all, two parents are better than one. The child is protected in the event of the death of one parent, and the sad case of the sudden disappearance of one parent from the child's life is avoided in the event of the breakup of the couple.

The relationship between a stepparent and the child in divorce is becoming more and more of an issue. In many of our modern families, a stepparent has a closer relationship with the child than does the noncustodial natural parent.

When the custodial parent and the stepparent terminate their relationship, often those children will suffer greatly. It may be difficult, but if the emotional needs of those children include seeing the stepparent, those visitations must be arranged. The custodial parent's anger at the stepparent or the stepparent's desire to punish the spouse by not seeing the children must be set aside to make way for the needs of the children. After all, this will be the second marital breakup for those children.

CHAPTER 10

ADOPTIONS

For an increasing number of women, adoption is the best way to have the baby they have always wanted. Even popular celebrities including Steven Spielberg and his wife Kate Capshaw, Jamie Lee Curtis and husband Christopher Guest, Tom Cruise and Nicole Kidman, Kirstie Alley and Parker Stevenson, Connie Chung and Maury Povich, and Michelle Pfeiffer and husband producer David Kelley are adopting children. There are also single celebrity moms adopting children including Diane Keaton, Rosie O'Donnell, Mia Farrow, Kate Jackson, Dianne Wiest, and Linda Ronstadt. The National Adoption Information Clearinghouse in Rockville, Maryland, reports that celebrities are adopting for the same reason many non-celebrities are adopting: infertility, postponed motherhood, and changing demographics that affect the lives of many American women, including changing attitudes. As one Hollywood manager says, "Women feel secure enough today to raise a child alone. You don't need a husband. That's creating an enormous comfort level." Whatever your reasons for adoption are, they are your own business, and here we will just talk about what may be involved on the legal side of adoption.

Adoption is a legal process as a result of which you assume the responsibilities and privileges of being the adoptive—not the natural—legal parent of another person. We say, "another person," instead of "a child" because it is possible to legally adopt most other people. You can adopt a grown-up and that occasionally happens, but most common is the adoption of a child.

A word of caution—every state has its own set of rules about adoption and its own system for doing it. In some states the system may be very complicated, long, and frustrating, which could lead you to attempt to take some shortcuts. The demand for babies is so high in some places that black markets dealing with both American babies and those from overseas have sprung up. You must be very careful about getting involved with these shortcut arrangements because you can be swindled out of substantial sums of money, perhaps become involved in illegal acts, suffer extraordinary emotional trauma, and still not come home with a child.

Most adoptions are either direct or through some legal adoption agency, which can be a state office or a private, licensed operation. Usually, you should go to an attorney who specializes in adoptions, and he/she will guide you on what is available to you where you live and the best approach to follow.

In a direct adoption, the deal is directly between the natural parent or parents and you. Usually, the state doesn't get involved in the process until the end when the you and the child go to court to have the judge issue the order of adoption. The state adoption system is more involved; public notice of your intent to adopt is often required. You may be checked out by the state adoption people to see that you are a fit parent and can give the new child a decent home.

Often adoption is construed as simply a couple taking on the care of an infant. It is much more complicated and often heartbreaking. Each natural parent has a chance to change his or her mind, and that may occur after you and your baby have been together for many months. A stepparent adoption, where a spouse adopts the child from a previous marriage of the other parent, is also becoming common.

There have been cases of adopting frozen embryos. Sometimes gay couples, prohibited in most places from legally being married, have sought to legally adopt each other. Because of the difficulty of adopting small children in the United States, many people seeking to adopt have turned to adopting children from overseas and from different ethic cultures. Ethnicity and religious choice have become issues in these overseas adoptions.

Whatever the circumstances of the adoption, the legal process consists of declarations by both the natural parents and the adoptive parents that set forth the willingness to give the child up for adoption and the acceptance of the child by the adoptive parents. However, sometimes it isn't possible to obtain the consent of both natural parents to give up custody and control either because one does not want to do it or because one cannot be located. In that case, the natural parent who is willing to consent to the adoption can go to court and attempt to convince a judge to rule that the other parent's permission and approval is not necessary.

Then, with the acceptance of the child's care and custody by the adoptive parents, the adoption is complete.

Traditionally, the records of adoptions were sealed and the adopted children never knew who their natural parents were. This was thought to be in the best interests of the children; however, times and attitudes change. Today, more and more adopted children are interested in finding their natural parents, and that search has been the subject of stories in newspapers, magazines, radio, TV, and the movies. It was the story in a 1996 TV episode of "Unsolved Mysteries" and in the 1996 movie *Flirting with Disaster* that brought together a child with her natural mother creating consternation within the adoptive family and a sense of bewilderment in the natural parent.

Many states now permit adoption agencies to contact the natural parents and to release the information of the adoption to the adopted child if those natural parents agree. Other states require the adopted child to petition the court; contact to the natural parents is made through the court to see if the natural parents will agree to a release of the information. Either way, it's essentially the same approach; the information can only be revealed to the child if the natural parents say it's okay to do so.

The principal thing to remember about adoptions is that the laws are different from state to state, and it is a highly specialized part of the law. You will need a lawyer who is an expert in the field.

Part Three

HATCHING YOUR OWN
NEST EGG

CHAPTER 11

BUYING, SELLING, AND HAVING PROPERTY

Buying a home or other real estate is often the biggest single purchase people make; usually your home is property that you will own for longer than most other possessions. Perhaps it is understandable why it is a complicated transaction.

Real estate is land and improvements on that land, possibly under it, on it, or over it. Buildings are attached to land. Under the land are minerals, water, and the right of passage such as for an underground pipeline. On land may be timber, crops, or the right of passage such as an easement for an above ground pipeline, trough, road, path, or walkway. And, what is over land are air rights. All of these elements of real property may be separated one from one another and each can be owned by a different person or entity. All of these things that exist in the land may collectively be known as a "bundle of rights." For example, the owner of a bundle of rights in a single parcel of land might sell or lease the mineral rights to a mining company; the right of passage or easements to a utility company to place power lines overhead; the right to raise crops to a farmer; and, the right to live in the house attached to the land to still another person.

The first real estate usually purchased by most people is a home. Traditionally, most of us want the security that comes from owning our own home. Often home ownership is a good investment; what would have been rental payments go to mortgage payments and building a nest egg. In recent years, however, some home values have not gone up as in the past or have, in fact, decreased, and people have been stuck with a negative investment in that their mortgage is higher than the current value of the home. Over the long haul, however, a home is generally a stable investment and the Federal tax laws help you buy the residence because the interest on your mortgage is tax deductible not only on your primary home but also on your second or vacation home. The dip in home values and the rise in foreclosures, of course, offers an opportunity for first time home buyers to make some good buys if they are willing to hold on to their new home for several years until market prices move up again.

Research shows that single women tend to buy a home later than single men do. Part of this may evolve from the lower pay scale in which most women find themselves. It is more difficult to save enough money for a down payment when your pay is lower than that of your fellow workers.

Homes can be purchased directly from the seller, of course, which may be the owner or a bank or the government. However, it most common for homes to be purchased from other private owners through real estate agents. Traditionally, real estate agents who list a property for sale and other agents who show the property to prospective buyers are actually and legally agents of the seller. It is important to remember that the agent you are dealing with is looking out for the seller, not for you, and will be paid by the seller from the proceeds of the sale of his or her home. As more buyers recognize this conflict, buyers tend to find their own real estate broker to represent them. Your agent will shop the market for you and have an obligation to be concerned for your best interests as the buyer. Your own broker will assure that you are made aware of the relevant facts about the property and the neighborhood in which your are considering buying. Who pays for the buyer's broker? The buyer's broker or agent may be considered a separate expense of the buyer, so the buyer not only might pay a purchase price that includes the seller's broker's commission but also a commission or fee to the buyer's broker. However, recent changes in the rules of the National Association of Realtors now allow the buyer's broker to share in the total commission paid; that is most often how the brokers are paid.

Do you need a lawyer to assist you in buying a home? Hiring a lawyer is probably not necessary when you first begin to look for a residence. However, depending on the jurisdiction you are in, a lawyer may be necessary when you are at the point of making an offer. Rights and restrictions are legal requirements that are involved in the sale and purchase of real property that must be considered before you buy; these include zoning laws, building codes, local covenants, easements, and the possibility of assessments due to required improvements or bond issues.

Compliance with applicable local, state, and federal laws is necessary when you are selling or improving your property. Your neighbors and your community also have rights and obligations that may affect your use of your property. That is why it is so important to know in advance of purchase all the codes, covenants, and restrictions (sometimes known as "CC&RS") that may apply.

Most municipalities have enacted zoning laws to keep residential and commercial properties restricted to certain areas. This means you don't have to worry about a car wash being built next door to your house. However, if you live on the boundary of a commercial district, you may be able to get a zoning variance if you wanted to start an antique shop in your home or open an office that may not increase traffic. Typical residential zoning laws usually allow for home-based businesses that don't impact on your neighbors (i.e., require exterior signs, increase traffic, create parking problems, etc.).

Building permits are almost always required when making alterations to your property, even for what you feel may be the most insignificant jobs, such as putting in a new fence. These laws are usually strictly enforced, so don't think you can just add on to your garage and no one will notice. In addition to paying fines, you could be forced to remove the noncomplying alterations, or you may have to nearly dismantle the new addition to prove that it does comply with local codes.

Other types of restrictions that may impact you are covenants designed to preserve certain aspects of a planned community, such as architectural guidelines and rules regarding square footage, paint color, and design style. Some of these covenants restrict residents from parking boats and motor homes in their driveways or from doing auto repair on the premises. These zoning restrictions are enacted with the hope of maintaining property values and forging good neighbor relationships. They can be a good thing; just be sure they don't impinge on your remodeling plans or you on them. Homeowners' associations can be sticklers for the rules, believing that if they grant an exception for one owner, they would have to do the same for all.

Be sure that a professional title search is part of your property buying process; that is the best way to uncover any easements. Your title search may disclose an easement on your property which gives another entity certain rights or access to your property. Once such easements are in place, they are difficult, if not impossible, to remove. These can include a neighbor's right to use part of your driveway or a power company's right to bury cable or to give the company access to their power lines in your backyard. There are some arcane laws about easements that vary by locality that can be enforced even when no rights have actually been granted. If a neighbor has been planting his vegetable garden on someone else's land for 30 years, even as a new owner you may not be able to prevent him from continuing. Your best protection is a title guarantee insurance from a reputable title company.

PROTECTING YOUR PROPERTY RIGHTS

If you have "good title" or "marketable title," that means you legally own your home and have the right to sell it if you so choose. Today, most lenders rely on title insurance for their protection in these matters. This type of insurance covers things that may have occurred before the effective date of the policy but were not discovered until later. You only have to pay this premium once for as long as you own the property, or until you refinance it.

In most states title insurance policies are standardized and include standard exemptions for such things as boundary disputes and unrecorded liens. Be sure to examine your policy carefully; you may need to obtain extended coverage for your situation.

There are several different types of deeds, and choosing the right one can have long-lasting significance. "Fee simple" is the most common form of ownership; when you own the fee simple in property, you are entitled to sell it, rent it, or bequeath it. The type of deed you choose is especially important in cases of joint ownership. The four basic types are: sole ownership, joint tenants, tenants in common, and tenants in partnership. In some states there is the additional option for married couples of tenants by the entirety and community property.

For couples, whether married or not, the most common form of joint ownership is joint tenancy. (More than two people can participate in this type of ownership, with each owning an equal share.) If two people have joint tenancy, and one of the couple dies, full ownership automatically passes to the survivor. This allows the surviving joint tenant to avoid having the property pass through probate. In most instances, it precludes the claims of others including heirs to the property. Parents can leave property to their children in this way and thereby avoid probate but not inheritance taxes. If three people own property in joint tenancy, the death of one of them terminates the joint tenancy, and the two surviving own the property in equal shares as co-tenants. Of course, they can convey the property to themselves as joint tenants.

If you prefer to have the right to sell or bequeath your interest in a property, then consider holding title as tenants in common. This gives each owner (and there may be more than two) separate legal title to an interest in the property. If one owner dies, the interest does not go to the other owners, but to the decedent's estate. This may be a choice for couples who have children from previous marriages and want them to inherit property that was accumulated during the first marriage.

For married couples, in some states (mostly in the eastern part of the country) there is the additional option of tenancy by the entirety, which includes aspects of the previous two types. There is right of survivorship, but also the ability to sell a half-interest in the property.

If you need to change the form of ownership on your deed, it's fairly simple. You just fill out a new one, have it signed by the people named on the deed as the owners of the property in the presence of a notary public licensed by the state to witness such transactions, and file it with the local recorder of deeds for a fee. However, if you have any doubts about proper forms or wording, be sure to check with an experienced real estate lawyer.

If you own property or are about to buy some, it is definitely time to make a will. That process could help determine which type of deed you choose for your property.

If you live in one of the nine states that have adopted community property laws— Arizona, California, Idaho, Louisiana, Nevada, New Mexico, Texas, Washington, and Wisconsin—you have other rights and obligations that may not be present in states that do not recognize community property. In those states there may be significant tax advantages of holding your home as community property rather than in joint tenancy. If you live in a community property state, be sure to consider all of your options carefully and seek professional guidance.

In divorce, 90% of such cases are resolved by the spouses and their attorneys out of court. If the case is left for the judge to decide, you will find that most judges today are more concerned with what is fair than whose name is on the deed. If there are minor children, the house usually stays with the custodial parent if sale can be shown to be detrimental for the children; if not, then property may be sold and the proceeds divided. Divorce decrees often have long-term impact on future rights to sell commonly held property. Pay close attention if you are buying property that is sold as a result of the seller's divorce; there are sometimes unsatisfied claims, debts, or liens that have not been divulged.

A lien is a claim against property to satisfy a debt. Refusing to pay the debt could cause the court to foreclose on your property and sell it to settle the debt. If contractors who worked on your property file a claim that is known as a "mechanics" or "construction" lien, you cannot sell your property until that lien is satisfied. Other liens that serve to cloud title may be filed in conjunction with a divorce decree to protect the interest in the property of the homeowner who is not living in the house. If you are divorcing and find yourself in this position, be sure your lawyer obtains a release of the lien should you later wish to sell the house.

If child or spousal support has been obtained against you, an abstract of judgment or the judgment itself may be filed in the county where you own property, and you will be precluded from selling that property until you can prove that judgment is current or satisfied.

To remove a lien, in addition to paying it off, you must have the payee sign a release-of-lien form or satisfaction of judgment to be filed either in the court or with the county recording office in order to clear your title. If you don't believe you owe the debt, consult an attorney about how to proceed.

HOMEOWNER LIABILITY ISSUES

If someone has an accident on your property, you are not liable unless it can be proven that you were negligent. Common examples of negligence include icy sidewalks, unfenced pools, obstacles near doors and on porches. Be especially careful to consider what trouble unattended children might get into on your property. Even if a child trespasses on your property and injures himself because of an unfenced hazardous condition, you could be liable. These are called "attractive nuisances," and that is why fences, locked gates, and pool covers can be essential to protecting your liability.

Damage caused to your property by your own children is usually covered by insurance—if the children are 13 or younger. All children need to be taught respect for property and the consequences of their actions.

For all their beauty and usefulness, trees cause many problems between neighbors. If you maintain your property and keep trees in good condition and a windstorm knocks a branch onto a neighbor's roof, that is usually covered by *their* homeowner's policy. If your tree falls on your house, then *your* policy should cover it. However, if you have failed to trim or cut a diseased or dying tree and it causes damage in a storm, you may be found negligent and therefore liable for your neighbors' damages. This applies to debris of any kind that may be on your property and then is kicked up in a storm and thrown at a neighbor's house. Again, prevention is always cheaper and easier on neighbor relations.

If you do not carry adequate liability insurance, you are asking for trouble. If you are sued for negligence and lose, you could lose your home to pay the damages awarded. In addition to liability insurance, your homeowner's insurance policy will also cover repair or replacement of your house and belongings. Be sure to consider which type of policy is best for your financial situation. Most

HOW TO HAVE A SAFE HOME AND NO LAWSUITS OR REGRETS

- Fix holes, uneven walks, steps, and weak railings.
- Wherever people walk, maintain a well-lit pathway.
- Salt walks and steps and clean snow and ice promptly.
- Keep toys off walks and steps.
- Replace slippery throw rugs.
- Don't have electrical lines crossing walkways.
- Put poisons, cleansers, and hazardous items out of easy reach.
- Fence and lock pools, ponds, and pits. Have an alarm on all these pools and ponds that goes off when a child falls in by accident.
- Don't leave ladders out for burglars to use.
- Keep weapons locked and stored away.
- Don't let guests drink and drive.
- Check house for exposed nails, screws, and sharp items.
- Childproof: Keep wall plugs covered, and keep breakables, poisons, and dangerous objects out of reach.

(continues)

basic policies only provide for the actual cash value of a house and belongings. If you need to rebuild your home, cash value might not provide sufficient proceeds to enable you to build a similar structure. There are policies that provide for replacement cost of your home and contents. Of course, this comes with a higher premium, but the peace of mind it brings may be worth it. Be sure to upgrade your coverage regularly, especially if you live in an area of rapidly escalating real estate values. There are even policies that increase coverage automatically. Consult your insurance agent for comparative policies.

The company who carries your homeowners insurance will handle most claims; only when they feel a claim is unreasonable or unfounded does the claim end up in court. Even if it comes to that, the company generally will pay all costs incurred if the company acknowledges coverage. Prevention through adequate insurance is the sure route to peace of mind.

Many homeowner policies have exclusions for floods, earthquakes, and home offices. If you have concerns about any of these, riders can usually be purchased for them.

Consider the need for workers compensation insurance if you are working at home or have a business you run out of your home and you have employees in your home.

HOW TO HAVE A SAFE HOME AND NO LAWSUITS OR REGRETS (continued)

- Install alarms and emergency lights. Absolutely have several smoke alarms and a carbon monoxide alarm. Night lights are important to avoid falls and ward off intruders. Also, emergency lights that plug into the wall and come on with the power fails are useful.

- Keep basement and outside doors locked at all times.

SECURITY ISSUES

Again: The buzz word is prevention. Maintain your home with deadbolts, exterior lighting, perhaps even a security system. However, in the event you should ever encounter a prowler on your property, always place the value of life over possessions. If you are able to escape to a safe place and call the police, then do so. If not, lock yourself inside. If you do come face to face with an intruder, try to remain calm and be cooperative.

Although you do have a legal right to protect yourself and your property, if you harm an intruder, you must be able to prove it was in self defense. This concept allows you to use "reasonable force" to defend yourself if you are being attacked—or believe you are about to be attacked. The key is what would be considered "reasonable" by a jury of your peers. If a single whack on the head stops an intruder, then you aren't justified in beating him to death. If a gunshot into the air drives off a prowler, you aren't entitled to shoot him in the back as he runs away. If you live in a high-crime area, consider taking a self-defense class. If you live alone and feel you must arm yourself, be sure to take classes in gun usage and safety, and practice regularly at a firing range.

KEEPING BURGLARS, RAPISTS, AND OTHER PREDATORS OUT OF YOUR HOME

The basic idea is to make it hard for intruders to get into your home or hide nearby without being seen.

- Have outside lights on all sides of your home.

- Cut back foliage near windows and doors so intruders can't hide there.

- Remember that privacy fences can also hide burglars from being seen from the street.

- Do not have outside doors with glass windows in them. An intruder can break the glass and be inside in an instant.

- Outside doors should be solid core doors at least 1¼ inch thick — not the kind of hollow core doors used inside. Hollow core doors can be broken down with one good kick.

- All outside doors should have a dead bolt inside the door that goes into the door jamb at least ¾ of an inch when in place. Door chains are essentially useless. The heavy chain is held in place by tiny screws, and one kick will rip the whole thing out of the door. Have a peephole in all outside doors. Never open the door for anyone you don't know. ALWAYS KEEP OUTSIDE DOORS LOCKED.

- Sliding glass doors and windows are easy to open from the outside unless you have special screw locks put on them. These are inexpensive and available at any good hardware store. The same kind of protection works on double-hung windows. Also, drilling a small hole through both closed double-hung windows and putting a nail in the hole works well.

- Iron bars or grating to keep intruders out can also trap you inside in a fire. Iron bars or gratings should be installed with release locks on the inside so you can unlock and push out the bars or grating from the inside if you need to escape.

- Intruders hate noises. Motion alarms and other types of inexpensive alarms are available at the hardware store. There are moveable motion alarms you can put anywhere and turn on when needed. There are also motion alarms that stick on sliding glass doors and windows and go off if someone opens the door or window. Get them and use them. Put stickers on your doors and windows warning that there are alarms. All these types of protective devices are relatively inexpensive and may save your life.

■ Never have your house keys on your car key ring where a parking attendant can duplicate them and sell them to professional burglars. Never have your name and address on your key rings so intruders know where to go if you lose your keys. Never hide a key over the door, in a fake rock in the planter, under the mat, or other obvious places. Burglars are not stupid. They know where to look. Best thing is to give a spare key to a trusted neighbor or nearby relative or friend.

SPECIAL SAFETY WARNING

If you ever come home and it looks as if the place has been burglarized, DO NOT GO INSIDE. Leave immediately and call 911. The intruder may still be inside.

■ Use timers to turn on outside and inside lights, including the TV, when you are gone. Curiously, everybody leaves a light on but turns off the TV. Yet, if you were really at home, the chances are that the TV or a radio would be on. Again, the burglar isn't stupid.

■ When you are away, have a friend come in to check your place, take in papers, and change the drapes or blinds and the lighting arrangement so that it looks as if you are there.

It is a good idea to make a list of all the valuable things in your home BEFORE you are ever burglarized. There are even computer software programs to help you do this. At the very least have a list of your valuables available with a description, serial numbers (where there are such numbers), and values. Some people even videotape everything that is in each room or take still photographs. All of this can make filing an insurance claim for loss due to burglary or fire or flood much easier. Of course, it goes without saying that you must not keep your inventory or photographs at home where they, too, might be stolen or destroyed. It is best to keep these valuable items at the office or at a relative's home.

HOW TO HANDLE PROBLEMS WITH YOUR MORTGAGE

Sometimes life's circumstances can make you unable to meet your mortgage payment. If you find yourself in that position, you need to act immediately. Ignoring the issue only makes it worse. Most lenders will work with you and try to arrange some interim solution to your situation. Foreclosing is not their first choice. If you cooperate with them, you can be able to make it through a rough patch in your life. A lender may choose to defer principal payments or may even refinance the loan to give you lower payments. A more desperate option may be to declare bankruptcy to avoid immediate foreclosure. You need an attorney.

If you exhaust all your options and are still unable to make your payments, then foreclosure will ensue. After that becomes final, you lose all rights to your property. Once a lender has filed for foreclosure you have very little time to reverse the procedure, short of paying all the arrearages and renegotiating your loan. If you have not yet done so, seek legal advice.

When you sell your home to another party and allow them to assume your loan, you may find yourself in another sort of dilemma. If the buyer defaults on the payments on your loan, you will still be liable.

TROUBLE IN THE NEIGHBORHOOD

Getting along with your neighbors can sometimes be a tall order, but resolving disputes in a friendly way should have a high priority. Typical causes of trouble are disagreements over pets, stereos, parking, trees, fences, and property lines. If you cannot settle the matter among yourselves, there are several ways to proceed.

If it's a zoning issue, you may be able to get help from the local officials. If it's noise and you live in an area with a noise ordinance, try the administrative offices of your police department. (Don't call 911 for a loud stereo!) If you belong to a homeowners association, the association may be able to help with enforcement if any of their rules are broken. If all else fails, there is always small claims court. In all cases, be sure your complaint is backed up by local laws. You can't get your neighbor to paint her house a different color if she violated no architectural guidelines. Sometimes just notifying your neighbor in a nonthreatening manner that he/she is breaking an ordinance will be enough to cause compliance. The very last, and most expensive resort, is to file a civil law suit against your neighbor. After this point has been reached, there are rarely ever any winners. Think long and hard before escalating the issue to that stage. Also consider hiring a mediator to help find creative solutions.

One rule of thumb courts use to settle nuisance complaints is that the parties are expected to be reasonable. If your neighbor has 10 big dogs that bark all night every night, that's clearly more than a nuisance. If the sound of one distant wind chime keeps you awake, get ear plugs!

Boundary disputes are best settled by a surveyor. Or, if the parties can agree that a certain tree or fence or even an imaginary line will serve as the boundary, then each can sign a quitclaim deed and file it in the county records office.

Another source of bad blood in neighborhoods is the one guy on the block who lets his place get rundown and fills the yard with junker cars and weeds. These eyesores decrease property values for many people; often the best approach is group pressure. Perhaps all this neighbor needs is some help to start on a cleanup program. A neighborly offer to turn his problem into a block work party could end up with everyone winning. In urbanized areas there are usually ordinances against extreme property neglect, but they are usually difficult to enforce. Sometimes, official notices from the city may be enough to shame the offender into action. Again, remember the rule about the complaint being reasonable. A few weeds in a flower bed do not an eyesore make.

One sad sign of the times is that it is becoming more common for residents to be aware that their neighbors may be engaged in illegal activities, such as drug trafficking. This is especially common if some of your neighbors are renters. The solution is simple: It is a job ONLY for the police. If you want to stick your neck out, you may provide some eyewitness evidence, but beware of the risks involved. The forfeiture laws are now strong enough to get these kind of tenants evicted and to force property owners to clean up their act.

One of the most emotionally charged neighbor troubles is pet disputes. People get very defensive about their pets and often have trouble believing that their little darling could possibly misbehave. If your neighbor's dog is fouling your petunia beds and Spot's owner doesn't believe it, a videotape is worth a thousand words. Most towns have an assortment of animal control laws that cover the common problems—barking, collecting doggie-doo, dogs off the leash. There is usually an animal control officer who will handle your complaints. If the problem persists after a few rounds of citations and fines, then you may need to pursue a civil nuisance lawsuit. Use that option as a last resort; once you've sued your neighbor, that's usually the end of any hope of civility. Remember what happened to the Hatfields and McCoys.

Next to yapping dogs, trees cause the most commotion in a neighborhood. The first thing to determine in any tree dispute is whose tree is it, anyway? A tree whose trunk stands entirely on the land of one neighbor belongs to that person. If the trunk stands on more than one piece of property, then it belongs to all the landowners in question. Someone who cuts down or harms a tree without permission owes the owner compensation. What if your neighbor's branches hang over onto your land? In that case, you may trim them up to the property line, but you need the owner's permission to enter his property to do the trimming. If you harm the tree in the process, you are liable for the damage. It is always the best policy to discuss your intentions with the tree's owner. It may well be that the owner plans to trim the entire tree and will thus save you the trouble or expense. You should also know that if your neighbor's tree drops apples onto your lawn, the apples still belong to your neighbor. On the other hand, if his rotten plums are ruining your prized lawn, then your neighbor is liable for damages. Tree roots are often frequent offenders. If the roots of your tree undermine your neighbor's driveway, for example, you are responsible for the damage. Prevention in these matters is always cheaper than the cure.

Imagine how you would feel if you had purchased your home for its wonderful view, then one day awakened to find that a neighbor's new fence obstructed your view. In most cases, you are just out of luck, unless you live in a coastal or other scenic area where view protection has been written into your deed either by easement or by city ordinance. If the view is of great importance to you, be sure to investigate your protection before you purchase. Never trust a real estate agent who tells you "that land over there will never be built on." If you have reason to believe the offending new fence was built maliciously to annoy you, you may have some recourse in court; consult a land use attorney.

The old adage about good fences making good neighbors may very well be true. It's certain that bad fences make for unhappy neighbors. First you should know that fence ordinances cover all types of fences, including hedges. Many zoning laws restrict the height of fences, even when they consist of living trees. Be certain what the laws are in your area before you construct a fence. If it is too high, you will most likely have to take it down, no matter how beautiful or expensive it is. Fences that sit on property lines are called "boundary fences" and are co-owned by the neighbors in question, who are all responsible for its upkeep, unless other agreements are made.

SHARED OWNERSHIP AND COOPERATIVE LIVING ARRANGEMENTS

Due to rising land costs and urban density, developers are getting more and more imaginative in finding ways to create common-interest communities. There are many confusing names for these type of arrangements, and they can vary in different parts of the country. Condominium is the best known term. Typically, you own the building or apartment itself and not the land beneath it. The land and all common areas are jointly owned as tenants in common and managed by a homeowners association, which assesses fees for maintenance, repair, etc. Another variation on this theme is a PUC or Planned Unit Community. In these subdivisions you own your home and the land it sits on, but the common areas, such as parks and playgrounds, belong to an incorporated association, which you are required to join. The association handles maintenance of common spaces and, in some cases, maintenance of the exterior of the homes, as well.

Beware that these communities often seek homogeneity and often have many rules and restrictions. For example, all pets may be forbidden. There are usually strict rules about what activities you can indulge in on the premises. Car repair, sanding a boat, building a chicken coop, etc. are often not allowed. You can be cited for hanging a towel over your balcony railing or anything else the association decides is unsightly.

As a rule, you are not allowed to make any modifications to the exterior of your unit. While you are often able to make interior alterations, you are also responsible for all maintenance and repairs, including appliances. There is no apartment "super" on call to fix your dishwasher. Condos often come with the problems of apartment living—noise, lack of privacy, shortage of parking spaces, too many kids in the pool, etc. The trade-off for single women can be a sense of security and community that comes from the presence of neighbors in very close proximity.

State and local laws governing common-interest communities vary widely. Even if you have owned a condo in another area, thoroughly research the stipulations of any such sale before you jump into a situation you may later regret. Also be aware that the resale market for condos can be fickle. Make it your business to know the long-term trends, especially if you suspect this may be a temporary home.

Generally these associations run a tight ship and have clear guidelines for dealing with almost any problem. Be sure to acquaint yourself with all the bylaws and procedures of the group. Homeowners who break the rules are usually fined. If the fines accumulate, the board may even file a lien against the property. It is sometimes possible to obtain a variance in the rules to do something ordinarily not allowed, but this is often an arduous process.

DISCRIMINATION IN BUYING A HOME

The laws covering the purchase of a house vary from state to state, and, even where the law forbids discrimination in selling a home, many early developers put restrictive wording in deeds that prohibited specific homes from being sold to certain groups of people, usually people who were not Caucasian. Federal laws prohibit discrimination, but it still exists informally in many places. Banks, for example, are precluded from discrimination in processing loans to buy a home and often advertise themselves as "An Equal Opportunity Lender." Translated into English this means "we lend mortgage money to nonwhites." It also should mean "we lend mortgage money to single women." However, the law and reality are not always the same thing. Civil rights groups, for example, occasionally test these laws by sending a white couple to a real estate office to shop for a home and then later sending a black or other nonwhite couple into the same office for the same purpose only to find out that the real estate people wouldn't show the nonwhite couple anything worth buying. Oddly, most civil rights organizations are still stuck on the race issue and don't go on crusades to obtain equality for single women or for women with children. The theory may be that, if you're white, you aren't discriminated against. Many single women know, from experience, that is simply not true.

Legally, these discriminatory practices violate Federal civil rights laws, but bringing a lawsuit to enforce your civil rights generally subjects you to a long process that could take many years, many dollars, and, moreover, doesn't give you a place to sleep tonight. However, if you can convince the real estate broker, the banker, the seller, and the others involved that you are a serious, determined buyer and intend to file complaints with every local, state, and federal agency you can find, this will get their attention. You may feel more comfortable having a lawyer represent you in doing this, and, of course, when a lawyer enters the picture, it is an indication that you are serious. A lawyer can explain the consequences to the people involved in terms of their reputation, time, money, and possible criminal penalties. This approach will certainly cause sellers to think twice before continuing patterns of discrimination.

It may sound silly or paranoid but you should be prepared to encounter discrimination before it happens. Even if you don't expect to be discriminated against when going out to buy or rent a home, we suggest you begin your quest as if you will be discriminated against and maintain a careful record from the beginning of your search. Keep a detailed diary of your search for a home with times, dates, names of people contacted, telephone numbers, addresses, car license numbers—every detail you can get. You probably want to record this confidentially or, if you are noting it in front of other people, excuse it by saying you have a bad memory or you are trying to keep all the places you see straight. You can still record important information about the property, the interest rates for your loan, and any information that a prudent buyer would want. Some people use a small, voice activated tape recorder concealed in their purse or pocket that can note what everybody says confidentially. Taking photos is also a good idea to "help you remember" the various places. Yes, yes, it all sounds quite paranoid and like 007, but if you face a problem of discrimination, your rational preparation may be the key to obtaining your loan or buying the home you want. Your lawyer will consider you inspired.

CHAPTER 12

CREDIT FOR WOMEN ONLY— A CAUTIONARY TALE

It has been difficult for women to obtain credit, enter into a mortgage agreement, even open a charge account. While things are getting better, most women still have trouble establishing their personal credit. The basic problem has been the practice of the credit issuers tying a women's credit rating to that of her father or her husband. In recent times, laws have been passed to alleviate that problem, but you should be prepared to help yourself as well.

Federal law provides that it is illegal to deny credit to anybody because of race, color, religion, national origin, sex, marital status, or age. Sounds good, but it doesn't always work. Basically, you need to prove to a company that issues credit that you are good for your debts, have a steady income, have sufficient funds to pay your bills, and have a record of good payment. First, try to get a credit card, open charge accounts, and open bank accounts in your name alone; whether you are single or married. If you are married and you and your husband open joint bank accounts, borrow money, take out loans or mortgages, assume that these financial assets are in both names, so you are establishing a credit history for yourself, not just your husband.

Build your credit rating by opening a savings account in your name with a bank that will issue you a Visa or MasterCard. Right there, you have established credit. Then, apply for charge accounts at various stores. Some may turn you down; if they do, find out why. You will be able to open accounts at some stores. Stores that sell appliances usually are among the easiest places to open charge accounts, but their credit terms are steeper than some other stores. Buy a small appliance on time from one of these stores and be aware of the extra interest you have to pay as part of the cost of establishing your credit. It may be worth it to establish your credit initially. Along with all the excitement of opening charge accounts and obtaining credit cards, you must be aware that you are entering into legal relationships and an obligation is created.

Careful and timely payment will establish your pattern which identifies you as a good credit risk when the time comes that you want to borrow big money for a house or car.

WHAT DO CREDIT AGENCIES WANT TO KNOW ABOUT YOU?

Generally, when you apply for credit, the tendency of banks and lenders is to ask you questions covering everything under the sun, but you don't have to tell them all. The idea is to give information that assures that you are a good credit risk and that you can and will pay your debt.

The creditor will ask where you work, how much you make, and how long you have worked. You may be asked about other charge and bank accounts to determine if other credit agencies have granted you credit. Inquiry into your living circumstances is fair. Do you rent or own your home? How long have you lived at one location? This information is an indication of stability. If you own your own home (with a mortgage, probably), it means that you are going to be around and that somebody else has lent you substantial money. You may be asked about the number of children or other dependents you have. The lender wants to know how many mouths you have to feed out of your paycheck, BUT no creditor can ask about whether you plan to have more children or whether you are fertile or if you are on birth control.

You do not have to tell the potential creditor about alimony or child support payments you receive unless you are relying on these payments to pay your charge account. If you are relying on court-ordered support to pay your bills, you must declare this on your credit application, and you may have to produce a copy of the court order. The creditor will also want to know if you have obtained credit under a different name.

The law has created different and sometimes conflicting rules for different credit situations. For example, when applying for a credit card or charge account, you cannot be asked about your race, national origin, sex, marital status, or age, but you can be asked those questions if you are applying for a home loan. That information is requested by the government to make sure the bank is not discriminating against groups of people in making home loans. (You generally are not **required** to answer those questions.) You are not required to give information about your husband or ex-husband unless he is going to use the account, pay the account, or you are relying on his alimony or child support to pay the account.

The creditor cannot require the signature of anyone else guaranteeing your account unless you have a bad credit record or no credit record. Finally, the creditor is allowed to know your immigration status because the creditor doesn't want to loan money to somebody who may have to leave the country precipitously.

WHEN WILL I KNOW?

After you apply for credit, the creditor will probably check with a credit reporting agency such as TRW to learn available information about your past credit record. The creditor must let you know within 30 days after your application is complete whether credit is granted or rejected. Be aware that some creditors don't start counting the 30 days until after they have received the report from the credit agency.

WHAT IF I AM TURNED DOWN?

If you are turned down, the creditor must tell you why or whom to contact to find out why and must tell you about your rights under the Federal Equal Credit Opportunity Act.

If the reasons you are turned down are not given, you have 60 days to request specification of those reasons, and the creditor has to tell you that within 30 days. If you have gotten a bad report from the credit checking agency, you are entitled to see a copy of that report. You may have to pay a small fee for this.

Read the credit report over carefully. Make sure that it contains no errors of fact and that it does not contain negative information about your husband's credit in your report. Also, check for any items that are over seven years old. Agencies love to keep information on you forever, but anything over seven years old is generally considered obsolete. Then, write to the credit agency spelling out each mistake, including your husband's information and the over-seven-year-old information and demand that it be removed from your record. There may also be information on the report that gives a former creditor's viewpoint without explaining your side of the story; for example, that you bought something and didn't pay for it (the store's side of the story) when it didn't work and the store wouldn't take it back (your side of the story). You can demand that your side of the story be included in the report.

If you think you have been discriminated against by either the creditor or the credit reporting agency, you should complain in writing to the right government agency. Most states have an Office of Consumer Affairs or Consumer Protection, or you may complain in writing to the Federal Trade Commission (see Appendix for the address of the office serving your state). If it is a bank that has refused you credit, complain to your state banking commission (if it is a state charter bank) or to the Comptroller of Currency (if it is a federally chartered bank) at:

Director, Consumer Examinations,
Comptroller of the Currency
Department of the Treasury
490 L'Enfant Plaza S.W.
Washington, D.C. 20219
202-447-1600

It is important that you do not let a bad credit report or being turned down for a charge account or a loan slip by if either is based on erroneous or inappropriate information. It may seem easier to throw up your hands and hope it will go away, but the problem will haunt you if you let it lie and do nothing about it. Fight for your rights, and become a pain in the rear for everybody if you have to because that is the way you will protect yourself. No one is going to do it for you. Remember the squeaky wheel theory.

CREDIT WHERE CREDIT IS DUE

Having the ability to buy on credit and maintain good credit is important to your financial well-being. You will need your good credit to make major purchases during your lifetime such as a home, car, or major appliances. If you have bad credit, you will be penalized because you may not be allowed to buy these major items on the installment plan, or, if you are able to buy them, you may be asked to pay substantially higher interest and other charges.

It is ironic that current economic problems have been so uncertain that more people than ever have had credit problems. This means that the credit industry—banks, savings and loans, insurance companies, mortgage companies, loan companies—has adjusted the rules somewhat and made it easier for people who have had credit problems in the past to obtain acceptable credit arrangements.

During recent years, the laws have changed to reflect changes in the national economic situation. The federal government has passed three laws specifically dealing with this. One is the Equal Credit Opportunity Act, the second is the Fair Credit Reporting Act, and the third is the Truth in Lending Act.

The Equal Credit Opportunity Act protects you against discrimination in the granting of credit based on age, sex, marital status, and religious affiliation. For example, for many years unmarried women had experienced problems obtaining credit. Creditors were and still are notorious for racial discrimination in refusing to give credit in so-called "red-line" areas, so named because creditors drew red lines around such areas on their maps and refused to make loans to people who lived in those areas. These areas are almost always predominantly nonwhite and poor.

The Fair Credit Reporting Act is designed to protect you against inaccurate reports on your credit record. Typically, if you have a dispute with a retail store credit department or some merchant, the merchant instantly threatens to report you to one of the major credit reporting services as a bad credit risk. This is a tactic used to intimidate you into paying whether the retailer's claim is correct or not. Later, another creditor checking this report may turn you down because of this inaccurate entry. The Fair Credit Reporting Act requires credit agencies to notify you in writing if you are turned down for credit and explain why you were turned down. You have the opportunity to ask that the incorrect information be changed. If the credit agency won't do that, you can turn to the appropriate state or federal agency for help.

However, you don't have to wait until you are turned down for credit to check on what is on you credit report. You can write a form letter to any or all of the three major credit reporting services (listed below) and ask for a copy of your record. Give them your name, address, social security number, phone number, and your work address and phone numbers. Notice that two of the three agencies have toll-free 800 numbers to call to obtain details about checking your personal report.

The credit reporting agency is allowed to make a small charge for their report (usually it is less than $20), but it's worth it because we can guarantee you that your credit report will surprise you. Credit reports are notoriously inaccurate, and you'll probably find all sorts of mistakes on yours. It is common that addresses, personal history, and credit experiences are incorrect, and sometimes the credit agency will confuse you with someone else with a name similar to yours. Although all reports are supposed to delete negative information that is over seven years old, they never seem to do that until you demand it. Again, you might find that negative information regarding the credit of your ex-husband is also reported in your file even though you are no longer married to him.

It is well worth the small fee and the trouble to check your credit report from time to time. Here are the addresses of the three main credit reporting companies:

TRW
P.O. 2350, Chatsworth, California 91313
800-392-1122

Equifax
P.O. 740241, Atlanta, Georgia 30374
800-685-1111

Trans Union
P.O. 390, Springfield, Pennsylvania 19064
312-408-1050

When you get your report, it should also include instructions on how to challenge negative or erroneous information contained in it. You can ask that outdated or inaccurate information be removed or that notations about credit problems with a creditor be double-checked. For example, as we pointed out earlier, some aggressive creditors routinely file a bad credit notation on you the minute they have any problem with you such as late payments or a dispute about a charge. However, when the problem is settled, that same creditor doesn't bother to notify the credit agency that everything is cleared up. You are allowed to file explanations for any credit problems on your record, and you should take advantage of that opportunity.

Finally, there is the Truth in Lending Act that requires any person or entity that lends you money, either directly or by financing your purchases, to explain the details of your loan. This will enable you to choose the most advantageous loan available and to protect yourself from being charged interest and fees you don't know about when you borrow the money. The law requires that you (a) be given the rate of interest you are being charged, (b) the nature of all other charges and how they are calculated, and (c) the entity to contact to correct errors.

This law also has two very important provisions for you. One is that if your credit card is stolen or lost and you report it to the company that issued it, you cannot be held liable for any illegal charges over $50. The other is that if you purchase merchandise that is defective and you are unable to work out a settlement with the seller, you can refuse to make payment. So, if you notify the credit card company that the merchandise is defective, they will not pay the charge nor can they charge you interest on a disputed charge.

GETTING A CREDIT CARD WHEN YOU HAVE BAD CREDIT

So many people have had credit troubles these days with layoffs and a tighter economy that the credit card industry has responded by making it possible for even people with poor credit to obtain a Visa or MasterCard. They have created the concept of the secured credit card. As usual, bankers don't want to take any chances, but this is a good solution for some women and men who want the convenience of a credit card for which they ordinarily could not qualify.

The procedure is that you open a savings account with one of the banks involved in issuing secured credit cards, and you get a credit limit equal to the amount of your savings account balance. You have to pay off your charges over that savings account balance as you would with any Visa or MasterCard. Your credit is identical to any other Visa or MasterCard and so there is no embarrassment when you use such cards.

To get a secured credit card, contact one of the following banks (there many be others who offer secured credit cards, but these are some we know of), and they will send you an application.

BANK	800 PHONE NUMBER	INTEREST RATE CHARGED
Orchard Bank	873-7307	15.25%
Amalgamated Bank	365-6464	16.25%
Chase Manhattan	482-4273	17.90%
Key FSB	228-2230	18.90%

An additional advantage of getting a secured credit card is that it lets you build up a new credit history showing that you do pay your bills on time. This will help you later in applying for credit from other sources.

THE BILL COLLECTOR COMETH

Bill collectors are among the most unpleasant people we can think of because they seem devoted to harassing and threatening us. This is not to say that every one of us hasn't gotten behind in paying our bills at one time or another for many reasons. To us, we are decent, law-abiding people who are in a temporary squeeze, and if given a chance, we'll get it all worked out. To our creditors we are cheating, lying deadbeats trying to bilk legitimate merchants out of their money and goods. So, assuming you aren't a deadbeat, but just in a temporary spot, and you want to pay your bills as soon as you can, what should you do?

PREEMPTIVE STRIKE

One of the first things you should do when you determine that you are in serious financial trouble is contact your creditors. Yes, that's right. You contact them before they contact you. Write them a letter explaining that you are having financial problems, and say why (lost your job, been seriously ill, or whatever). Make it clear that you have every intention of paying them in full, and you want to keep your good credit rating but need some temporary help. Then, ask the creditor for suggestions as to how the creditor can temporarily ease your financial problems. If the creditor is reasonable and sensible, he/she will try to work out something you both can live with to get your debt paid, such as providing for installment payments on account.

DEALING WITH THE COLLECTION CREW

However, creditors are people, and some of them are dumb, vindictive, or skeptical of whether you are telling the truth. These types will aggressively try to collect the debt you owe them before you can hide, spend your money, or declare bankruptcy. Either the creditors themselves will try to collect or may turn the job of collecting your debt over to a professional collection agency.

If your debt is turned over to a collection agency, you can count on it being routinely reported to a credit agency with the consequent detrimental effect on your credit rating. You can also count on the collection people being very aggressive and sometimes nasty—that's how they earn their living and the commission, often 50% of what they can collect from you. Even when a collection agency becomes involved, you may still be able to work out extended or reduced payments, but it is tougher than working it out with the original creditor because collection agencies are, as we noted, interested in collection and not financing your spending habits any further.

If the collection agency cannot easily collect by being demanding and aggressive with you, it will probably move fairly quickly to sue you in court. Their objective is to obtain a judgment against you in small claims court (if your debt is within the dollar limit for small claims court) as soon as possible so they can attach your property, your bank accounts, or garnish your wages.

WHAT THEY CANNOT DO (LEGALLY)

You do have legal protections against overly aggressive or unscrupulous collection agencies through the Fair Debt Collection Practices Act, which is a Federal law that does *not* cover the creditor—only the collection agencies. Your original creditor may be covered by laws in your state and you need to check that. The Fair Debt Collection Practices Act states that the collection agency people cannot threaten you, be abusive, or harass you. This includes badgering you on the telephone at odd hours—essentially, they must call only between 8 a.m. and 9 p.m. They can't harass you at work or publicize your financial condition. What they are supposed to do is send you a letter spelling out the details of your debt—who you owe, how much you owe, and for what you owe it. You are given a month to reply and contest the claim, and if you don't answer, that is as good as admitting the claim is correct.

ZAPPING THE ZAPPER

Just because the collection agency is legally required to behave in a certain way doesn't mean it will. Some collection agencies operate on the assumption that the tougher and meaner they are, the more frightened and confused you will get, and the easier a mark you will be.

We suggest that you respond equally aggressively. If a substantial amount of money is involved, you should engage the services of a lawyer who specializes in credit matters. However, be careful about engaging the services of so-called "credit counselors" who may be scam artists. Credit counselors are people who represent you in reorganizing your finances and negotiating with your creditors to work out a plan for payment. Unfortunately, there are some people who take advantage of people in financial trouble and drain them of what little assets they have. So, as with any product, you need to shop for a good credit counselor. Trustworthy credit counselors may include nonprofit organizations; Credit Counseling Centers of America is one of them, respected by creditors in your area. In fact, you may want to contact one of your creditors and ask advice to find who is an honest credit counseling service in your area.

If you use neither an attorney or credit counselor, move aggressively to protect yourself. For example, tape telephone calls, keep a diary of everything said and done by everybody involved, write letters offering to work out a deal, challenge everything that is charged against you that is incorrect, and complain immediately about any breach of the Fair Debt Collection Practices Act. You can do that by contacting the

Federal Trade Commission (FTC) listed in the telephone book under, United States Government, or check the Appendix of this book for the numbers of the regional FTC office serving the state where you live. The FTC enforces the Fair Debt Collection Practices Act.

THE DREADED "B" WORD FOR YOUR CREDITORS

The one word that none of your creditors want to hear is "bankruptcy." In theory and in practice, if you declare bankruptcy your credit problems are wiped clean and you get a fresh start with no debts. You can do this under one of two procedures in the federal bankruptcy law named after the places they occur in the law, Chapter 7 or Chapter 13. Baseball coach Tommy Lasorda says that there are two theories about how to handle a screwball pitch and neither one works. In a way, that is also true of bankruptcy.

It is tempting when you are in financial difficulty to file bankruptcy to wipe out your debts. The problem is that there are some debts NOT wiped out by filing bankruptcy. For example, even in bankruptcy you are still required to pay court-ordered alimony and child support, student loans, taxes, money owed the government, and money owed people who were hurt by something you did such as in a car accident. However, you may be able to obtain an order lowering your support obligations and work out payments with the government for student loans.

Another drawback to bankruptcy is that it is on your credit record for at least seven years or more and can impair your ability to borrow money in the future. We have heard of some lenders who prefer lending money to people who have gone through bankruptcy because it means they are free of other debts and sometimes in a better position to repay a loan made after declaring bankruptcy. That is an imaginative view, but we doubt if many lenders will operate on that basis.

An advantage to declaring bankruptcy is that when you contact your creditors to confirm the details of what you owe, you will get their blood racing at the sound of the "B" word, and because of that, the creditor may decide to offer you a settlement deal if you don't go bankrupt.

The process of declaring bankruptcy, which is usually done under the terms of Chapter 7 and is referred to as a "straight bankruptcy" by many experts, involves several steps. You start by filing a bankruptcy petition with the court. On this petition you must list all your creditors. To assure yourself that you are absolved of all your debts you must assure that all your debts are listed in the petition. Your creditors are notified in writing. The court will appoint a trustee to oversee your bankruptcy, and sometimes you will be allowed to supervise your own bankruptcy. The trustee will call a meeting of your creditors. Between the time you file the petition and the meeting of creditors, all legal actions against you by your creditors are stayed. No court orders can be obtained against you until a bankruptcy judge says that the litigation may proceed. At the creditors meeting the trustee decides who gets paid and how much, assuming, of course, that you have some assets with which to pay. The trustee will also decide if you get to keep any of your property. Usually, you will have to sell your property to pay creditors. If you have money owed to you, the trustee will decide if litigation should be pursued against your debtors. The plan is then approved by a bankruptcy judge.

You might consider a Chapter 13 bankruptcy if you have a regular income and you don't have more than $250,000 in personal, unsecured debts (personal loans, credit cards, etc.) plus $750,000 in secured debts (house, car, etc.) Under this Chapter 13 plan you have to be making enough money to pay for your reasonable living expenses and have a surplus that can be used to pay off these other debts in full. The procedure is essentially the same as with Chapter 7 except the trustee works out a pay-off plan for your creditors, and you agree to adhere to it. A Chapter 13 plan also lets you keep the property you have.

Bankruptcy does not cure all of your financial woes, although it does allow you to start over with a clean slate except as noted above. Bankruptcy is a mark on your financial history that you should prefer not to have.

ESTATE PLANNING FOR WOMEN ONLY

WOMEN AND INHERITANCE– PROPERTY RIGHTS

More women are becoming more wealthy and are owners of substantial property; it's important that women with wealth or who expect to have wealth understand the basics of financial planning. We know a very prominent family in the entertainment business. The old-world bred father who controlled the entire company died, leaving nothing to any of his sisters or daughters. Instead, he left all his extensive property to his son because, in the traditional world in which he lived, the son would be morally obligated to take care of his sisters and aunts. Well, "morally obligated" doesn't pay the rent anymore, and women are not only entitled to their fair share of the family property, they must insist on being treated equally with males in the family. Financial control is security, and women should not be forced to beg for money to which they are rightfully entitled. So, here are some basics about owning property that all women need to know.

First, property is divided into two categories that have their genesis in the beginnings of civilization: real property and personal property. Real property is land and things attached to it including, a home and other buildings that may have been built on the land. Personal property consists of moveable items such as your car, your clothes, your lava lamp, your makeup, your money and bank accounts, and your back issues of *McCall's*, as well as intangibles such as the right to sue someone or a right to receive assets in the future.

Personal property is itself divided into two types: tangible and intangible. Tangible means you can see it, feel it, and sense it. Generally, when we speak of tangible personal property, we are referring to that which we can see, feel, and/or wear. However, ideas, patents, copyrights, and artistic concepts are also very valuable—sometimes more valuable than anything else you might own—but you can't always perceive them with your six senses. These are what we call intangible personal property.

There are several ways you can own property, the differences among them generally having to do with time and other people. Here we need to be aware of some old English words that are sometimes confusing. We would like to simplify them; but, because these are words that are used in the law, you need to know them as they are, or you won't understand what the law is about. There are several different ways of holding title:

1. Several or sole tenancy

2. Joint tenancy

3. Tenancy by the entirety

4. Tenancy in common

5. Community property

The first one, several or sole tenancy, is confusing right off the bat because the word "several" sometimes means more than one. However, in the old English language of the law, it means the opposite. It means the ownership is "severed" or cut off from everybody else. You are the only owner if you hold title to the property in "severalty." So, the first way to own property is all by yourself, in severalty or sole tenancy.

The second, joint tenancy, is easier to understand because it means what it says. You have ownership jointly with somebody else. It could be one other person or more than one other person. The tricky part of joint tenancy is that every joint owner has the unrestricted right to use all of the property equally with every other joint tenant. In other words, each joint tenant can use the entire property, house, bank account, car, boat, TV set, swimming pool, etc., as if it were entirely hers. In addition to the unrestricted joint use of joint tenancy property, there is one other important angle to title by joint tenancy. If a joint tenant dies, her share automatically goes equally to the other joint tenant or tenants; it is divided among them. So, if you are joint tenant with another person owning a house and the other person dies, you become the sole owner or owner in severalty of the house. The joint tenancy form of ownership is severed by the death of a joint tenant. It can be severed during the joint tenancy by any joint tenant conveying her interest in the property to herself as a tenant in common.

The third way of holding title is by tenancy by the entirety. It is a special form of tenancy that applies only to married couples. It is a joint tenancy limited to two people only and they must be husband and wife. This special arrangement also has the right of survivorship, but with a nice twist. When one of the tenants by the entirety dies, the surviving tenant gets full ownership, and the property is NOT subject to the debts of the tenant who died. If you are married and your husband owes other people money, his creditors cannot come after your home as long as both of you are alive. If he dies before you do, the creditors still can't come after the house because the total ownership has shifted to you, and they are not your debts. If you died first, however, they could come against the house because it would now be his house alone. The exception here, of course, is if you should foolishly make your husband's debts your debts by co-signing on loan papers or other documents that say both of you owe somebody money. It is most difficult for a married couple to separate their debts in this manner because usually the married couple is the beneficiary of the contracts or purchase which resulted in the debt. However, through careful pre-marital planning you may be able to protect yourself against your husband's foolish and/or non-productive debts.

A fourth method of holding property is by tenancy in common, which is much like joint tenancy and tenancy in the entirety in that more than one person has the exclusive use of the entire property with you. The significant exception is that it doesn't carry with it the right of survivorship. Each tenant in common can will his/her property to whomever he/she wants to leave it. If the deeds or other ownership papers you hold to the property don't say what kind of ownership or tenancy is involved and there is more than one owner, it is assumed that it is a tenancy in common. Title to all property you own should specify that it is held in joint tenancy or tenancy by the entirety or tenancy in common.

A fifth method is available in some states: Spouses may hold property as community property, which is a type of ownership that gives each spouse an equal coexisting interest in the property.

Some miscellaneous ownership points are: If you are the sole owner, you are free to sell it, give it away, lease it, or do whatever you like with the property. If, however, you have a joint ownership interest, you must have the signature approval of the other owners to do those things. Or, you can end the joint arrangement. For example, if you are in a joint tenancy or tenancy by the entirety, it is ended when one of you die or when you both sell or when the two of you are divorced. A tenancy in common can be sold separately or willed separately because it doesn't carry the right of survivorship. However, it is difficult to sell a partial interest in property. Another way of changing the ownership arrangement that applies only to joint tenants (who don't have to be married) and tenants in common is to simply divide the property. (Sometimes this is called "partition.") If, for example, it's a bank account, divide the money. If it is real estate, sign over new deeds dividing the property—if that is physically possible to do. If it's a joint tenancy or tenancy in common and one owner wants to split up the property, but the other owner refuses, you can go to court and petition a judge for an order to divide things up. This is a "partition" order. If the property can't be divided because of physical characteristics, the judge may order that it be sold and the money from the sale be divided instead. This, of course, doesn't work with tenancy by the entirety or community property because the two tenants have to be married for tenancy in the entirety to exist, although in most states spouses can enter into contracts one with another that can have a profound effect on the ownership of their property. The best advice is to see a lawyer.

There are other kinds of exclusive uses of property that are a form of ownership related to time. Some of these have to do with the disposition of your property when you die, and we'll talk about that in the section on wills and inheritances.

You can have temporary "ownership" or the exclusive right to use certain property for a limited amount of time by renting or leasing that right from the sole or joint owners of the property. When you have the exclusive right to use property for a limited time, it means that the exclusive right to use that property will pass or revert to someone else in time. For example, you might be renting an apartment, a boat, a store, a car, or a house, which gives you the exclusive right to use that property for the term of your rental agreement. When your rental term or lease expires, the exclusive rights revert to someone else, probably the landlord or person who leased it to you called the "lessor." These temporary ownership rights can be very valuable. For example, if you open a business at a good location in a store you leased for many years, you own the lease and the exclusive right to that property within the terms of the lease, for the term of the lease, and that can be a valuable asset of yours depending on the terms of your lease. If you ever sell the store, for example, and if you have a very good price on your lease, the remaining term may be a valuable business asset particularly if the location is important to the success of the business.

INHERITANCE, WILLS, AND TRUSTS

Through the use of inheritance laws, wills, and trusts, the law allows us to impose our desires on other people after we're dead. A will, for example, sets forth your directives about how you want what you own distributed at the time of your death. The law recognizes your right to do this and limits its involvement to making sure you knew what you were doing when you made your will (competency) and that the document is really your will and not a forgery. The law is also designed to protect the rights of the living who may not be able to look after themselves. The state has an interest in assuring that your will comports with "public policy." For example, if you left money with instructions that the funds were to be used to put a contract out on individuals you didn't like, that would be against public policy. Or, if you left behind a infant child without providing for that child's support, that would be against public policy. If someone forged your signature or imposed on you to make a will when you were confused and incompetent, that would be against public policy and might constitute fraud under the law.

Your will may list your specific property, real and personal, and state who gets what. Some wills just make a sweeping designation saying that ALL your property is to go to a certain person or to be equally divided among all your children. Other wills can be quite specific. For example, when the super-rich Dodge Brothers, founders of the Dodge Motor Company that ultimately became the Chrysler company, died, their wills specified who would get each article of clothing—their pants, underwear, shirts. Either method of disposition is acceptable and often a will may include specific gifts with the balance (residue) after payment of the specific gifts going to others. You must name someone you trust as executor to carry out the terms of your will. If you don't make a will or don't name an executor, the law of the state in which you reside at your death will do it for you.

HOW TO ASSURE THAT YOUR WILL IS VALID

Most states require that you be competent to make a will to assure a valid will. You must be of legal age (usually 18), be of sound mind, and intend the document to be your will; you'll indicate that you intend the document to be your will by signing it and having at least two other people sign it as witnesses. The witnesses either have to see you sign the will or have you tell them that it is your will and your signature or both. In most states it is acceptable that the witnesses be beneficiaries—they get part of your property—under the will. It is recommended, however, that you have your signature witnessed and attested to by individuals who have no interest in your estate or by a public official who does that professionally, that is, a notary public. This costs a few dollars and takes some extra time, but after you are dead, it may be hard to locate personal witnesses or they may be dead, too.

SOME OF THE USUAL QUESTIONS— CRAZY AND OTHERWISE

Q. What about making my own will?

A. This can be done, but it's usually foolish to do it. Having a lawyer prepare your will costs a little money, but it is less than it will cost your estate after you are gone if your will is challenged. Understand that your heirs may fight over your property when they see the terms of your will. Some will not agree on your decision about who gets what. The author and newspaperman, Ambrose Bierce, noted years ago, "It not over when you die. First, they bury you and then there is the blood-letting over the inheritance."

However, it is possible to prepare a simple holographic will. For validity, it must be in your own handwriting and signed by you and dated at the end. No witnesses are needed for a valid holographic will.

Q. What about those form wills you can buy in the store?

A. These inexpensive will forms can be the most costly you ever bought. The terms are not geared specifically to you, your property, and your wishes. These may be better than dying without a will if you specifically wish to disinherit someone who, otherwise would be entitled to share in your estate. But, again, some of the heirs won't be happy, and these kinds of store-bought wills may be easier to successfully challenge than one specifically drawn up for you.

Q. Suppose I die without making a will?

A. The laws of the state in which you die or in which you reside at your death will dictate how your property is divided. An administrator will be appointed who can be a member of your family or a public official. You may not like how the law provides for distribution of your estate, however, which is why you should make a will.

There are, of course, methods of giving away your property without a will or in spite of a will. For example, we mentioned earlier that property you hold in joint tenancy or tenancy in the entirety automatically goes to the survivor or surviving husband or wife. This applies to real estate and personal property held that way. You may also dispose of your property through life insurance or retirement plans or trusts. The proceeds of the estate go to the beneficiaries you name in the insurance policy, retirement plan, or trust. For example, even if you provide in your will that you want the proceeds from your life insurance policy number 12345 with XYZ Insurance company to go to Aunt Gertrude, it will go to whoever is named in the insurance policy as beneficiary regardless of what you say in your will. This is also true for your retirement plan that is likely designated for your spouse, your trusts, and other investments that have a named beneficiary.

There is also the living trust arrangement that we mentioned in the section on owning property. We said property ownership could be connected with time and that is the way it works with a living trust. Some parents, for example, will set up a living trust that gives them complete, exclusive use of their home while they are both alive; that's called a "life estate," but the ownership is passed to their children or grandchildren or some other person while the parents are still alive. The management of the trust is put in the hands of a "trustee" who is often the parents themselves or a trusted friend. When the beneficiaries of the trust, the parents in the example we are using, both die, their "life estate" also expires. What is left of the estate is called "the remainder estate," which passes to whomever is designated. This life estate and remainder estate are not affected by the provisions of your will.

A trust is an arrangement between three groups of people. First there is the trustor or "settlor" who puts his or her property into the trust. That is you. Then, there is the beneficiary who receives the property from the trust at a later time such as when the trustor dies. And there are also trustees. Generally you will be the trustee of your trust until your death or incapacity (you may be sharing this duty with your spouse) and upon your inability to act as trustee, your designated successor trustee will take over. The successor trustee may be a friend or advisor such as a banker or a lawyer who succeeds to the position of trustee of your property. You may also designate a bank or a trust company to act as trustee. All trustees have the obligation to manage your property reasonably. During your lifetime generally all income and principal as needed is paid to you or for your benefit. Upon your death, the trustee administers your trust estate according to your wishes as described in the written instructions in your trust agreement.

Often married couples will establish a family trust with the two spouses as trustees during their joint lifetime; upon the death of one spouse, the other spouse becomes the trustee, and at that spouse's death, the trust estate is distributed to the beneficiaries established at the time the trust was set up originally. The trust also can be set up as revocable or irrevocable. If it's revocable, you can change your mind later and eliminate the trust or change it. Conversely, if it is irrevocable, you're stuck with it as you originally set it up. There are tax reasons behind nearly all this testamentary plan, and you should consult an estate planning lawyer to determine what is right for you.

Q. How can I change my will?

A. You can change your will by making a new will with a later date and following the same requirements, including witnesses, as with the earlier will. Or, you can simply add new provisions to the old will. The addition is formally called "a codicil" and should be dated, signed, and witnessed just like the original will was.

Q. What is the legal status of my children upon my death?

A. In most states, your children do not automatically share in your estate (unless they are minors and you die intestate—without a will) if you don't mention them in your will or if they are not the beneficiaries of your insurance, retirement, a living trust or joint ownership arrangement.

Q. What is probate?

A. Probate is the court process of settling your estate after you die. The executor of your estate is responsible for marshaling and distributing your assets, that is, if you left a will and named an executor. If not, it's done by an arm of the state government. The idea of the probate is to pay all the bills you legitimately owe, and to provide legal deeds (for real property) and bills of sale (for personal property) to the people you have designated to receive your assets. It is done through court process to assure that your wishes as expressed in your will are honored.

When you die, your executor files a petition with the court for probate of your estate. The probate is advertised in the newspapers, and copies are sent to all the beneficiaries named in your will or who are your natural heirs. Then, after a sufficient period of time for claims to be made, a hearing is held to hear claims against your estate and to approve the distribution contained in your will or according to the court's distribution of your estate if you didn't leave a will. This whole process takes at least one year or sometimes longer, depending on how complicated your estate is or whether there are challenges to your will. The costs of this, including the fee paid to the executor are, in most states, set by law and based on a sliding scale percentage of the value of the estate. Extraordinary fees can be sought both by your executor and the lawyer for the executor depending on whether there is work to be done that is out of the ordinary such as participating in litigation.

There are ways of to avoid probate, but each has drawbacks. For example, you could give all your property away while you're still alive (you can give away $10,000 each year to each "donee" and the first $600,000 of your estate is not taxed as a gift or in your estate); you can put property into a joint ownership with right of survivorship; and, you can put property into a living trust. Remember, avoiding probate does not avoid taxes. Uncle Sam always gets his share.

Q. What is not included in the probate?

A. The only property involved in a probate is the property you owned and left to others in your will. Joint tenancy property, insurance policies, remainder estates, and trust property are not included in the property to be divided by the will.

YOUR HEIRS AND HIS NEXT WIFE—CHANGING SITUATIONS

Life being what it is, your financial and living situation may change after you have made a will. Thus, it is important that you review your will or your estate plan from time to time to bring these documents up-to-date with your wishes and your life situation. This may be anticipated by dividing your estate among children, natural or adopted, or other heirs whose situation might change. Many people write wills requiring the heirs to do certain things before they are able to receive any of the estate such as: remain married, complete school, get married, have a child, move, buy or sell something. As a rule, heirs that don't want to do what is required by your will while you were alive won't be any more anxious to do those things when you're dead. Your efforts to control your heirs from the grave to conform to your whims or wishes may trigger resentment and cause some heirs to rebel by challenging your will.

Many wills are challenged by unhappy heirs who failed to get what they thought they should from you through your estate plan or what they thought that you wanted them to have and would have so provided had you not been weak, under the influence of nefarious forces, or taken leave of your senses. They may go to court to say that your will isn't valid. When multibillionaire Howard Hughes died leaving one of the largest estates in the history of America, several different wills surfaced, and, after years of investigation, the court declared them all invalid and decided by itself who the heirs to this enormous estate should be. In a bizarre ending, the court finally ruled that certain people would get Hughes' money even though the judge said he was pretty sure that these were the wrong heirs, but he couldn't prove it!

So, your will can be challenged. Usually, there are three reasons for the court setting aside your will after you're dead:

- You were incompetent to make a will, that is, crazy or feebleminded.

- The will is a phony and a fraud, the result of undue influence or duress.

- The will was not created pursuant to legal requirements.

To prove you were incompetent to make a will, the will busters have to show the court proof through testimony, documents, witnesses, or videotapes to establish that you didn't know how much or what kind of property you owned or who your family and heirs are. Or, they may attempt to establish that you were literally insane or so feeble minded that you didn't know what you were doing when you made your will.

To prove the will is a phony and a fraud, the will busters might try to show undue influence or duress on you by certain heirs. For example, they will try to establish that you were forced to sign the will by others who used their relationship with you to cause you to sign a will, which you would, under other circumstances, not have signed. To prove the will isn't legal, the will busters also might try to prove you didn't sign it, or there were no valid witnesses.

WHAT ABOUT ESTATE TAXES?

Starting January 1, 1982, the federal estate tax was changed so that you can leave all your property to your spouse without paying any federal tax. Currently, the first $600,000 worth of property that you leave in your will is free of federal estate tax. Many states, however, also have an estate tax.

GUARDIANSHIP

There are times when a guardian is needed for either a person or property. Usually this occurs when an adult is not competent—an elderly parent or a mentally impaired relative, for example—or possibly a minor child who is not legally competent to run her affairs.

GUARDIANSHIP OF A PERSON

Most often, legal competence to handle one's own business and financial affairs comes with the age of majority. However, there are exceptions. The unique Howard Hughes Jr. became an orphan at the age of 17 and was left valuable property by his father. Instead of letting a guardian be appointed to run his affairs, Hughes went to court in Texas, and the judge declared that young Hughes was competent to run his own affairs. This is an unusual case. In most states this process is called "emancipation." If a guardian is appointed by the court, the child who the guardian is appointed to protect is called the guardian's "ward."

The court can appoint anybody it thinks appropriate to be a guardian and that guardian has the same powers that a competent parent in the same position would have. Usually, the guardian of the person takes care of the living arrangements of his/her ward including housing, feeding, clothing, medical care, education, and all the usual needs a child may have.

While you might be the guardian for an elderly parent or a minor child, there is the possibility that YOU may be the person who is incapacitated or incompetent, In other words you may not be the guardian. You may be the ward. You may be in an accident or become ill and generally be unable to care for yourself and for others who have been depending on you. To assure that your guardian is the person you want to handle your affairs, you can make advance provisions for the appointment of a guardian to take care of you if you need one and to take care of others, too, such as your minor children or your parents. You can do this through preparation; let your wishes be known, and execute a durable power of attorney. For example, you can specify guardians for your minor children in your will, assuming that your spouse is not living or available to take the children. You can assign such a power of attorney to a trusted relative or friend in which you appoint that person your legal guardian under certain circumstances. This is a precaution to consider when you are in good health and competent to make these decisions. Remember each of us is just one accident away from physical or mental incompetence.

GUARDIANSHIP OF PROPERTY

At times a guardian of property or an estate is needed. This need may arise when a minor or an incompetent adult inherits or is awarded damages or gifts and prizes. Personal living needs may be taken care of, but a person who may be capable of seeing after her physical needs may not be capable of managing her property. Such a person may not have the knowledge or experience necessary to manage the property she has inherited. In this situation, the court may appoint someone guardian of the property or estate only. The court may appoint a relative or friend or, possibly, a corporation such as a bank or investment firm. Most states have specific requirements about who can be a guardian of property.

The difference between a guardian of a person and of property is that the guardian of property controls the management of the property only, not the personal life of the protected person. While the guardian of property has the power to buy, sell, rent, give, and do almost everything an owner can do, the law says the guardian of property must act prudently. Technically, they call this living up to the "prudent person standard." That means the guardian can't do crazy, irresponsible things. Of course, just as in the case of executors of wills and trustees who perform duties for others, the guardian is entitled to be paid a reasonable fee. The fee is usually set by the court.

Here again, you may want to designate a guardian of your estate in advance of an event that causes you to be unable to manage your property. It is also wise to pick not just a guardian, but a successor guardian in case the first one refuses to take the assignment or herself is incapacitated or deceased.

CHAPTER 14

INHERITANCE AND OTHER LEGAL RIGHTS FOR LESBIANS

Equal rights for lesbians and gays is a concept that generates a lot of emotion. Being lesbian or gay is not illegal, and sexual orientation cannot legally be a reason for discrimination in most instances. There is, however, discrimination against lesbians and gay men, and there is no Federal law such as the Civil Rights Act of 1964 that forbids discrimination on the basis of sexual orientation. Discrimination on the basis of sex is illegal, but not on the basis of "sexual orientation." If you are fired from your job or refused the rental of a home because of your sex, that is illegal and you may have the basis of a lawsuit. However, if you are fired or refused a rental because of your sexual orientation, in most states you would have no similar right to sue.

This same philosophy applies to benefits and inheritance rights between homosexual partners. In some jurisdictions, local governments are allowing live-in partners to obtain some joint health and retirement benefits, but this is not the norm. In fact, private industry is ahead of the government on this issue with major companies such as Disney and IBM providing for joint health and retirement benefits for homosexual partners. In the area of inheritance law, if one homosexual companion dies without a will, his or her estate does not automatically go to his or her homosexual partner. Unless other formal arrangements are made, the estate will go to the deceased person's family. So long as the legislature refuses to act to change the law to protect the surviving same-sex partner, the solution is to make a formal disposition of your property: Make a written will, transfer property before death into a trust or joint tenancy, or one of the other many arrangements we have discussed in the sections on estates and real estate.

The key to domestic partners taking care of each other is to put everything about their relationship into writing. Often, for example, when a person dies, the heirs may quibble over the inheritance, and sometimes become quite vicious and unforgiving. So, put all your legal arrangements in writing. Some of the documents same gender couples may want to consider include:

- **Will or Living Trust.** Usually, the law allows you to pass your property to anyone you want even outside your biological or legal family. The Living Trust is somewhat like a will and permits property titles to pass from one to another without going through probate.

- **Living Will.** Sad to say, but in this time of AIDS this could be a very important document because it specifics the extent of treatment a person wants even after he or she is no longer able to competently communicate with doctors.

- **Health Care Proxy or Power of Attorney.** This is also very important since same gender companions technically have no legal authority to direct or agree to health procedures for someone who is stricken. This allows each partner to make medical decisions and to speak on behalf of the other partner.

- **General Power of Attorney.** As the name implies, this gives each partner the right to transact business and make decisions on behalf of the other partner, such as signing documents, paying debts, executing forms, and so on. It can also be limited to instances of emergency or when the other partner is disabled.

- **Joint Tenancy.** As explained in other parts of this book, if you and your companion buy property and take title as joint tenants with the right of survivorship, the entire title passes to the survivor in the event that one of you die. If you take title as tenants in common, the deceased person's share goes to whomever is designated in his/her will.

- **Partnership Agreement.** In some ways this is like a prenuptial agreement between a heterosexual couple; it can spell out how your assets will be divided and handled in the event the relationship splits up.

- **Insurance.** For decades, insurance companies have insisted that anyone taking out insurance on the life of another have an "insurable interest." That is, the owner of the policy must be able to prove a legally recognized loss if that person dies. Some insurance companies are now willing to recognize that there is an insurable interest between gay couples. However, a simpler way of handling life insurance is for each person to take out a life insurance policy on himself/herself and name his/her partner as the beneficiary. In other kinds of insurance, such as homeowners and car, the marital relationship of the insured usually doesn't matter.

For more information on the issues concerning lesbian and gay couples, you may want to refer to such books as:

Financial Self-Defense for Unmarried Couples by Larry M. Elkin, published by Doubleday, New York.

The Living Together Kit: A Legal Guide for Unmarried Couples by Toni Ihara and Ralph Warner, published by Nolo Press.

A Legal Guide for Lesbian and Gay Couples by Hayden Curry, Denis Clifford and Robin Leonard, Nolo Press.

Personal Financial Planning for Gays & Lesbians by Peter M. Berkery, Jr., Irwin Professional Publishing.

CHAPTER 15

WHAT YOU NEED TO KNOW ABOUT TAXES

FEDERAL INCOME TAXES

Everybody in the country is subject to Federal income taxes, but not everybody has to pay taxes. Our income tax laws are filled with loopholes (although they are rapidly being closed), exceptions and exemptions, and a bewildering array of details so that almost no one clearly understands it all. In some ways, the Federal income tax is like the airline fare where two people leaving from the same place and going to the same destination may be paying vastly different fares. It is money in your pocket if you understand some of the basics about the Federal income tax. For example, what is your *filing status?* This is very important because it helps to determine how much tax you have to pay.

One of the most important things in determining your personal filing status is your marital situation on the last day of the year—December 31st for most people who file personal income taxes based on the calendar year. So, what is your marital status on the last day of your tax year? You are, for the tax collector, either Single, Married, or the Head of a Household.

You are Single if you are one of these:

- You have never been married.

- You are a widow whose husband died more than two years ago. More details about this below.

- You have a final decree of divorce, separation, or annulment. A special note about annulment in a minute.

You are Married if you are one of these:

- You are married and living with your husband.

- You are married and living separately, but there is no final decree of divorce or separation.

- You are separated under an interlocutory divorce decree, but it is not final.

You are a Qualifying Widow with a Dependent Child if you are ALL of these:

- Your spouse died within the past two years and you did not remarry within this year.

- You have a child, stepchild, adopted child, or foster child whom you can claim as a dependent.

- This child lived in your home for all of this year.

- You paid over half the cost of keeping up your home.

- You could have filled a joint return with your spouse the year he died, even if you did not.

You are a Head of Household if you are ALL of these:

- You pay more than half the household cost.

- You are not married or you are a "surviving" spouse.

- Your home is the main residence for a dependent relative, such as a child, for more than half the year.

REPORTING AND PAYING YOUR FEDERAL TAXES

Federal income taxes are, as we all know, complicated, but we have to file them nevertheless. Here are some pointers that will make it easier for you.

STANDARD DEDUCTIONS

Everybody is entitled to deduct a certain amount from their so-called gross income depending on filing status. This can be changed by Congress every year, but as a guide, these were the standard deductions in the 1997 tax year:

SINGLE—4,150
    If blind or 65 or over—5,150
    If blind and 65 or over—6,150

SURVIVING SPOUSE

MARRIED FILING SEPARATELY—3,450
If blind or 65 or over—4,250
If blind and 65 or over—5,050

MARRIED FILING JOINTLY
Additional deduction for over 65 and being blind
If 1 additional deduction—7,700
If 2 additional deductions—8,500
If 3 additional deductions—9,300
If 4 additional deductions—10,100

HEAD OF HOUSEHOLD—6,050
If blind or 65 or over—7,050
If blind and 65 or over—8,050

OTHER FEDERAL TAXES

Besides standard federal income taxes, there are some special taxes that deal specifically with property and what happens if the owner of the property dies.

ESTATE TAXES

These are the taxes paid on property that changes hands because somebody died. The tax is like income tax in that a sliding scale applies based on the size of the estate, and it applies to all property owned by the deceased person upon his/her death, whether he/she distributes his/her property by a will or tangible trust or insurance or even if he/she fails to prepare documents that sets forth his/her plan for distribution. The effect of the law is that the first $600,000 worth of property is free of Federal state taxes, but there may be a state tax based on a different minimum.

If you leave property to your husband or he leaves it to you, the value of that property is subtracted from the total value of the estate, and there are no Federal taxes on it. This is called, "the marital deduction." This is an excellent way of deferring estate taxes that may have to be paid when you or your husband die. If your wills are drawn carefully, your husband may be able to pass your joint marital property to you without you paying any estate taxes. Since women traditionally live longer than men, this is very important to you. Check with your attorney on this, but generally your marital property is held as "tenants by the entirety" (see chapter 13 above) or as joint tenants with the right of survivorship, provided you and your husband are the **only** joint tenants or as community property.

CHAPTER 16

THE NASTY TRUTH ABOUT YOUR PENSION

Even though women are in today's workforce as much as men are, today's working woman will get a much worse deal on her pension.

A recent study[1] shows that women end up with a lot less money in their pensions than men do. In the first place, men tend to stay at one job longer than women do on the average—4.8 years for women versus 6.5 years for men. This means that women gain fewer retirement points and, in many cases, don't qualify for a pension at all if they have to stay on the job for five years in order "to vest" or be eligible for any pension.

The result is that, while 47% of retired men received pensions from their previous employer, only 20% of retired women did. Here again the wage difference between men and women, wherein women get paid less than men for the same work, affects how big the pension will be. The sad news is that, in recent years, women's pensions have *dropped* in comparison to men's. In 1989 the average women's yearly pension was $4,330 compared with the average man's yearly pension of $9,460. So, in 1989 a woman got a pension that was 46% as large as a man's, but 11 years earlier in 1978 a woman's pension was 51% as large as a man's.

So, one of the first things you want to do when considering a job is find out the details of the company pension plan, if any. Find out whether it will apply to you and when and how you become eligible. If you are married, you may be covered under your husband's pension plan with his employer. However, you should find out all the details of his plan. For example, if you outlive him, does the pension continue to

---

[1] Martha Priddy Paterson, *The Women's Guide to Retirement Planning*, Prentice-Hall, Englewood Cliffs, New Jersey, 1993.

be payable to you? Some employers offer a choice of several pension options to their employees. For example, one plan might pay the same amount to both you and your husband for as long as either of you is alive. Another plan, however, might stop paying when whoever has the pension dies, or it may pay out a reduced benefit when whoever holds the pension dies. You need to know this so you can plan accordingly.

What about your husband's pension benefits in the event you and he divorce? Are you cut out entirely or are you still eligible for some benefits? This might be something your divorce lawyer will want to include in the divorce settlement.

You need to educate yourself about IRAs, 401 Keogh savings plans, Social Security, and all the other pension options available to you, and you need to do it long before you retire so you can make the adjustments and arrangements necessary to have a safe and comfortable retirement. The U.S. Department of Labor has a free pamphlet on "Women and Pensions." Just call (202) 219-9247 and they'll send it to you.

CHAPTER 17

ASSURANCE ABOUT INSURANCE

Unfortunately, too many people think insurance is insurance, and there is no difference from company to company. This is not true. Insurance is a commodity just like anything else and you need to shop carefully to get the kind of insurance policy that is best for you.

To begin, you need to understand what insurance is. The idea of insurance is as old as civilization, and it works like this. Over time, statisticians determine that a certain number of people will have bad things happen to them. For example, out of every thousand people, a certain number will have an automobile accident, be hurt in an accident, have their house burn down, be robbed, or die. We know what percentage will suffer these tragedies, but we don't know who they are. The concept of insurance is that a large group of people pool their money by paying "premiums" to cover the cost of the accidents that will occur to some of them. Insurance companies make money, in theory, by charging an administration fee plus making a profit by investing this pool of money. In theory, the total cost of insurance that everybody in the pool divides up should be the sum of three things: the amount of money paid out to victims, the administrative costs of running the pool, and a profit for the people running the pool.

This simple arrangement becomes complicated when some insurance companies try to increase their profits by charging higher premiums than are needed to cover costs and reasonable profits. Some may wish to avoid paying a victim's losses. And, sadly, it has happened that insurance companies refuse to pay claims made and ultimately close their doors and disappear with the money.

The point is that you need to investigate before you choose an insurance company to assure that you get the best protection from your insurance company at the lowest reasonable cost. Before you buy insurance for you car, life, home, and other things, shop around. Talk to other people who have insurance to determine what their experience has been with various companies, check consumer protection articles in local newspapers, and consult the state agency that regulates insurance in your state. In the library, you can consult *BEST'S Guide* which rates certain insurance companies.

Many insurance companies try to cut the risks that they will have to pay claims by avoiding certain kinds of customers. For example, some companies charge more for drivers who drive in certain geographical areas, who have bad driving records, or are male and under 25 because statistics show that those drivers tend to drive recklessly. Companies also often prefer not to insure the lives of smokers, excessive drinkers, airline pilots, and sky jumpers, for example. Most insurance companies require that the insured take some part of the loss—this is the so-called "deductible." Others cut their exposure by refusing to pay for preexisting illnesses.

Review the information you gather very carefully because it will be important, perhaps critical, to you at a time when you are weak, sick, even incompetent, and you need all the help you can get. That's when your choice of an insurance company will be critical. Often, insurance may be obtained through work, unions, credit unions, or organizations to which you belong. Check all these sources carefully.

CHAPTER 18

OTHER AVAILABLE BENEFITS AND HELP

WOMEN AND SOCIAL WELFARE LAWS

There are a number of government programs to help you when you are in need, and we outline some of them here. However, the political climate is changing rapidly and programs are being added, dropped, and altered, so you need to check out the current situation and the appropriate government agency.

SOCIAL SECURITY DISABILITY BENEFITS

If you are the main wage earner in your family and you become TOTALLY disabled, you may be able to collect disability benefits from the federal or state government. To obtain these benefits you must be under 64 and have a serious physical or mental problem that has kept you from working for more than a year or that may ultimately kill you. You must be unable to work at any kind of job—never mind the job you previously had—any kind of job. Finally, you must have a certain number of what are called "work credits" from your previous jobs. You receive one work credit for every three months or every quarter of a year you had a job earning at least $500.

The next requirement for social security disability payments is based on your age and the number of these credits you have earned. If you are 23 or younger, you must have earned six credits since you were 20. If you are between 24 and 31, the formula is more complicated. Count the number of quarter-years (three month periods) between your 21st birthday, and the date you became disabled. Divide that by two and that's the number of work credits you must have. If you are between 32 and 64, there is a sliding scale for calculating the number of work credits you must have with the minimum being 20 work credits in the 10 years before you became disabled.

If you apply for disability payments and are turned down, you have 60 days to appeal that decision. The Social Security Administration will review its decision, and, if it still turns you down, that second rejection will be reviewed by an administrative law judge. If he or she turns you down too, it goes to a hearing before a Federal district court. So, you have four shots at getting federal benefits if you believe you are totally disabled.

MEDICARE BENEFITS

This is a program of medical insurance coverage for those over age 65 and, in special cases, some under 65. This insurance is for both medical care and hospital stays. The program is run by the Social Security Administration.

The hospital aspect of the program has two parts and covers hospital care, nursing home care, hospice, and home health care. Hospital insurance may also be available to your widower, widow, divorced spouse, and children or parents who are disabled or dependent upon you for support. The two parts are hospital insurance with a premium and hospital insurance without a premium.

To be eligible for hospital insurance with a premium you have to be 65 or older, a citizen and resident of the U.S., and not eligible to obtain the other hospital insurance. To obtain the hospital insurance without paying a premium you have to be 65 and on Social Security for at least 25 months or have serious kidney disease. Just as with Social Security disability benefits, the government has established an appeals process in the event you are turned down for hospital insurance. You must file your appeal within 60 days of receipt of the letter denying you coverage, or you're out of luck. Non-U.S. citizens can also apply for medical insurance if they are over 65 and have lived in this country for at least five years.

The medical aspect of Medicare insurance covers doctor's fees, medical supplies, clinic visits, ambulance service, and tests, plus some drugs and things such as pacemakers. It also covers home health care and outpatient services, physical therapy, nursing, and psychological care.

Normally, to obtain your initial coverage under Medicare you need to sign up at one of two times. One is called "initial enrollment," and that is the three months before you technically are eligible to be on Medicare. For most people without serious kidney disease or other disability, that would usually be the three months before your 65th birthday. If you miss this "initial enrollment" period, you have to wait and enroll during what the government calls the "general enrollment" period, which is January 1 through March 31 of every year.

The Social Security Administration is quite efficient, and when you sign up for Medicare, you will be guided through your choices for medical and hospital insurance because you have some choices available to you. Remember, Medicare does not cover everything and you may want to consider supplemental health insurance from a private insurance company. There are many of these and each has its pluses and minuses; each will cost you a premium so study such plans carefully before you decide.

SOCIAL SECURITY: SUPPLEMENTAL SECURITY INCOME

This is a payment program for people who are poor and whose total assets are less than $2,000 per person or $3,000 per couple. Besides being poor you must be unable to work, aged, disabled, blind, or a child under 17. In addition, you cannot be getting more income from such things as pensions, food stamps, or earnings than that which the supplemental security income will pay.

WELFARE RIGHTS

"Welfare" is becoming a dirty word in America because welfare programs have been demonized by politicians who like to paint welfare recipients as lazy people who just want to be paid for not working. Undoubtedly, there may be some people on welfare who fit that description; but the reality is that there are millions of young children who are on welfare, and it doubtful that we will ever do away with it entirely. However, as this is written, there is much turmoil about the welfare system, so it's important that you check with your local welfare agency on the latest rules concerning welfare to see how they may have changed. As we write this, Congress has passed and the President has signed a bill that significantly changes the welfare system. No one is sure just how it will all sort out, so check with your local welfare agency to find out the current status of the system where you live.

UNEMPLOYMENT INSURANCE BENEFITS

Unemployment insurance is money paid temporarily to people who are out of work through no fault of their own. It is administered in most cases by the state of residence and has basic requirements that must be met by those who wish to collect unemployment payments. Essentially, you must apply for unemployment insurance benefits and register with the public employment or human resources office as one who is looking for work. You must be, as they say, "ready, willing, and able" to work. Usually, you have to have worked at least six months during the previous year and have earned a certain minimum amount of wages. Normally, there is a wait of at least a week before you can start collecting unemployment benefits.

Some of the reasons you would NOT be eligible for payments include that you quit your job without a good reason, are getting unemployment payments from some other source, lied about being eligible for unemployment benefits, or refused to try to get another job.

WORKER'S COMPENSATION

This is a program that provides a payment to you if you are injured on the job. Usually, you have to have been working at a paid job—not volunteer work or work as a personal servant—in order to qualify. The rules of what is "work" have been expanded over the years and should apply to anything you do related to your job including on-the-job injuries and going to or from work when you are engaged in work-related activities off the work site. You may receive worker's compensation benefits as a result of injuries sustained by someone physically attacking you because of your work or if you contract a disease as a result of your work.

There is one aspect of Worker's Compensation that makes it different than other benefits available to workers: It is paid from a fund financed by employers. Employers pay a certain percentage of their payroll into the Worker's Compensation fund, which is use to pay benefits to injured workers. The percentage of the payroll that the employer pays is on a sliding scale based on how many claims each employer has that must be paid. The fewer the Workman's Compensation claims paid to a employer's workers, the lower the amount he or she has to pay into the fund. In theory, this was designed to make employers more safety conscious, and it probably does to some extent. However, it also makes employers fight against many claims because, if your employer or ex-employer can get your claim turned down, it is beneficial to the employer. As with other compensation programs, Worker's Compensation has strict time limits you must observe, and it has an appeal procedure by each employer and employee if either is unhappy with any ruling on a claim.

Part Four
GETTING THROUGH THE DAILY PROBLEMS

CHAPTER 19

HOW TO SURVIVE APARTMENT LIVING

At one time or another in our lives most of us live in an apartment or rental unit; perhaps, for some us, apartment living is a way of life. You should always have a written agreement, lease, or rental contract because it will save a lot of hassle and expense for everyone. Ideally, everyone—landlord, you, and the other tenants—will all get along just fine and live forever in peace and harmony. However, ideally doesn't often happen, so it's sensible to hope for the best and prepare for the worst by having everything set out in writing.

LANDLORD-TENANT AGREEMENTS— ORAL V. WRITTEN

The law varies from state to state, but generally, lease or rental agreements are legal whether they are oral or in writing. However, you are foolish to rely on an oral agreement because any dispute that comes up, and we guarantee one will, becomes a vitriolic exchange of "he said, I said, they said, we all said," and it may be difficult to resolve your dispute without court intervention. Even a written agreement may not be perfect, but it will set to rest those matters with which it deals. If the landlord doesn't want to put the terms of your rental agreement in writing, that is a red flag that you may be headed for trouble. He may be offering a quick rental at a good price to you while holding open the option of throwing you out with minimal notice; you may have trouble getting your deposit money back or getting your furniture out when you leave. Take the New England approach where they have said for hundreds of years that "good fences make good neighbors." Written contracts make for fewer misunderstandings. Tell the landlord that "just to keep things neat or orderly we ought to jot down what our arrangement is."

DON'T FALL FOR THE OLD "STANDARD AGREEMENT" TRICK

You can expect that the landlord will want you to sign a printed lease form he got from the stationery store or the Board of Realtors or a lease usually drafted to favor the landlord. He will tell you, "This is just a standard agreement," as if it were created by God and were perfect in every way. There is no such thing as a "standard agreement." Every agreement was originally drawn up by somebody, and usually it is drawn in the favor of one side of the deal or the other. So, do not just sign any "standard agreement" without carefully understanding what it obligates you to do and pay. Your best approach when confronted with this "standard form" is to accept it and stall for time so you can study it alone without the landlord hovering over you. Make some excuse such as that your brother-in-law is an attorney, and he won't let you sign anything—ANYTHING—that he doesn't read first. So, you will bring the "standard agreement" back later with his suggested modifications.

Read the landlord's agreement very carefully indeed. You may want to have a friend or a lawyer review it, particularly if it is going to commit you for a long time and involves a substantial monthly payment and security deposit. Here are some of the main things you and the landlord have to agree upon even before you get to the written agreement.

ADVANCE INSPECTION AND INVENTORY

You must always inspect the property you are renting in advance to making any deal. Open all the drawers, cabinets, doors, and try all the faucets, toilets, gas outlets, lights, and other utilities to make sure everything works. If there is any furniture belonging to the landlord in the place, make a careful descriptive list that both of you will sign as a part of the lease. It is an excellent idea to have a friend do this with you and for you to take notes and photographs. Doing something as simple as that can save you tremendous irritation and possibly thousands of dollars later on if there is a dispute.

AMOUNT OF UP-FRONT MONEY (DEPOSITS, CLEANUP)

Most landlords want money from you up front. Be sure you understand how much up-front money you have to pay and when it is to be paid and what it is supposed to cover. For example, it is normal for the landlord to want the first and last month's rent in advance. In addition, it is common for the landlord to ask for a cleanup or security deposit. Everybody must understand just exactly what each of these is. Normally, the last month's rent is just what it says, the last month's rent. A cleanup deposit is usually also what it says. It is money to pay for cleaning up the apartment after you move out to make it ready for the next tenant. However, this is often a rip-off gimmick because too often, even if you leave the place immaculate, the landlord will say he had to have it cleaned up and he is, therefore, keeping your cleanup deposit. Be tough. Don't let the landlord push you around at the end of your term. To assist you in avoiding this, spell out in the lease just exactly what "cleanup" means. For example, you might specify that you are to repair and replace any damages (including holes in the wall from picture hooks), wash the windows and tile, and leave the floors vacuumed or mopped clean. Then, you are both to inspect the property *before* any of the cleanup deposit is used, and if you are unable to agree on whether the place needs repair or cleaning, you both call in a third-party arbitrator to settle the question. The security deposit is another name for cleanup money or for last month's rent, and we recommend against paying that if you are also putting up cleaning money and last month's rent.

An important question about this up-front money comes from the fact that it is legally your money all the time until the end of your lease. So, who is going to hold it? Usually, it will be held by the landlord, but it is not technically his/hers unless and until you fail to do what you are obligated to do upon vacating the premises, such as cleaning up the property satisfactorily or unless you skip out on your lease. It is an increasingly accepted practice that this money is deposited in a landlord's trust account at a bank or savings institution and that you are entitled to the interest it earns while there.

IF YOU WANT OUT OF THE DEAL

Things change, and we try to prepare for change as much as we can. At the time you entered into the lease for your rented home, you may have intended to stay there at least for the length of your lease. Still, circumstances change, and you may find that you want or have to move before the end of the lease term or you are unable to comply with other terms of the lease agreement. Thus, you may want to have an escape clause in the lease; if not, you may legitimately be held responsible for paying the full amount of the lease payments until the end of the term even if you are not living there anymore. So, we recommend that the lease have a clause that permits you to sublet the property on the same terms, except for the rent and deposits, on which you are renting the property.

REPAIRS PROMISED BY THE LANDLORD

Even with new property there are repairs that need to be done. Generally, most states require that the landlord rent property in "livable" condition, which usually means that all the appliances, the gas, electricity and water, and bathroom facilities are in working order. If other maintenance items need repair to assure that the premises are livable or are desirable and the landlord agrees to do them (such as repairs to floors or walls or windows or painting), it is preferable to have him do those things before you accept the premises and move in.

Remember, if the landlord does not maintain the premises in livable condition, you can have the repairs made and deduct the reasonable cost from your rent.

RENT

Most of the time, unless your lease says differently, the rent is due when it's due with no grace period. The amount of the rent is set in the written agreement and can't be changed by the landlord or you without changing the written agreement. However, if you are foolish enough not to have a written agreement, the landlord can raise the rent by any amount at any time, usually with no more than a month's notice. This is one of the many reasons you should have your understanding with the landlord in writing. Another reason is that, in most states, if your rent is paid up, you have the exclusive use of the property and privacy, so the landlord cannot come into your place without your permission. Essentially, while you are renting the place and paid up, it is your place, not his/hers. Some lease agreements spell out exceptions to this; for example, if your lease is ending and you are moving out, some agreements allow the landlord to come in to show the place to prospective new tenants. Usually the landlord has the right to enter in case of needed repairs or an emergency. However, all this should be spelled out in your agreement so you're not standing there, just out of the shower and wearing nothing but a smile when the landlord barges in with 16 of his/her relatives.

TERM OF THE LEASE

Your agreement should spell out how long the arrangement between you and the landlord lasts, that is, the term of your lease. Read this carefully because the details on the term of the lease often have automatic provisions that you may or may not want, but in any case should understand. For example, it may say that if you don't notify the landlord in writing at least 30 days before the end of the lease that you are moving out, the lease agreement is automatically renewed. For example, if you have a one-year lease and you plan to move out at the end of it, if you don't notify the landlord in writing at least a month before the end of your lease, it automatically puts you on the hook for another year. Look carefully for such a clause BEFORE you sign the lease and try to negotiate out of it.

KEEPING THE PLACE LIVABLE

Usually, it is the landlord's duty to keep the place livable with the toilets working, the water running, the electricity and natural gas connected, and free of insects, vermin, and rodents. Also, you may want the landlord to be responsible for repainting, recarpeting, and major cleaning. Make sure the lease specifies these as the landlord's responsibility. It will probably also call for you to take partial responsibility by not ruining equipment, storing flammable or dangerous chemicals, or by having annoying pets. If something gets clogged, broken, and damaged because of negligence by you, you will have to pay for fixing it. Ordinarily, you are allowed what is called "fair wear and tear," but not major damage and ruination.

LANDLORD REPOSSESSION, LOCK-OUTS, SEIZURE, ETC.

There are times when the landlord can repossess the property, seize your belongings, and lock you out. These are usually extreme circumstances and must be detailed in your rental agreement. If, for example, you haven't paid the rent and the landlord has served a legal notice on you (he might have posted the notice on the door of your apartment) to quit or get out of the rental, he then may have the right to come in, change the locks, and grab your furniture and personal belongings.

RETURN OF DEPOSITS

Most states have laws specifying when your deposits must be returned. You should also insist that money paid as a cleanup deposit or security deposit and held by the landlord be put in an insured savings account paying interest and that you get the interest. This is the law in many states or local communities.

PETS AND ANNOYANCES

You should be sure that the landlord has the same limitations in all the leases in your building on types of pets, noise, and other activities that are permitted. Yes, this is a restriction on you, but it should also be a restriction on your neighbors so you can enjoy living in the building. Thus, rules forbidding jungle animals, snakes, and vicious dogs as pets and limiting parking, noise, storage of dangerous chemicals, and so on are usually in your best interest. It should apply to everyone. The lease may contain rules regarding whether you can run a business out of your home, and if so, what kind of business it might be. In general noisy, hazardous enterprises as well as those which attract crowds are banned and, naturally so are illegal and immoral enterprises.

SUBLETTING OR ASSIGNMENT

It is often good to have the right to sublet or assign your lease because, if your circumstances change and you want to be released from the lease, this offers a way. In subletting, you are still primarily responsible for the main lease, but you can rent the place out to someone else. However, if you do this, make sure that your sublessee signs a sublease agreement with you holding him/her to the terms of your original lease. Thus, your place is taken by someone else to whom you may assign or transfer the lease if that is possible in your lease agreement. If your original lease does not allow an assignment, as it most probably will not without the lessor's approval, you may try to negotiate a sublease. If you can make a valid assignment, you are out of the deal. The assignee has taken your place, and you have no further privileges or responsibilities. If you cannot assign you may be able to sublease, again probably only with the landlord's approval. When you sublease, you are still responsible to the landlord pursuant to the terms of your original lease. Most landlords will specify that they must approve of the sublease or assignment. Such a provision is a protection for the other tenants and thus is desirable in most leases.

LANDLORD/TENANT DISPUTES

As a tenant there are various issues that may arise for which you may seek redress from the landlord. You may file a complaint with the appropriate local or state agency. If your dispute involves money, as is likely, you have the option of suing the landlord in small claims court. Suing in a higher trial court, such as municipal or superior court is probably too complicated and expensive unless you are talking big money. See our section on small claims court for limits and details.

CHAPTER 20

BUYING AND OPERATING A CAR

BUYING A CAR

Cars cost as much as homes did in the not so distant past. Buying a car is a major investment, and it is also a necessity in some parts of the country where it is the only practical form of transportation. Because an automobile is such an important investment, you should take the time to thoroughly investigate and research the market. First, get a clear understanding of what you want and what you need. Discuss it with friends, review *Consumer Guide* magazine and other magazines that will assist you in determining what is the right car for you considering affordability and upkeep. The first decision is whether to buy a new car or a used car. Each has its advantages. Obviously, the new car is supposedly more stylish and in better mechanical condition while the used car is less expensive to buy.

Here are a few considerations to think about when deciding to buy a new or used car.

- **Bait and Switch.** Unfortunately, some new car dealers resort to "bait and switch" tactics. This means they advertise one car that sounds almost too good to be true (probably because it IS too good to be true) to bait you into coming to their showroom. Once you are there, they switch you to a more expensive or less desirable car. If that happens, you should just leave the showroom and not do business there. You might want to report a bait and switch to your local consumer protection agency, but whatever you do, just say "no" and leave.

- **Sales Contracts.** When you make a deal to buy a car, it should be in writing. In every state except Louisiana, there is some variation of the Uniform Commercial Code that says anything bought and sold for $500 or more requires a contract in writing. A written contract will provide a protection for you if you find that you have to go to court over the deal. Some of the items that should be in the contract and/or bill of sale include:

- Vehicle identification number (on the dashboard of the driver's side of the car).

- Details of the car: year, make, model, and mileage.

- Status of the car: new, used, rental car, taxi, demonstrator.

- Price, terms of sale, trade-in received, payments, annual interest (called the "annual percentage rate of interest" or APR), and term of the loan.

■ **Warranty details.** Often the seller of a used car wants to sell it "as is," which means just that. It is not advisable to buy a used car "as is" unless you can have it inspected by a mechanic you trust to make sure of its condition. No legitimate seller should object to this. Be careful, some sellers will lie and say the car comes with a warranty when, in fact, it doesn't. Get the warranty in writing with the signature of the responsible party.

■ **Buyer's Guide.** If you buy a used car from a dealer, he or she is forbidden to misrepresent the mechanical condition of the car and is required to post a "Buyer's Guide" on the side window of the car. A dealer is anyone who sells six or more used cars a year. The Buyer's Guide tells you if there is a warranty on the car and what it covers or if it is sold as is. It also warns you to have the car inspected by your own mechanic and to get all promises in writing.

■ **Lemon Laws.** Some states have laws to protect you if the car you buy turns out to be a "lemon." Check with your state consumer protection agency to see if your state has a lemon law and what the details of it are. We know that California, Florida, New York, Pennsylvania, and Texas all have lemon laws, but each has different details. Basically, if you buy a new car and it doesn't work right, the manufacturer is allowed several tries—usually three or four— at repairing the problem. If it can't be fixed and certain other requirements are met, you are entitled to a replacement car or a refund of your money.

■ **Monroney Label.** Another protection for you is called the "Monroney Label" in the business. It is a sticker that the makers of the new car must put on the window of the car listing the base price plus the price of the extras that have been put on the car and the mileage that the car is supposed to get. Only a buyer is allowed to take the Monroney Label off a car.

■ **New Car Warranty.** When you buy a car from a dealer, you are entitled to see the written warranty on that car so you can see just what is covered and what is not. This federal law, the Magnuson-Moss Act, has been law since 1975 and applies to all cars made after 1975, but not if the car is sold "as is."

■ **Leasing.** Leasing is a method of having the use and control of a car without buying it. Whether leasing or buying is right for you is something that you should carefully consider. It depends on your personal needs and your financial condition. On the plus side, leasing usually means lower monthly payments; there is generally a minimal or low down payment and no sales tax. Your lease payments may be tax deductible if you use the car in your work not including going to and from work. On the negative side, you are not building any equity in the car, and when the lease expires, your options generally are to buy the car or release or buy a different car.

There are two types of leases: "closed-end," which means you walk away from the lease and the car at the end of the lease with no further expense unless you have abused the car or "open end," which calls for you to pay the difference between the appraised value of the car and what you have paid in lease payments. If the car is worth more than what you have paid in applicable lease payments, you owe nothing. So, in essence you are gambling on whether the car will hold its value or be worth less at the end of the lease. The advantage of the open-end lease is that the monthly payments are smaller than the closed-end lease. However, understand that the monthly payment you make is not entirely a payment on the car lease, it probably also is a payment on an insurance and maintenance contract. Of course, in some deals —usually open-end leases—you can get a lease with the option to buy the car at the end of the lease period. In this case, the company leasing the car to you must specifically detail the purchase price or how it is to be calculated in the original lease. Recently dealers have advertised leases which include the right to simply turn in the car at the end of the lease if you have not exceeded a set mileage rate.

OTHER CONSIDERATIONS IN OWNING AND OPERATING A CAR

Most of us appreciate the advantages of having a car and the increased convenience and mobility it gives us, but having a car can also bring you problems. We'll alert you to some of them in this section.

WHEN YOU ARE STOPPED BY THE POLICE

Driving is among one of the most regulated human activities. Regulation assures that we are able to go from place to place with a minimum of hazard. Because it is heavily regulated, driving may be the one activity of your life during which you and millions of other Americans are under the surveillance of the police. You should understand your rights and theirs. First, the police have the right to stop you if they believe you are driving in a hazardous or unlawful manner such as speeding or making dangerous moves with you car.

When the police stop you, they have the right to request proof that you are licensed to drive and that the car is legally in your possession. Most of the time you will be stopped by an officer in uniform, and it is always wise to pull off the road to a place that is safe from the other traffic but that is always in full view of the other traffic. If you are stopped by a person who is not in uniform in an unmarked car, insist on seeing his or her identification or badge. If the stop is at night, pull off the road into a lighted location such as a gas station or convenience store or some place where there are other people.

After you are satisfied you are being stopped by a bona fide police officer and you have shown him/her your driver's license and vehicle registration to prove you are driving legally and that you have the right to be driving the vehicle, you may find yourself confronted with the following issues. For example, the police officer may want to search your car. Some people may take the position that, "If you have nothing to hide, you shouldn't object." That is nonsense. It is not a question of whether or not YOU have anything to hide, it is a question of assuring that the police officer has legitimate grounds for searching your vehicle. If the automobile is not yours or is used by others, you do not know what is in the car. The officer normally can search your car under these conditions: with your permission or with a search warrant or if he or she has "probable cause" to believe that there is evidence of a crime being committed in the car such as if the officer smells the odor of marijuana smoke or sees weapons or blood or if he/she believes a search is necessary to protect himself. A police officer may search the vehicle if you are stopped and accused of a crime for which you must go to jail, such as driving under the influence of alcohol or drugs or being involved in a serious accident. In that case, he/she can not only search your vehicle but you, too. With probable cause, the police may search the immediate area around where you are seated in the driver's seat plus any area that you can reach including the glove compartment and under the seat.

Generally, the Supreme Court has been more relaxed about searching your vehicle than the search of your home because it has determined that the constitutional protection against unreasonable searches doesn't extend as rigidly to your vehicle. The idea is that most people don't expect it to be as rigidly enforced in the case of vehicles as it is in the case of one's home. For example, the police are not required to ignore anything they can see in plain sight from where they are standing outside the car. If there is a packet of drugs or weapons in open sight on the back seat, the police can seize those.

Although the law varies from state to state, the U.S. Supreme Court has upheld police use of drunk-driving road blocks, check points, and radar. If you are caught speeding by radar, you should either pay the fine or hire an attorney who specializes in that kind of case. His first line of defense is usually that the radar gun was not working right or the officer wasn't properly trained at using it. Also at a police stop the police have the right to administer a field sobriety test to make a preliminary assessment of your ability to drive. Walking a straight line or a breathing test can be done at the scene. Blood and urine testing come when you are transported to the police station.

ARRESTED BY THE POLICE

If the police stop you and a warning or a citation isn't the end of it and you are arrested, there are several things to understand. Ask if you are under arrest, and make sure that the police answer your question, although, if they handcuff you and put you in the patrol car, it is obvious you are under arrest. From the instant you are under arrest, refuse to answer any questions and—repeatedly and insistently—demand an attorney. Keep alert and note the names and badge numbers of the police who arrest you. Most important always be polite to the police and everyone you encounter in this process. Politely refuse to submit to a lineup or to answer any questions about what happened until you are provided with an attorney.

The police are allowed to do what is necessary to get you under control and to transport you to the police station. There you go through the normal arrest or booking process including giving your name and address. Your photograph is taken and your personal possessions removed and catalogued. You may be video taped in the station or even during the stop and arrest out on the road. Each state has different laws about chemical tests to which you must submit, but in most jurisdictions police are allowed to give you a breath test without your consent. There, state law says that when you applied for a driver's license, you voluntarily agreed to take such a test in the future should the police demand it. This is called the "implied consent" rule. However, blood testing is a more serious test because this presents more accurate and stronger evidence in court. In some states, you cannot be forced to take a blood test, and, unless you are certain you haven't had much or any alcohol or drugs in the last hour or two, it is best not to submit to a blood test. Some people stall by saying they want the advice of their attorney and have to wait until he/she arrives at the jail before deciding. This may allow blood levels of alcohol or drugs to fall as time passes, and these substances are metabolized.

After you have been processed and have met with your attorney, he/she can give you a better sense of what your situation is and the options open to you. You may have a winnable case or be facing a fine, jail time, or your driver's license may be suspended or revoked, depending on the laws of your state, how serious the transgression is of which you are accused, and your own background.

WHAT ABOUT BEING INVOLVED IN AN ACCIDENT?

Most people know what to do when they are driving a car and have an accident, but just to review: Pull over to a safe place so you and the other driver or drivers can exchange information. You all should trade your driver's license numbers, address, phone, vehicle registration, and information about your insurance company. You should be sure you have all the information noted down carefully before you leave the scene of the accident. Obviously, if someone is injured, getting help for them is the first order of business, but aside from that get the needed information. Also note down for yourself the time, place, and road and weather conditions at the time, as well as, the names and badge numbers of any policemen at the scene.

As we have advised in connection with other situations where you might be in conflict with the law or with others, be quiet about blame or fault. In the stress of the moment it is often difficult to know exactly what happened or who is at fault. Keep your own counsel until you are represented by a lawyer who can advise you how best to approach the possibility that you may be at fault and facing monetary damages or jail. Notify your lawyer as soon as possible.

All states have laws requiring certain accidents to be reported to the appropriate authorities. All states require that the accident be reported if anyone was hurt or killed. Since someone is likely to be hurt even in a minor accident, the chances are that you will have to report the accident. Other than death or injury, you are also required to report the accident if the amount of the damages exceeds a certain dollar amount. This amount varies from $200 worth of property damage in Michigan, Kentucky, and Pennsylvania and $250 in Alabama, Arkansas, the District of Columbia, Georgia, Idaho, Illinois, Mississippi, New Mexico, and West Virginia to $1,000 in Colorado, Connecticut, Massachusetts, and South Dakota. The number of days in which you must report the accident varies from state to state and ranges from immediately in Delaware, Idaho, Kansas, Michigan, North Carolina, North Dakota, and South Dakota to as many as 30 days in Ohio, Missouri, and Arkansas. Check your local regulations. Usually the accident report is filed with the local police. If you don't file an accident report as required, that is a separate crime— usually a misdemeanor—that might result in your losing your driving privileges.

Some other points about automobile accidents you should know are: You must show that you used reasonable care in operating your car if you are to be found free of negligence and possible penalties after an accident. If you hit a parked car, you are required to try to find the owner and leave a note for him/her identifying yourself if you can't find him/her. An interesting aspect to the laws in most states that many people are unaware of is that you might be at fault in an accident even if you were not driving! If you own or have control of a car and you let someone use it who doesn't know how to drive or isn't capable of driving safely at the time, you can be held liable for any accident. If, for example, you give the keys to a child or an inexperienced person or someone who is under the influence of alcohol or drugs, you are responsible for what happens. This is also true if you let someone drive your car when the car is not in driveable condition, for example, the brakes don't work.

CHAPTER 21

GOING TO SCHOOL

WOMEN AND EDUCATION

According to Title IX of the Higher Education Act (20 U.S.C. SS. 1681–1686 [1982]) women are entitled to equal education in schools that receive federal funding. This applies to the entire school, not just specific departments. The rule of equality applies to education, admissions, financial aid, employment, medical treatment, discipline of students, housing, and athletics. If you are discriminated against in your school, you can complain either to the U.S. Department of Education for administrative relief or sue in court. A well-publicized recent case involving the right of women to equality in education involved The Citadel and the Virginia Military Institute in 1996. Both of these schools receive public funding and, as such, must comply with Title IX. Finally, both have done so and have admitted women, albeit grudgingly.

One of the major concerns about going to college is paying for it, and this seems harder each semester. The best place to start looking for help with tuition and other college costs is your high school and college counselors since they are normally well versed in available sources of college funding. Check with your local librarian; most libraries have informational books to guide you. One of the government agencies you want to contact is called "Sallie Mae," which is a financial services corporation that specializes in student loans and currently funds about 40% of the legitimate student loans in the country. A bank will make you a student loan and then sell it to Sallie Mae, which can sometimes give you repayment options and borrower benefits that were not previously available to you. College Answer is a service Sallie Mae has for college-bound students and their families. College Answer can provide information on college costs, financial aid programs, eligibility for financial assistance, and how to process your application. College Answer representatives can provide help in completing and submitting the Free Application for Federal Student Aid (FAFSA).

You can reach College Answer at (800) 239-4269 or if you are computer literate, it is on the Internet at http://www.salliemae.com.

The Federal Trade Commission and Sallie Mae are both concerned that student loans and fraudulent scholarships services prey on women wishing to finance their education. There are legitimate companies advertising that they can give students access to lists of scholarships in exchange for an advance fee that ranges from $10 to $400. Others charge an advance fee to compare a student's profile with a database of scholarship opportunities and provide a list of awards for which the student may qualify. These companies **don't** guarantee or promise scholarships or grants.

However, some scholarship search services do misrepresent their services, guaranteeing that they can obtain scholarships on behalf of students or that they actually do award scholarships to students for an advance fee. In these cases, consumers receive only a list of scholarships or grants for which they can apply. Usually, all consumers receive that same list, regardless of their qualifications. The search companies that offer a "money back guarantee" usually require students to apply for each scholarship or grant they have listed and then offer proof that they've been denied by each one. Other companies may provide nothing for the student's advance fee, not even a list of sources. Still others tell students they've been selected as "finalists" for awards that require fees to be paid first; these scams usually ask for the student's checking account number to "confirm eligibility for an award" and then debit the account for larger fees.

Here is a list of telltale lines used by fraudulent operators and whom the FTC warns you to avoid:

- "The scholarship is guaranteed or your money back."

- "You can't get this information anywhere else."

- "I just need your credit card or bank account number to hold this scholarship."

- "We'll do all the work."

- "The scholarship will cost some money."

- "You've been selected by a national foundation to receive a scholarship," or, "You're a finalist" in a contest you never entered.

Sallie Mae recommends that the best place to start looking for a student loan is with the college's financial aid office. Ask for the Sallie Mae recommended list of lenders.

CHAPTER 22

THE IRRITATION AND MAGIC OF SMALL CLAIMS COURT

Small claims courts exist in every county of most states and can be useful in settling minor problems between people. In like manner, if you are a defendant, the small claims court can be a major headache. Small claims courts are designed to settle minor disputes between people without using lawyers; in fact, most small claims courts preclude the use of lawyers. You represent yourself.

Small claims courts usually have a financial limit on the amount that you as a plaintiff can seek. This varies from state to state in the range of $1,000 to $15,000. The process begins with the filing of a complaint against someone who owes you money. You pay a small filing fee, probably around $40 to $50. Then, you usually have to pay a process server—in some locations it can be a county marshal and elsewhere it is a private party—to serve a notice on the other person (the defendant, you are the plaintiff) whom you are suing. Once you have served the official summons and a copy of the complaint on that person, he or she has a certain time in which to file an answer to your charges with the court. A date is set for a hearing; both parties appear and tell their version of the event to the judge—there is no jury. The judge, who is often a lawyer sitting as a temporary judge, decides who is right and who is wrong. A former presiding judge of the Superior Court for the County of Los Angeles, Judge Joseph Wapner, became a television personality after his retirement from the bench when he played a small claims court judge in a very popular TV show.

Next we look at small claims court from each side: the plaintiff and the defendant.

THE PLAINTIFF'S SIDE

You are probably suing for the payment of money owed to you, perhaps return of a rental security deposit, or damages for repair work that wasn't done right or because an appliance that you purchased or had fixed doesn't work or someone to whom you loaned money has failed to repay you. Perhaps your boss has not paid what he/she owes you. There are some nuances of small claims court that you should know.

BEFORE SUING

Before you go to court, there are several things we recommend you do. First, contact that other person in writing by certified mail with a return receipt showing your letter was delivered. Tell the other person what your problem is and how much money you think you are due. This is called a "demand letter." Specify the amount you are owed and that you expect payment by a certain date. In many states, the courts will insist that you send such a letter and prove it was delivered to show you have tried to collect what was due you before enlisting the aid of the court. Of course, if you and the other person come to a settlement as a result of your demand, that settlement should be spelled out in writing and signed by both of you as a protection for both parties.

In your small claims complaint you may claim the money owed (within the small claims court limits) plus the cost of suing and appropriate damages. Damages may include the post judgment interest (interest earned after the judge's ruling) on money you are owed and replacement cost of items destroyed or damaged. Damages other than the amounts owed are extremely limited in small claims court.

Before suing, be sure you can sue. Each state has regulations limiting who may sue in small claims court. There are limits on time and the amount of money you can seek. Many states do not allow collection agencies or money lenders or people or organizations to whom a claim has been assigned to sue in small claims court. In addition, corporations are not allowed to use small claims court in some states. Most states also limit the number of times you can sue in small claims court each year. There are actions that cannot be settled in most small claims courts, for example, criminal cases, libel and slander cases, malpractice, and certain types of cases involving tortious conduct.

Realistically, you must consider whether it makes sense to sue in order to collect what is owed you. The person you sue will be angry with you for a long time afterward, and the question is, do you care or will your law suit injure you in other ways such as the termination of a friendship? If you are suing a friend or relative, are you willing to suffer the consequent damage to your relationship with that person? Is the hatred worth the money? Or, if the person is not a friend or relative, can they harm you later in other ways? Can they affect your job or your well-being or that of your family?

Beyond these considerations, there is also the practical question of whether you can collect the judgment from the defendant. After you have gone through the hassle of bringing that other person into court, presented your carefully prepared case, and jubilantly won justice, so what? If the other person is broke or "judgment proof," what have you won? You have the judgment, but to obtain payment the other party has to have money or assets which you can get to enforce your judgment. However your judgment is usually good for several years (this is another of those things that varies from state to state). The question is, can you collect? Does the losing defendant have a job so you can garnish his or her wages? Keep in mind, in most states, a part of a person's wages is protected from garnishment. Or, does the judgment debtor have property or a bank account or something you can file a lien or execute against? Give some thought to how you will collect before rushing to the courthouse because you're ticked off at having been cheated.

SUE PROMPTLY

There is a limited time after you suffered the loss during which you can sue. This is technically called the "statute of limitations" and is designed to put an end to claims that are too old or "stale" as is known in the law. You can sue on the basis of a written agreement or an oral agreement that you think has been broken. However, you have less time to bring your law suit if you are suing on an oral agreement rather than a written one. The statue of limitations varies from state to state, so check with your local small claims court on the statute of limitations in your county. You should also check on the monetary limits for claims filed in small claims court. If your claim is for more than the monetary limit in your county or state, you either have to sue in a higher court or reduce your claim to the small claims court limit. Don't try to get cute by trying to split up your claims so you can sue the defendant twice over the same incident for amounts less than the limit. You can only sue a person once for each incident. Here are the small claim limits in various states at the time of this writing:

Alabama	$1,500	Idaho	3,000
Alaska	5,000	Illinois	2,500
Arizona	1,500	Indiana	6,000
Arkansas	3,000	Iowa	3,000
California	5,000	Kansas	1,800
Colorado	3,500	Kentucky	1,500
Connecticut	2,000	Louisiana	2,000
Delaware	15,000	Maine	3,000
District of Col.	2,000	Maryland	2,500
Florida	2,500	Massachusetts	2,000
Georgia	5,000	Michigan	1,750
Hawaii	3,500	Minnesota	5,000

Mississippi	1,000	Pennsylvania	5,000
Missouri	1,500	Rhode Island	1,500
Montana	3,000	South Carolina	2,500
Nebraska	1,500	South Dakota	4,000
Nevada	7,500	Tennessee	10,000
New Hampshire	2,500	Texas	5,000
New Jersey	2,000	Utah	5,000
New Mexico	5,000	Vermont	3,500
New York	3,000	Virginia	1,000
North Carolina	3,000	Washington	2,500
North Dakota	5,000	West Virginia	5,000
Ohio	2,000	Wisconsin	4,000
Oklahoma	2,500	Wyoming	2,000
Oregon	2,500		

Keep in mind that many states are considering increasing the limits, so you should always check with your local court.

SUE THE RIGHT PERSON

When you sue, you must carefully and correctly identify against whom you are filing. Be sure you have the individual's name completely and accurately. It might be that this person operates as a corporation or under a business name, and you should be suing that business entity in addition to the individual. If you are suing for breach of a written contract, it is easy enough to check the names as stated in the contract. But consider whether some persons who may not be named in your contract should also be sued. If it is an oral contract, you also need to be assured that you are suing the right defendant. You may need to sue somebody you don't even know. For example, if you are suing as a result of a car accident, you might be suing both the driver and the registered owner of the car. Or, if a company is involved, you might be suing an individual and the company. If you are suing someone who is not legally competent to make a contract, such as a minor or mentally ill person, you must also sue the parents or guardians of the incompetent individual. Minors, children under 18, for example, cannot be held liable for contracts. Of course, more confusion is created where you are trying to sue a government agency or the estate of a deceased person. You should talk to a lawyer before beginning your lawsuit. The clerks who work in most small claims court offices are of great assistance in filing your claim, but they are not lawyers and cannot give you legal advice.

WHERE TO FILE YOUR SMALL CLAIMS LAW SUIT

It is important to decide early where to file because you may have several options for place of filing. A claim in the small claims court can be filed either in the county where the defendant lives or works or in the county where the event occurred. So, if your complaint involves return of rent or a security deposit, it could be filed in the county where the property is located or the county where the landlord lives. If your complaint is work related, it should be filed in the county where the defendant resides or where the work-related event occurred. After you have completed the paper work and filed in the small claims court, the court issues you a summons notifying the defendant that he, she, or it, if it's a company, is being sued by you and giving the defendant 30 days after service to answer you charges. Now, it is up to you to see that this summons is served properly so that you can prove the defendant received it. The most reliable method of serving the other person is by having a "process server" deliver it personally to the defendant. The process server might be the local county marshal or a private person (an adult), and it will, of course, cost you a fee. If you are suing more than one person, every person named as a defendant must be served individually with the complaint and summons even if they are all living together. Different states have different levels of proof about a summons being served. In many places, the process server only has to touch the body of the defendant with the pleadings, and even if the defendant refuses to take the summons in his or her hand, it is considered served if it is left on the floor or anywhere in the vicinity of the defendant.

YOUR NOTIFICATION THAT THE DEFENDANT HAS BEEN SERVED

After the papers have been served on the defendant, the process server must notify you in writing that the summons has been properly served. The process server will give you a document called "Proof of Service" that sets forth exactly what defendants were served with what document, where, and when. You *must* have this with you when you go to court to show to the judge. The judge won't hear your case unless you can prove the other side has been served and has had the requisite number of days to respond to your charges. This procedure is all in the interest of fairness and due process to the defendant. Even if the defendant doesn't show up in court, if he/she has been properly served, the judge can go ahead with the trial. But you must be able to prove to the judge that the defendant has been served.

GETTING READY FOR COURT

It is very important that you personally visit the small claims court to see how the court operates; you should obtain copies of all the forms you need and acquaint yourself with the court rules. Find out the court hours, where to park, the best route to get there, and how to respond to the judge's questions. Sit in the small claims court for an hour or two and observe how the cases are handled, how the people are dressed, the questions the judge asks, and what kind of evidence and presentation the winner has. Since most people never have been in small claims court before they sue or are sued, observing small claims court hearings is an extremely valuable experience.

You may just luck out, do everything right, and the defendant decides not to show up. Some judges will just rap their gavels and give you a default judgment. However, some will still demand that you present your evidence so they are convinced that a judgment in your favor is just.

You should write out and rehearse what you are going to say about your case. Make it simple and short. Start at the beginning of the event and move quickly through your evidence because judges are busy and don't like meandering, rambling stories that don't get to the point. For example, in a case to recoup your payments where there has been shoddy workmanship, you need to say: I hired this person to do something, it was done badly (go into detail), and I want my money back. Or, this person asked me for a loan and signed a note, I gave him the money, and now he refuses to pay me back. Or, I rented this apartment with a security deposit, I moved out on time and left the place clean, and now the landlord won't give me my money back.

To help establish that you are telling the truth, you should have corroboration: documentary evidence and witnesses with first-hand knowledge of the facts. Evidence is anything that proves your side of the story: It may be written or oral. Examples of written evidence are: contracts, leases, canceled checks, letters, and even telephone notes may be admitted into evidence with proper foundation. You might also use photographs, video tapes, or sound recordings. For example, you may play audio tapes from your telephone answering machine with messages from the defendant on it. Or, you may show photographs or video tapes of work that was done, the apartment you occupied, the car that was damaged, or whatever supports your facts. Sometimes it is a good idea to prominently display a current newspaper with the date clearly showing so you can establish the date the photographs or video tapes were made. You might even bring into court other physical evidence that shows things are broken or unworkable. One word of caution though, the court often will want to keep all the physical evidence you bring into court to support your case as part of the file and in case it is needed for the appeals judge, so make copies of everything you need to have for yourself.

Witnesses are people who can testify to what they saw, heard, and personally experienced that has to do with your claim. Usually the judge will limit these witnesses to what they know of their own personal experience and will not let them testify as to what somebody else told them. That is called "hearsay" and such evidence is considered unreliable. Also, there are experts in various fields you might bring in to testify who did not experience what happened, but can support your case. However, this is relatively rare in cases in small claims court because there usually isn't enough money involved to justify hiring an expert witness. If you have a witness who cannot appear in court when the hearing is scheduled, you might be able to obtain a sworn affidavit from the person, and the judge may accept it. However, many judges will not accept affidavits because it is only fair that the other side have the chance to cross-examine your witnesses after they testify for you. If you have someone you want to testify in your case and they are reluctant to appear, you can get a subpoena from the small claims court office that requires them to appear and testify before trial at a deposition or at trial. This has to be served by a third party such as a marshall or process server just as the summons was at the beginning of the case. You can also subpoena evidence that you may need in your case by subpoenaing a company's records.

THE HEARING IN COURT

Here are some simple tips for making the best impression on the judge when you appear in court:

- Dress neatly and conservatively. A woman should wear a conservative, dark dress—no hats, wild makeup, or flamboyant accessories.

- Always stand up and be polite when talking to the judge. Try to be yourself, and don't try to act like Perry Mason or Matlock.

- Try to avoid reading a prepared statement. Instead talk naturally referring to your notes as needed.

- Never interrupt the judge or others. It's very important that, when the judge talks, you remain silent. Don't interrupt your opposition. You'll get your turn.

- Do not lose your temper, yell, or curse. No matter what the other side says about you, keep cool. It's the secret to winning.

When the time comes for your hearing in court, you must appear and present your evidence and your witnesses. If you don't appear, you will lose the case by default and not be allowed a second chance in most small claims courts. By the same token, the defendant must be there to answer the charges and present his/her testimony, evidence, and witnesses to show you are wrong. By not being at the hearing, he/she may lose by default. Each side can question or cross-examine the witnesses of the other side. Again, we emphasize small claims court is informal, and there isn't a lot of time to present your case. Keep your presentation short and simple with direct evidence and witnesses to support your position.

THE DEFENDANT'S SIDE

Now, let's look at the other side of the small claims court case where you are defending yourself against a plaintiff who claims you owe him/her money. What can you do? First, read all the previous material and understand the process and what the creditor may be trying to do. Go to small claims court to sit and observe the procedure just as your opposition did.

Notice that if you do nothing—if you don't answer the summons and complaint or you don't show up in court, you will lose by default. At the beginning, when you become aware of the other person's claim, you need to decide if you are going to pay or contest the claim. If you decide you're going to pay, you may want to try to enter into a payment plan with the plaintiff.

If you decide to pay, you pay or work out a payment plan; that's the end of the matter. If you decide to pay but can't afford to pay the entire judgment in one payment, and you can't work out an installment payment plan, then you should come to court and plead your case and your poverty to the judge. You may tell the judge that you agree you owe the money, but you cannot pay it all at once and ask that the judge order an installment plan. Even if the plaintiff does not agree to such a plan, the judge may recognize that you have no possibility of paying the entire judgment and may fashion an installment plan so long as you can offer some security. A successful plaintiff may insist that you defray the costs of filing and the service of the complaint.

On the other hand, if you decide to fight the claim, your procedural options are limited. We do not suggest that you try to dodge the process server. He/she will eventually serve you and, if you lose, you may be ordered to pay the extra costs of service. When you are served, file your answer with the court immediately. Deny the charges and prepare to contest them at the trial.

You must follow the same drill as described above for the plaintiff. You must anticipate the plaintif's evidence and prepare to refute it with evidence and witnesses to support your position. There are usually two approaches. One is to deny any blame and force the other side to prove their case. The other is to admit fault but to claim that the amount of money the other side wants is unfair, unreasonable, and or the alleged damages cannot be proved.

Another approach that will often throw a curve at the plaintiff is to take an aggressive stance and countersue. You can file your own complaint and counterclaim against the plaintiff with your own set of charges and demands following the approach we outlined above. In your countersuit you may claim damages against the other person, and you may sue other people besides those who are initially suing you so long as the two claims, yours and the plaintiffs, are related. This is often tactically appropriate because third parties come into the case whom the plaintiff may not have wanted to bring into the case. In this circumstance the plaintiff may be induced to resolve the case short of trial.

AFTER THE HEARING

When the hearing is over and the judge has ruled, the loser has a chance to appeal. As before there is a time limit, forms to fill out and file, and fees to be paid. These vary from state to state, and if you are the loser and want to appeal, carefully check out the local procedure.

If you are the plaintiff and you win, the next step is to collect the judgment that the court ordered. You can take several courses: One, you can work out a payment plan with the loser. Be sure you get some security for payment. Two, you can do nothing for the time being because your judgment is good for quite some time, usually 10 or 15 years. Some winners want to wait until after there has been a ruling on the appeal if the loser has appealed. In many states, the winner can collect during the appeal time unless the person making the appeal posts a bond guaranteeing payment if the appeal is denied. Certainly, you don't want to wait too long with your judgment in hand because the losing party may use that time to clean out his or her bank accounts, sell or hide whatever he/she owns, or move out of town to make it more difficult to find the debtor or his/her assets. Even successful parties who decide to delay their efforts to collect should record a lien against the loser's property—home, business, or bank accounts—so the winner is sure to ultimately get his or her money.

Three, you can move immediately to collect the money due to you by attaching the loser's bank account, wages, stock brokerage account, or whatever hard assets you find. Attachment of any of these sources is called "garnishment" or "execution." In this procedure you are claiming that assets in the name of the judgment debtor held by a third person—banker, employer, stockbroker—should be turned over to you. You garnish by filing a document, usually a court form, with the small claims court clerk giving details of who has the asset and where it is located. Be specific as to account name and number. Then, the marshal or sheriff serves notice of garnishment on the third party who must freeze the account and pay you what you are owed under the judgment. When you are paid, you may be required to sign documents acknowledging that you have been paid in full (satisfaction of judgment), and the garnishment is lifted. You can have the marshal or sheriff seize personal property and this is called "execution" or "writ of possession." Another alternative is to place a lien on real estate that will remain until the claim is paid off or the property is sold, and you are paid out of the sale price.

However, there may be a limit on how much money can be levied upon at one time or which kind of property can be garnished. These limits vary from state to state and, in some ways, are related to America's early history. In general, you have to leave the loser with whatever he or she needs to survive and earn a living. You can't take all of his or her wages. In western states you can't take the loser's horse—now extended to include his or her car—because to be without a horse in the early days of the West was to be stranded and to "die." You can't seize tools necessary for the debtor to work. This includes some clothing, and today it might mean that a computer is exempt, just as mining tools were in the old days.

THE CASE AGAINST DEFECTIVE GOODS

One of the kinds of issues that often ends up in small claims court is that of defective products and personal injury. There are various ways of handling these situations, which do not always have to involve going to court; we will outline some of them here for you.

DEFECTIVE CONSUMER GOODS

If you found that a product you bought either is defective or it injures you or some-one else, there are several things you can do. First, it is important that you document your experience carefully with photographs, a written statement of what happened, the names, addresses, and statements of witnesses. Of course, keep the defective product so you can show it to the authorities.

If you charged the purchase, you should immediately notify the card issuer, whether it is the store or the bank such as MasterCard or Visa. In most cases, the Fair Credit Billing Act permits you to stop payment for the item until the dispute is settled.

Your first step after carefully documenting the defective product or the injury is to notify the store and manufacturer in writing. It is important that this be in writing because you are building a case to present to a judge and he/she doesn't want to know about he said, she said, or they said. The judge wants to see written records. So build a written record. We recommend that all correspondence you have with the store and the manufacturer be send certified mail with a return receipt requested. Again, you are building a provable record to present to a judge if it comes to that.

Often stores and manufacturers will be smart enough to respond quickly and do whatever is necessary to correct the situation, unless there is a lot of money involved. In the case of an injury situation, a great deal of money may be entailed if someone was seriously injured. If that is the case, you should immediately document every-thing as we have said and consult a personal injury attorney.

If it is less serious, such as a defective product that caused no hurt or only minor injuries, the store and manufacturer should respond quickly and correct the prob-lem. If it does not, then you have several other choices. First, check your local phone book under the listing for your city, county, and state. Often, they have a consumer protection agency you can contact and they can get action for you based on your carefully documented record. Every state has laws against unfair and deceptive trade practices and they apply to practically every consumer sale. They are flexible in interpretation and can be quite powerful since they usually call for triple damages. A word of caution: The defense against many consumer complaints by stores and manufacturers is that you misused the product or that you failed the "reasonable person" test. This means that you broke the product or hurt yourself because you did something with it that no reasonable person would do. In other words, the law will not let you hide behind your own stupidity or lack of common sense. So you should be prepared to prove that you used the product as it was supposed to be used and that you acted in a reasonable, common-sense way and, yet, it still broke or injured someone.

Another alternative to filing suit in small claims court is checking out radio and TV stations and newspapers; they often have a consumer advocate who can help you get the matter settled.

CHAPTER 23

READY-TO-WEAR, OFF-THE-SHELF LAW

ONE SIZE DOESN'T FIT ALL

The temptation is great, we know that. Lawyers can be expensive and intimidating and they deal with a confusing bunch of laws and rules. So, we often would rather not go to a lawyer or dentist or car dealer or police station if we can handle things ourselves. That's why there is a large market for preprinted, stock legal documents you can buy in the stationery store or bookstore. Buy the form, fill it in yourself, and your legal problem is solved. Keeping up with the electronic age, there are also a number of computer software programs to guide you in solving your legal problems. Not so fast—legal forms do not resolve each and every problem; sometimes the use of a legal form exacerbates the situation and you must hire a lawyer for much more money to untangle it.

Here we offer some guidance in using legal forms if you insist on doing so.

■ First, for some simple transactions, the preprinted forms may be fine. The bill of sale for some personal property, for example, may be all you need for that transaction. It depends on the amount of money involved and the amount you can afford to lose. If you're selling a used camera or patio furniture set, it is not the same thing as buying or selling a 10-carat diamond ring.

Legal forms are probably all right for other simple transactions such as promissory notes for small personal loans or uncomplicated short term leases. However, if you are loaning or borrowing tens of thousands of dollars or are entering into a complicated long term commercial lease where the success of your business may be in jeopardy if you make a mistake, you should consult with an attorney.

Also, you may want to try a variation on this theme by filling out all the details of your transaction on the store-bought form and then hiring an attorney to simply review it. Many attorney's will do this kind of consulting for less than the cost of their drawing up all the documents themselves.

In summary, if the transaction is important and involves a lot of money or the possibility of very serious loss, you are well advised to hire a good attorney before the transaction occurs. When you hire your attorney after the transaction has been botched, the cost can be much higher and the chances of saving your situation much lower.

■ **Don't Be Suckered by the "Standard Agreement" Gimmick.** When someone presents you with a preprinted store-bought legal form and says, This is our standard agreement, don't accept that. Every agreement ever created was originally written up by somebody, and it usually was designed to protect his best interest—not yours. Thus, the document becomes HIS/HER standard agreement that he or she wants everybody else to sign. It is not your standard agreement. You must carefully read and understand what you are signing and modify it to fit your situation.

■ **Don't Ignore What You Don't Understand.** One of the great dangers of the preprinted store-bought legal form is there may be wording in it that you don't understand, but agree to anyhow. This is like sitting down at the roulette table and making bets blindfolded. You are literally gambling that nothing will go wrong and that you will just be lucky and will not be caught up on something you agreed to, but didn't understand. Later, of course, if it turns out that something you didn't understand but committed to anyway is costing you a ton of money and you want to get out of the deal, you will have to hire an attorney and pay a top dollar to extricate yourself from the situation, if that is possible. If you don't understand something in the contract or agreement, either don't sign it or cross it out and have everybody initial the deletion to show that it isn't part of the deal.

■ **Is the Form Right for Your State?** Many preprinted, store-bought forms are printed and distributed to stationery and book stores in more states than one. Since the laws can vary vastly from one state to another, the preprinted form may not be the best or even valid in your state. Check it out. Here again is good reason to have your deal at least reviewed by an attorney who knows the applicable laws of your state.

■ **Be Sure the "How" Is Included.** A great weakness of some preprinted, store-bought forms is that preprinted forms is all they are. They are the what of your intended deal, but they often have very few instructions and don't tell you the why of the deal and exactly how the forms should be filed out and the contract executed. If you are going to use these preprinted forms, try to tailor them for your specific transaction.

SETTLING DISPUTES WITHOUT GOING TO COURT

Because Americans are the most litigation-oriented people on earth, our courts, both civil and criminal, are overloaded beyond expectation. In civil lawsuits, where you and somebody else are feuding over a relationship, custody of a child, property rights or money, damages to a car, or personal injury, you may have to wait several years to bring your matter in front of a civil court judge who will decide your matter. This is why there is a growing movement toward what the lawyers call Alternative Dispute Resolution (ADR). It often involves lawyers, sometimes retired judges, or commissioners and is a way of settling a dispute between two or more litigants without the long and thus expensive court process. All sides must agree to use ADR and then jointly select the trier of fact.

These procedures are relatively new and may differ from state to state. Be sure you understand how ADR works in your state before agreeing to it.

Alternative Dispute Resolution comes basically in two forms: mediation and arbitration. Mediation is where both sides agree on somebody to mediate their dispute, acting as a go-between to help the parties reach their own agreement and resolve their own dispute. In arbitration, both sides pick an arbitrator and agree beforehand to be bound by whatever the arbitrator decides. It is more akin to going to the public court, but it is done in a private setting at a time and place decided by the parties. Of course, the parties must pay the judge.

In most contracts, there is an arbitration clause. It will provide that if there is any disagreement over any part of the contract and the two sides cannot settle it within so many days (usually 30, 60, or 90 days), the dispute will go to arbitration, and both sides agree in advance to abide by the arbitration ruling. Sometimes, it calls for simply hiring a professional arbitrator from an organization such as the American Arbitration Association. Another approach is for each side to pick whomever it wants as an arbitrator, and the two arbitrators who are selected then jointly pick a third arbitrator, and this panel of three makes the decision.

Mediation is more freewheeling, with the mediator often shuttling back and forth between the two sides who are in separate rooms and trying to work out a deal to which both will agree. Of course, it may not be possible, and the mediation could fail. Then, the two sides have to resort to either going to arbitration or going to court.

You should be prepared in either case to present and prove your case as carefully and as thoroughly as you would if you went to court. However, understand that you do not have the secrecy of the attorney-client privilege between yourself and a mediator or arbitrator. Whatever you tell him or her may be repeated to the other side. You may be represented by a lawyer during mediation and arbitration. Having a lawyer represent you and be present is important, particularly if the mediation fails or the arbitrator's award is appealed. Three professional organizations also provide arbitrators. You can find them in the local phone book, or you can call their national headquarters and get a local referral. They are:

American Arbitration Association
140 West 51st Street
New York, New York 10020
212-484-4041

Academy of Family Mediators (for family disputes)
1500 S. Highway 100
Golden Valley, Minnesota 55416
612-525-8670

Society of Professionals in Dispute Resolution
815 Fifth Street N.W.
Washington, D.C. 20005
202-783-7277

Part Five

DON'T BE A BUG ON THE WINDSHIELD OF LIFE

CHAPTER 24

SO, WHOSE BODY IS IT– REALLY?

WOMEN AND CONTROL OVER THEIR OWN BODIES

BIRTH CONTROL

A variety of birth control devices is available to women who want them. These include the birth control pill, the diaphragm, and the IUD (intrauterine device) and usually require a doctor's prescription. Other contraceptive items are spermicide foam, the Today™ sponge, and condoms, none of which require a prescription nor parental consent.

ABORTION

There is no more controversial subject in America today than abortion, laden as it is with strong religious and constitutional overtones. From the legal viewpoint, women in the U.S. still have the right to have an abortion. The landmark case was *Roe v. Wade* in 1973, which was reaffirmed by *Planned Parenthood v. Casey* in 1992. However, note that although both U.S. Supreme Court rulings stated that women have a constitutional right to an abortion in the early stages of pregnancy, control of **how** abortions are done still rests with the states. A late-term abortion performed when the fetus is able to live outside the womb may be banned by state law unless the mother's life or health is endangered. While the *Casey* decision upheld *Roe v. Wade,* it did allow states to require a 24-hour waiting period before getting an abortion, and it also allowed states to require underage girls to have the consent of at least one parent or a judge for an abortion. There is the issue of whether your employer's health insurance must pay for an abortion. Generally speaking, the answer is no. There is a Pregnancy Discrimination Act passed by Congress in 1978 that bars sex discrimination because of pregnancy or childbirth. However, it specifically excludes an employer's health insurance being required to pay for an abortion unless the life of the mother would be endangered by carrying the fetus to term or unless additional medical care becomes necessary as a result of complications arising from an abortion. Abortion laws vary from state to state so check our Appendix to see what laws apply where you live.

CAESAREAN SECTION

The Caesarean form of child delivery is also called a "C-section." In this procedure the baby is delivered through an abdominal incision. We bring it up in this book because the legal implications of childbirth have encouraged Caesarean deliveries. Natural childbirth through the vaginal canal sometimes results in injuries to the mother or child. When there is injury—either to mother or child—in the process of childbirth, litigation sometimes results; the mother or child may sue the physician and the hospital. As a result, some physicians, when the birth looks at all risky, pre-fer to do a Caesarean rather than wait out the normal delivery process.

Obviously, a Caesarean section is major surgery with the concomitant dangers of any major operation as well as complications resulting from anesthesia. For many years doctors believed that, once a baby was delivered by C-section, succeeding births had to be similarly treated. It was thought that the scar from the first Caesarean would split from the pressure of a normal delivery. For the past 15 years or so, however, obstetricians no longer believe that "once a Caesarean, always a Caesarean." There are now two national organizations working to reduce the num-ber of unnecessary Caesarean deliveries. These are the Caesarean Prevention Movement, P.O. 152, Syracuse, New York, 13210 and Caesarean/Support Education and Concern, Inc., 22 Forest Road, Framingham, Massachusetts 01701.

A Caesarean delivery cannot be done without your written permission, just as is required with any major operation. Still, there have been court cases in some states where the court has ruled that the unborn child has rights that must be protected, and a Caesarean has been ordered to protect the life of the baby. This has not become a widespread practice, but it has occurred. This is part of the complicated legal and philosophical debate over when life begins that is fundamental to the pro-choice and anti-abortion debate.

HYSTERECTOMY

There is a lively debate both within and outside the medical community about when a hysterectomy is indicated. A hysterectomy is also major surgery. In recent years, the number of hysterectomies done in America has skyrocketed. In 1968 a total of 47,000 were done, but by 1980—just 14 years later—that figure had leapt to 649,000, and some studies claim that from a third to a half of these should not have been done.

A hysterectomy is the removal of the uterus from your body. This procedure is combined with removal of the ovaries and Fallopian tubes if these structures are diseased. It is the ultimate form of birth control. Sometimes physicians recommend hysterectomy as a cure-all for non-specific, persistent gynecological problems. Some of these operations are not indicated and as such, form the basis for a malpractice claim. This operation is so frequently abused that insurance companies often insist on a second medical opinion before they will authorize it.

The operation cannot be done without your written consent, and it is not something to which you should agree without carefully considering your medical options. As with any major surgery certain complications may arise: adverse reaction to anesthesia, infection, and hemorrhages. Possibly, through misdiagnosis, the operation will not solve the complaints you presented to your physician. From disappointing results lawsuits arise. When a hysterectomy turns out badly, the patient may turn to the courts by filing a lawsuit against the physicians and the hospital seeking damages for injury whether real or not. This is a delicate area, and you need to discuss your particular case carefully with your attorney and a physician who is an expert in analysis of lawsuits involving hysterectomies. There is a national organization that helps women facing hysterectomies called Hysterectomy Education Resources at 501 Woodbrook Avenue, Philadelphia, Pennsylvania 19119.

ACCESS TO YOUR MEDICAL RECORDS

Whether or not you can have copies of your medical records depends on what records are available and where you live. You should have copies of your medical records to help you understand your physical condition better and to make it easier to explain to others when it's necessary. Medical records kept by doctors in federal hospitals are normally available to you if you ask for them. Other private medical records may not be available to you depending on what state you live in, but most states do not allow automatic access to state medical records. Certainly, in litigation and even in anticipation of litigation, your medical records must be copied and made available to you.

Ironically, while you may be unable to obtain copies of your medical records in some states and under some circumstances, there are other people who can obtain your medical records. The villain is the computer. Your doctors, insurance companies, government agencies, hospitals, and laboratories are all computerizing their records including what they know about your medical history, thus opening a window to your past medical history to practically anyone with a computer. To demonstrate, 730 different insurance companies pooled all the information they have on medical examinations of people who applied to them for insurance. Now these 730 companies have information that the insured thought he or she was giving to only one company.

Your personal physician knows a lot about you that you have told him or her in confidence; that information finds its way into your physician's computer. This may include information on your social life, sexual behavior, drug and alcohol use, smoking, illnesses, mental and personality problems, and everything else that is private in your life, information you thought you shared with your physician alone. From the doctor's office information may slip into the computers of hospitals, clinics, or Health Maintenance Organizations with which the doctor my be affiliated. Remember, generally when you file an insurance claim, apply for insurance, make application for a government loan or program, or seek a job or a professional license, you are required to sign a release that allows the entity to which you are applying to look at your medical records. At that point, the information becomes available to anyone who knows how to work the computer system. One solution is to decline to sign such a release, but that may mean you are unable to obtain the insurance coverage, the job, or the license you need.

Another partial protection is to limit access to your medical information by allowing that person or agency to see your medical records only for the purposes for which you are applying and to specify that this is not a general release of your medical records. Of course, that limitation then requires someone to make a determination of what's relevant for the purposes for which you are applying.

CHAPTER 25

DOMESTIC VIOLENCE AND WHAT TO DO ABOUT IT

Domestic violence is a complex issue upon which our system of justice and society has focused in recent years.

Case workers, policemen, women, and mental health professionals who work with battered women and deal on a daily basis with domestic violence insist that, at the first hint of abuse or physical violence, the victim must immediately decide that this conduct is unacceptable and that it will not happen to her or to her children.

Several recent notorious cases widely reported in the news have underscored the extent of domestic abuse, usually of women by men. Certainly, the O.J. Simpson case, the Darryl Strawberry case, and recent accusations against 80-year-old actor Harry Morgan remind us that domestic abuse is a widespread blight on our society. The TV movie *Burning Bed* was one of the first for TV on the subject and its ramifications. Many relationships today involve some form of abuse. There are cases of woman abusing men, but the overwhelming majority of these incidents are of men abusing their girlfriends, live-in sweethearts, wives, daughters, and female children of the girlfriends and wives. Many of these have resulted in tragic deaths, to say nothing of debilitating physical and emotional injury.

Our objective here is to support you in obtaining assistance through realistic and practical tips. One of the first things to understand is that it is not just lower-class, blue-collar men or professional athletes who abuse the women in their lives. For decades it has been clear and proven time and again that domestic abusers come from all walks of life. They are doctors, college professors, policemen, ministers, and shoe clerks. Abusers are found in every ethic group, nationality, profession or job, cultural background, and age group. Often abusers have been abused themselves as children and frequently have a problem with alcohol or drugs. One common fact is that they rarely can deal with their abusive behavior by themselves, and they usually need professional help. Until they get that help, however, wives, sweethearts, and daughters will continue to be the daily punching bag.

Generally, abuse is classified into five categories, and it's useful if you think about these and understand what may be happening to you. First, is the obvious physical trauma involving your being punched, slapped, cut, burned, stabbed, clubbed, kicked, choked, and generally knocked around.

Second, there is abuse by intimidation, threats, and harassment where you are threatened with harm to yourself, your children, family, or friends. This harassment can take place anywhere—at home, work, or in public places. He can be constantly telephoning you, stalking you, showing up unexpectedly, yelling at you, and flashing weapons with the implication that he will use them on you or people around you. Sometimes this intimidation may involve his threatening to kill himself.

Third, sexual abuse occurs when he forces you to have sex with him at times, places, and in ways to which you object. If you are married, this could be marital rape, a crime not recognized in all states. It could be forcing you to perform sexual acts with him that are offensive to you or forcing you to perform aberrant sexual acts against your will.

Fourth, there is psychological abuse in which you are humiliated and belittled, called nasty names, and, over time, robbed of your self-esteem. Interestingly, many women complain that this is the worst treatment that they receive from abusive boyfriends or husbands. They are told they are ugly, fat, dumb, a bad wife and mother, idiotic, and repulsive sexually. These men will openly have affairs with other women because they perceive you as unworthy of their attention.

Finally, there is the isolation treatment where the man you are with tries to cut you off from family, society, and adult society by refusing to let you see your friends, your family, use the car, have money or credit cards of your own, and wants you or forces you to be, instead, wholly dependent on him.

It is most important to understand that abuse will not stop until the abuser admits he is an abuser and seeks help to change this devastating pattern of life. Equally important is to understand that you do not have to take abuse. You have a right NOT TO BE ABUSED and so do your children and family.

Here are ten things you should do if you find yourself the victim of abuse:

1. **Report to the Police.** File a report with the police about the occurrence including details of any other abuse you have suffered from the same man before. Sometimes the police don't want to investigate such a report unless you are willing to press charges. Don't accept that. Insist that they file the report, and if they won't, go to their superiors and supervisors; keep making noise and moving up the ladder until you get your report filed and law enforcement begins to do something about it. For future protection it is

often important to show there has been a pattern of abuse. If the police will not cooperate, go to the district attorney's office, and if you don't get help there, go to your local elected official and keep notes all along the way of whom you talked to in the police department and the district attorney's and other government offices with times, dates, and what was said and done. If nobody helps you, turn to the daily newspaper or local radio/TV station in your area for help in getting out your story about how you tried to obtain the cooperation of the authorities and were refused.

2. **Get Medical Attention.** It is important to establish a medical record of physical or psychological abuse. See a doctor. Take photographs of bruises and marks on your body from physical abuse. It is a good idea to show a daily newspaper in some of these photographs with the date plainly displayed so you can establish the date of this abuse. If you can't afford a private doctor, go to the emergency room of the local hospital. Again, be sure to make notes about who treated you, the nature of the treatment, when they treated you, and what course of action was recommended.

3. **Set Up a Haven.** If you are going to stay with this man who abused you despite the abuse, you must, at the very least, arrange for a haven that you can run to the next time he abuses you or your children or threatens you. Check local battered women shelters and how to get in one and exactly where it is located so you can find it in the middle of the night, which is when you are most likely to be fleeing an abusive man. Many battered women shelters are vastly over crowded, and there may be a long waiting period before you can get into one. This is not helpful when you are out on the street looking for a safe place to hide. You need to arrange for a safe haven well in advance. The natural tendency is to ask a friend if you can stay with him/her in an emergency. However, your spouse or boyfriend may look there first for you. Try to make an arrangement for a safe haven with someone with whom the abuser is unfamiliar. You might consider having a storage locker or hiding place you can get to 24-hours a day in which you keep spare money, car and house keys, a change of clothes, and important legal documents. This preparation will enable you to go to a motel for a few days where he can't find you and the kids.

4. **Contact Family Court for TRO.** The instant the abuse starts, take your children and leave the house in which you are living with the abuser. The next working day, contact the family or domestic relations court in your community and obtain a Temporary Restraining Order (TRO). Be sure you seek custody of the children and "stay away" orders, which will warn him to stay away from you and the children. If you have such a TRO, you can demand police action against the abuser. Realistically, that TRO, which is an order signed by a judge, cannot and will not keep a crazy, obsessive

abuser away from you. In real life, many women have been murdered by their abusers while they had a TRO in their purses. However, such an order does make police action possible because if he threatens you and the police arrive in time, they have the legal grounds to arrest him and put him in jail. That raises another important point about making the TRO work to protect you and your children: You must be totally intolerant of any breaches of the TRO. From the minute you have it, call the police INSTANTLY whenever he shows up on your doorstep or takes any threatening action against you. Teach him that the slightest infraction of the TRO will bring the police. Don't let him sweet talk you into just "sitting down to see if we can work things out." That is pure manipulation and will soon result in you or your children's being brutalized again.

5.   **Start a Private Diary.** If the abuser begins to get help and you decide to stay with him, begin keeping a private diary. In your daily diary, note what happens in your relationship with the abuser. Detail names and phone numbers; the times, places, and kinds of abuse you and your children experience; as well as other threatening behavior such as drunkenness, sexual abuse, drug use, fights with other people, and his general behavior pattern. The fact that you are keeping this diary must be secret because, obviously, if the abuser finds this diary, it may be the trigger for another beating or other abusive behavior. Keep it hidden away and, preferably, not at home where he might accidentally find it. For example, keep it at a friends house whom you can call and who will take notes on what you tell her. Perhaps a family member or friend with a telephone answering machine will keep the tapes made when you call and record your message detailing the abuse. This diary may also involve photographs and recordings of your life with this man. The secrecy of your diary will not need to be maintained long because we assume that you will take our advice and that of nearly all professionals that at the slightest sign of continued abuse, you leave this man.

6.   **Separate Your Money.** Money is important to assure your freedom from abuse. No matter how small it is, have your own bank account, credit card, or cash stash. Keep putting away every penny that you can and that family and friends will give you so you and the children can escape if it becomes necessary. Again, this must be your secret, or it means another beating or losing your savings to your abuser. Abusive men, surprisingly, are often very insecure and are afraid of losing you. That is why they try to keep you subservient through physical and psychological abuse and by denying you money, family or friends, or places where you can run.

7.   **Tell Friends and Family.** Abuse happens in secret only if you let it happen in secret. Sometimes you may be humiliated and bewildered. You may not understand how the man you love, who may be a respected and highly

regarded person in the community, can treat you as he does. His slaps, taunts, ridicule, punches, and torture are very real, and you must discuss his behavior openly and immediately with your friends and family. Some of them, including your own family, may suggest that it's your fault that he treats you badly. This is part of the disbelieving, "What did YOU do to make him act that way?" routine. Don't let that intimidate you. No matter what you have done or said, there is no excuse for a man to brutalize and torment you. You are a grown woman; you are not a punching bag. Ignore friends and family who have such an attitude, and turn to those who are supportive and can help you. Knowledge of the abuse will enable others to help you. We suggested that you avoid seeking shelter with friends and family unless you are sure the abuser can't get to you there because your friends and family are the first people he would expect you to turn to for shelter. However, if the home of your friend or family member is secure and safe from break-in, you may consider it. Or, your friend or family member might have, in turn, another friend who your abuser doesn't know about and where you can stay safely—at least overnight.

8. **Get an Attorney.** Even if you are not prepared to file a divorce action, you should establish a relationship with a family or domestic relations attorney so you can obtain competent legal guidance. This kind of contact is important BEFORE YOU NEED IT. An attorney is like a fire extinguisher. You hope you never need it, but it is essential if flames break out.

9. **Contact a Battered Woman Program.** Most metropolitan areas have some kind of battered woman program. We list a number of them in the Appendix of this book. The instant you start having a problem with an abusive boyfriend, husband, father, brother, or anyone, contact a battered woman program. Learn where it is and how to get there and what services and guidance it can offer you. It may offer you and your children shelter, training in handling conflict situations, self-defense, legal remedies, and other useful information.

10. **Protect Your Children.** Protecting your children physically and psychologically are, of course, your top priorities, although you may believe that you need to get away and survive yourself to be there later for the children. Be careful how you act with the children. They will know about the abuse because usually they are in the same house, seeing and hearing it all. It is important that your children have counseling from someone who is qualified to give it. If you can afford it, you should get them professional psychiatric counseling. Your lawyer, people at the battered women's shelter, people at your children's school, your family, friends, the domestic law courts, or your church may be able to help you obtain counseling for both yourself and the children.

Research shows children who live in a home where there is violence and abuse, even if they are not the victims of it directly, are seriously damaged emotionally. They may have nightmares, become aggressive, have irrational fears and terrors, be unable to sleep, and become bed-wetters. Ironically, boys from homes where they observe males who engage in violent and abusive behavior tend to become themselves violent and abusive to the women in their lives. The violence and abuse becomes ingrained in them as a way of life, as normal behavior for men toward women and children that they will imitate.

If you leave your abuser, be sure the personnel at the children's school—both teachers and administrators—know the situation so they will not release your children to your husband or your boyfriend. Check with your attorney or counselors at the battered women's shelter or the family or domestic relations court office to assure the directive is carried out.

Always take the children with you if you possibly can when you decide to leave an abusive situation. Mental health professionals, lawyers, judges, and others who deal with victims of abuse will invariably advise you to TAKE THE CHILDREN WITH YOU.

Here are some of the reasons that YOU MUST TAKE THE CHILDREN WITH YOU. If you don't take them with you:

1. You risk losing them to the abuser or to the state. You may have to go through a very tough and expensive trial to regain custody.

2. The children's father may claim that you abandoned the children to him. Or, the county or state may claim that you left the children in a dangerous situation and are not a fit mother. The children may go to a foster home.

3. The judge may believe the abuser when he says you are a selfish woman and you don't care about anybody but yourself. The abandonment of your children is proof for some judges. (Don't forget, anybody can be an abuser.)

4. The children and your abuser may disappear, and it may be a very long time, possibly never, before you see your children again.

5. Your children may be sorely damaged and traumatized, and THEY may believe you have deserted them. They may become hateful and angry toward you, causing them to testify against you in court or decline to return to you.

6. If you abandon your children and the father obtains custody, you may have to pay child support.

Finally, it is very important you understand that times are changing throughout society. Things are different today than they were 25 years ago when it was naturally assumed by courts and judges that the mother was the appropriate custodial parent. More and more men, on occasion, even men who are abusive to their spouses, are awarded custody of their children. Part of the reason for that is the change of philosophy that women are always the more nurturing parent. Part of it is that there are some judges who don't regard a man's beating his wife as a reason to keep him from having custody of his children. Many abusers can be charming and very convincing in the courtroom while you may be on edge and crying. Many of these violent men do not appear to be dangerous and aggressive or to sport the type of image associated with a wife beater. Many are doctors, college professors, policemen, attorneys, public officials, even judges themselves, who appear before the judge in expensive suits and ties and speak articulately about their wacko, emotionally out-of-control wives.

This is why we suggested earlier that you make official police reports, keep private diaries, photos, tapes, and talk to your potential witnesses who will support you if you have to fight for the custody of your children. Go into it as if there was a good chance you might lose and as if it was the fight of your life. It just might be.

One final, non-legal, important bit of advice that many of you who read this will ignore at your peril: DO NOT GO BACK TO HIM. It doesn't make any difference what he promises. NEVER GO BACK until he has completed a rehabilitation program and the physicians say he is has been able to curb this abusive behavior. But cure is unlikely. Distance is a safer bet.

CHAPTER 26

WHEN AND IF YOU ENGAGE IN A CRIMINAL ACT

It is possible that, at some time, you may yourself become entangled on the wrong side of the law through your involvement in alleged criminal activity. The following is a basic overview of how the system works. This section will not deal with the entire criminal law process, a topic that would fill several books. We will focus on the possible initial experiences you may have with the criminal justice system beginning with arrest and possibly before you have an attorney to represent you.

If you find yourself charged with a crime, your first step is to immediately ask for a lawyer. Until a lawyer is appointed for you or you hire private counsel the rule is to **volunteer nothing, say nothing, agree to nothing, and demand an attorney over and over again until one is appointed for you.** Nobody you meet in the criminal justice system is looking out for you. You are on your own until you get an attorney!

Crimes are divided into two categories, depending on how serious they are: misdemeanors and felonies. Misdemeanors are relatively minor crimes while felonies are major crimes. In some states felonies are crimes involving more than a certain amount of money (perhaps $500) or carrying penalties of more than a certain amount of jail time, such as over a year in the local jail. There are, of course, exceptions, such as stealing a car. In most states, stealing a car is a felony even if the car is worth less than the minimum amount of money set for felonies.

Crimes usually get into the court system because a citizen has reported a criminal occurrence or the police or prosecutor after investigation has uncovered a crime. Of course, you may also be caught in the act. You may become charged with a crime in one of three ways: an information by a prosecutor, a grand jury indictment, or a citation by a police officer. An information is a written charge by a public prosecutor claiming that you have committed a crime; a grand jury indictment is a charge made against you by a group of citizens brought together by a court and who have heard evidence sufficient to cause them to issue an indictment against you; a citation by a police officer is usually a lesser charge such as a traffic violation.

POINTERS

Your rights vary with your situation. The United States Constitution provides maximum constitutional protections for those accused of a crime whether they have committed a crime or not. The police have the right to stop, briefly detain, and question you if they have "probable cause" to believe a crime has been committed and you may be involved. Ask if you are officially under arrest. From the moment you are under arrest, say nothing except to ask for an attorney. Answer all questions by demanding an attorney and be careful to memorize the police officer's appearance and badge numbers and name tags. Be polite at all times.

SEARCHES

There are various kinds of searches as well as differing circumstances, and we outline them here for you because it is important to know your rights in a stressful situation where the police want to search you.

TELEPHONES

The police may tap your telephone, but only with a judicially approved warrant. This is usually given only for serious crimes such as treason, drug dealing, and fraud. Besides a voice telephone tap, the police may also get a "pen register" tap which only records the numbers dialed from your number, but doesn't let them listen in on your conversations.

BODY SEARCHES

If you are not under arrest, the police sometimes need a judicially approved warrant to search you. They have the right to stop and frisk you if they have "probable cause" to suspect that a crime is in progress. Police also may search you and the area immediately around you if you give them permission to do so. Some police will say to you, "if you are innocent and have nothing to hide," you'll let them search you. This is leading you down the primrose path to your possible destruction. Never agree to a search because the search will include you and the area around you, and evidence you don't even know about might be found on your premises linking you to a crime in which you were not involved.

HOMES SEARCHES

Even when the police have a warrant to search, you need to know your rights. A warrant does not erase every constitutional right you have.

WITH A WARRANT

The Fourth Amendment of the Constitution provides you with a great deal of protection in your home, considered to be a most sacred place. The Constitution prohibits the police from invading and searching your home except under carefully detailed rules. A judge will grant a search warrant for a home if the police can convince him or her that you are hiding evidence of a serious crime there. The police may use secret information they have from informants to justify the warrant to the judge. The police must spell out what they are looking for, where they are planning to look, and that must be reasonable. If they say they are looking for a long-barreled shotgun, they may not look in small drawers or the refrigerator freezer where such a weapon could not reasonably fit. On the other hand, the police are not required to ignore anything that is in plain sight. If they are searching for a long-barreled shotgun, for example, and see drugs or drug paraphernalia sitting out on the kitchen table, they may seize the contraband and arrest you even though drugs were not mentioned in the original warrant.

WITHOUT A WARRANT—WITH YOUR PERMISSION

You and others may give permission for a search of your home without a judicially authorized warrant. Consent for the police to search your home without a warrant can be given by you, your spouse, or your adult child. Again, it is not wise to give police permission to search your home without a warrant because they may find something that you did not know was there but for which you will be held responsible. For example, if the police find drugs that a relative has placed in the house without your knowledge, under drug seizure laws the police may seize all your assets and your home even though you are innocent of drug use or dealing and didn't know the drugs were there.

WITHOUT A WARRANT—WITHOUT YOUR PERMISSION

There are times when the police can search your home without a warrant and without your specific permission.

For example, the police are allowed to search your home without a warrant if there is an emergency and they must act immediately. An emergency occurs when someone's life is in danger or when a criminal suspect might escape or evidence might be destroyed. Even though such searches are allowed, it is the burden of the police to later prove to the court that it was a true emergency and, thus, justified. If the judge doesn't agree with the police, the evidence they obtained from such a warrantless and unjustified search cannot be used in court against you. This is the effect of the "exclusionary rule," which has been in effect since 1914 in federal courts and 1961 in state courts.

When you are arrested or detained, arrangements are made for you to appear in court. A police officer may arrest you on his or her reasonable suspicion that you have committed a crime. "Reasonable suspicion" means more than a blind hunch but can be less than absolute proof. The officer can hold you temporarily, usually no longer than 48 hours. After the temporary period of time has passed, he or she must either release you or bring you before a judge to be arraigned or charge you with a crime.

KNOCKING AND STALE WARRANTS

If the court gives the police a warrant to search a home, they must not allow it to go stale: That is, they must not delay acting on the warrant because the circumstances that justified the issuance of the warrant initially may have changed. The police are expected to exercise the warrant and search the designated location in a timely manner after the warrant has been issued by a judge.

The issue of knocking has been around for a long time. Some judges insist on requiring the police to knock and announce who they are before entering a home to search. However, because some police searches can be dangerous to the police, some judges and some states allow "no knock" warrants. The police are allowed to force entry into a home without knocking or announcing who they are. Such conduct would be justified, for example, in drug raids where the officers' lives might be in danger if they knocked first and announced who they were. However, executors of no-knock warrants must show that the search was made in a dangerous situation.

The legal concept known as "Stop and Frisk" gives an officer the right to stop and question you if you are acting suspiciously and it appears that a crime is in process in which you may be involved or that you are about to commit a crime. If you are acting as though you are about to burglarize or engage in an armed holdup of a store, police can stop and question you. And, if the police suspect that you are armed and dangerous, they have the right to frisk you. If they frisk you and feel a hard object that might be a weapon, they have the right to remove that from you.

POLICE STOPS

The police have the right to stop you if they see you driving in an erratic or unsafe way. If they have reasonable cause to think you have been drinking alcohol or using drugs, the police are allowed to ask you to take what is called a "field sobriety" test; e.g., walking a line or performing certain motions. Some police officers are now equipped with flashlights that have a breathalyzer device on them; when they flash the light in your face, they are also testing you for alcohol. In some jurisdictions there is some question as to the legality of the use of these tests. The police can ask you to take a chemical test to determine the amount of alcohol in your system. These tests vary from state to state but generally are either a urine, blood, or breath test conducted at the police station. You are not required to take any of these tests because they can be used against you in court. However, in most states if you refuse to take one of these chemical tests, your driver's license will be suspended immediately for a period of time.

BEING ARRESTED

The fact that the police arrest you does not mean you are guilty of anything. It merely means that the police have reason to suspect that you are guilty of a crime. However, the police cannot arrest anybody anywhere. There are rules.

Obviously, if the police see you commit a crime, they can arrest you on the spot. This is a common type of arrest. A police officer may also arrest you if he or she has a reasonable suspicion that you committed a crime, i.e., they observed you running out of a store holding a gun, a bag of money, or a TV or acting in a way that indicates you have done something criminal such as running or acting furtively. These kinds of arrests in a public area such as the street or a mall or in a facility open to the public do not require a warrant.

However, you normally may not be arrested in a private place— a private home, for instance—unless the police have obtained a warrant. Again, there is an exception in the case of emergency where a life may be in danger or where the suspected criminal may escape or take someone hostage. Otherwise, the police must have an arrest warrant—which is different than a search warrant—that permits them to enter a private place and take you into custody. This does not stop the police from waiting outside the private place into which you have fled until you come out into a public place. As in the case of search warrants, the police can give the judge information they have gotten from informants or other sources to justify the arrest warrant.

IMPORTANT POINT

In spite of all the TV shows you have seen in which the actors playing police officers solemnly chant the Miranda Warning ("You have the right to remain silent," etc.) the police are NOT required to cite the Miranda Warning *unless they are planning to question you.*

THE ACTUAL ARREST

The police may arrest you without telling you what crime you are charged with committing. They are not even required to announce that you are under arrest. However, the law defines being under arrest as being handcuffed or confined and not able to leave the scene at will. Normally, however, the police will tell you that you are under arrest and specify the crime with which you are charged. In making the arrest, the police are not allowed to use excess or brutal force, only the amount necessary to take you into custody. This, of course, has been the basis of some infamous arrest cases such as the Rodney King arrest and several others that have been recorded on video tape.

AFTER ARREST

If the police arrest you and take you back to the police station or barracks, you are legally required to supply your fingerprints, handwriting, and voice sample. This is done to identify you and determine whether you are wanted on other charges. You may find yourself as part of a lineup with other people to determine if witnesses to a crime can identify anyone in the lineup. However, the lineup must not be rigged. That is, all the people must be of the same physical characteristics. Police may not suggest to the witness that you might be the criminal. In this situation, you are permitted to have a lawyer present. However, if the police use a photo lineup in which they show the witness several people's photos including a photo of you, your attorney need not be present each time the photo lineup is used.

Before police or any authority can legally question you about a crime for which you may have been arrested, they must give you the Miranda Warning, which says exactly the following:

> "You have the right to remain silent. If you give up the right to remain silent, anything you say can and will be used against you in a court of law. You have the right to an attorney. If you desire an attorney and cannot afford one, an attorney will be obtained for you before police question."

TAKE THAT ADVICE! Remain silent and demand an attorney immediately. Some people foolishly think that anything they say to the police **before** being given the Miranda Warning or after asking for an attorney cannot be used in court against them. This may be technically true, but in reality it can be hard for your attorney who comes on the scene after you have been arrested to suppress confessions or incriminating statements that you have made before he or she got there to protect you. Again: Remain silent and demand an attorney and continue to demand an attorney until you get one. Your lawyer may be your only salvation.

CHANGING YOUR MIND

This is important: Assuming you have not followed our advice about keeping quiet and asking for an attorney, you can change your mind about making a confession or not wanting an attorney even after you have started talking to the police or other authorities or started confessing to the crime. You can simply stop talking and say you have changed your mind and demand to have an attorney present. This, again, is your right.

GETTING AN ATTORNEY

If you already have a private attorney, you are fortunate. If you don't have an attorney, call a friend or family member and have them get you an attorney. Or, you can call the local Bar Association referral service. If you cannot afford an attorney, tell the authorities and demand that an attorney be provided for you.

CONFESSIONS

Sometimes people who are arrested for a crime feel the need to confess, to the police or district attorney. This is not a legal requirement. If you do confess, remember a confession does not have to be in writing. A verbal confession can be used in court against you, the police and others witnesses testifying as to what you said. It also may be tape recorded. If you don't keep your mouth shut and you talk to the police before you have a lawyer, what you say can be used against you. In some limited situations you can withdraw your confession if you can prove it came before you were given the Miranda Warning or after you demanded an attorney, but before you had an attorney on the scene.

WHAT TO DO WHEN YOUR ATTORNEY ARRIVES

When your attorney arrives, tell him/her everything you know or think you know about the circumstances of your arrest. What you tell your attorney outside the presence of others is privileged communication; that is, it is protected against disclosure and cannot be revealed. It is important that you be honest with your attorney so he/she can defend you properly.

However, understand that your lawyer also has a legal duty to the court not to lie for you. A lawyer's career is in jeopardy if he/she lies for you, and an attorney has an ethical obligation not to lie for you. The practical effect is that your attorney must take into account what you tell him/her when he/she speaks for you in court. If you tell your attorney that you murdered or robbed or beat up somebody, he/she cannot tell the judge that you didn't do it and were miles away when it happened.

If you are given a citation, the police officer has a right to detain you until you promise in writing to show up in court. There is a release called an "OR" release that stands for on your "Own Recognizance." This is legal jargon for your promise to show up.

On more serious criminal activity or grand jury indictments, after your arrest a judge will decide if you can be released on bail. Bail is a sum of money put up by you to guarantee your appearance in court at a later date. If the judge decides you are not likely to show up, you will be denied bail and locked up until trial. Many courts will allow you to put up 10% of the required bail and then release you. If you can't raise the money for bail, a bail bondsman may post bail for you in exchange for your signed pledge of property you own or 10% of the bail in cash as a premium. If you don't show up in court, the bail bondsman has to pay the forfeited bail and can seize the property you pledged. If you do show up, the bail bondsman keeps the premium payment.

The day of trial you must appear in court to answer the charges against you. For minor traffic violations many people represent themselves, but for a more serious violation you must have an attorney. If you cannot pay for a lawyer yourself, the court will provide one at public expense—a public defender. In many cases, the charges against you are settled in this first appearance by a plea of guilty or no contest (nolo contendere), which means you don't admit you're guilty, but you won't challenge the charge against you. From the legal viewpoint, a plea of nolo contendere is the same as a guilty plea. See the expanded explanation below.

SOME FINAL POINTS

Before we leave this subject, following are listed some criminal law concepts you should understand in order to enable you to know what's going on and to help you protect yourself:

- **Names and Titles to Understand.** The "defendant" is the person accused of a crime by the people of the county or state or the U.S.A. The "prosecutor" is the lawyer representing the people. His/her job is not so much to convict a particular person but to determine who is responsible for the crime and then work toward a conviction of that person. The "defense attorney" or "public defender" is the lawyer representing the defendant. "Witnesses" are people who have observed the crime or the defendant and can be called by either the defendant or the prosecutor to help make the case. The "judge" is the neutral person who oversees the court trial, and if the defendant is found guilty, the person who sets the punishment. The "jury," if there is a jury in the case, is a group of ordinary citizens—usually 12—who decide, based on the evidence presented at trial whether the defendant is guilty as charged by the prosecutor. "Dismissal" means that the charges are dropped for a variety of reasons such as there being insufficient evidence that you committed the crime.

- **Attempts Can Be Crimes, Too.** You need to understand that trying to commit a crime can also be a crime. For example, if you try to rob or murder or assault somebody and you don't succeed, you are still involved in a crime. The crime of attempting a crime is usually not punished as severely as if you had succeeded, but it is punished. There are, of course, some obvious exceptions usually coupled with some other crimes such as the attempt to commit murder and the crime of bodily assault.

■ **Conspiracy—The Crime of Planning a Crime.** If two or more people get together and plan a crime, that planning is a crime in itself. This is separate from the crime that was planned. You may be charged with both the crime and the planning of the crime, which results in two charges, two crimes, and two penalties.

■ **Accomplices—The Crime of Helping a Criminal.** Helping a criminal either commit a crime or escape arrest and punishment is a separate crime. This offense is more common among women than you might think because, while you personally may not be disposed to assaulting or murdering, you may feel constrained to protect a boyfriend or husband who robbed, assaulted, or murdered, and begs you to hide him or assist his escape from the police. Of course, you might actually take part in the crime itself by acting as a lookout or getaway driver. In that case, you may be considered as guilty as the actual perpetrator, and you may be punished as severely or, possibly, more severely.

■ **Pleas.** When you appear before a judge after your arrest, you are given the opportunity to enter a plea about your guilt or innocence of the charges against you.

■ **Guilty.** This means you admit to the crime and so the only job for the judge is to determine your punishment. However, the judge is not obligated to accept your plea of guilty, and most will not accept it unless they are convinced you understand what you are doing and that you are doing it of your own free will having been advised by competent counsel. In some parts of the country, the judge must also be convinced that the facts of the case show that you are guilty. This is designed to prevent mentally or emotionally unstable people from pleading guilty to a crime they didn't commit, for example, to prevent an individual with a psychological desire to be punished from being punished for something he/she didn't do or to preclude someone from taking blame for another. A mother, for example, may plead guilty to protect a child who actually committed the crime.

■ **Nolo Contendere.** This is one of those Latin phrases sprinkled throughout the law, and it means that you do not contest the charges against you. It is different from pleading guilty. If you plead guilty, the victims of your criminal conduct may sue you for money damages in civil court—that's different from criminal court. However, if you plead nolo contendere and you are sued in civil court, the plaintiff has to prove you committed the crime before he/she can collect. The burden of proof is less in civil court than in criminal court: preponderance of the evidence versus a standard of clear and convincing evidence that proves an accused person guilty beyond a reasonable doubt. An example of the difference between criminal charges and a civil suit for damages is the murder case against O.J. Simpson. There, even though the defendant was found not guilty in the criminal trial, he was sued for money damages by the parents of Ron Goldman and Nicole Brown Simpson in civil court. Many criminal cases are settled with a guilty or nolo contendere plea. Often this is because of a "plea bargain."

■ **Stand Mute.** In some courts—not many—the defendant may chose to "stand mute" or not enter a plea. His or her attorney would then tell the judge that his or her client stands mute. In that case, the judge will enter a plea of "not guilty" on behalf of the defendant. The point of standing mute is that the defendant may then attack everything that has happened in the legal proceedings to that point. He or she might, for example, attack the arrest, the jailing, the questioning, the charges, and all proceedings as being improper or illegal. If the defendant is right, the charge is dismissed.

■ **Plea Bargain.** The practice of entering into a bargained plea with the district attorney is common in today's overloaded court system. Until the recent "three strikes" law came into effect, just over 90% of most criminal cases settled this way. There are dangers. The idea is that the prosecutor and the defense attorney, with his/her client's permission, make a deal. To save the people the cost of a lengthy trial and the possibility of a very tough sentence, the defendant agrees to plead guilty. In return, the prosecutor agrees to reduce the charge to a lesser one with a less onerous penalty. Naturally, this deal has to be approved by the judge, and it usually is. As a matter of bargaining, the less work the prosecutor and the courts have to do, the better the plea bargain deal for the defendant. That means the best plea bargain deals are made very early because the options become less attractive as time passes and the trial date approaches.

The advantage is a lighter sentence for the defendant. However, there are some real disadvantages from the defendant's viewpoint. Even innocent people wrongly accused of a crime may plea bargain. This occurs when an accused person is so frightened of the system that a plea bargain is more appealing than uncertainty—even if you are innocent.

A plea bargain means that you will have a criminal record and that can, if you don't already have a criminal record, seriously affect you throughout the rest of your life. For example, if you are convicted of another crime later, the punishment for this second crime might be harsher because you already have a criminal record. In some states where they have a "three strikes" law, three felony convictions means that on the last one you will spend a minimum of 25 years to life in prison. Each felony conviction has great significance in and of itself. Also, being a convicted criminal can affect your credit rating, your ability to be licensed to do certain work, to gain custody of children. It becomes a permanent blot on your life; there is more at stake than there may first seem.

■ **Not Guilty.** You are telling the court that you did not commit the crime with which you are charged. At that point, it is up to the prosecutor to prove that you did do it. You don't have to prove you are innocent; the prosecutor must prove you are guilty beyond a reasonable doubt.

■ **Dismissal.** There are several circumstances in which the charges against you may be dropped entirely, and this is called, as we saw above, "dismissal." For example, the prosecutor may find proof that you couldn't have done the crime or the evidence isn't strong enough to convict you. Or, witnesses may have died, disappeared, or simply not show up in court. Or, perhaps you are technically guilty of a crime, but it may be a useless act to prosecute you, so the charges are dismissed "in the interests of justice." A typical example is if you broke a law to save another person's life.

■ **Immunity.** In a number of cases, the prosecution may have difficulty successfully prosecuting a crime without one participant testifying against the others who also are accused of the crime. The prosecutor may convince the judge to give one of the suspects immunity so the prosecutor has a better chance of convicting the others. Women are more likely to be offered immunity than the male defendants involved in a crime.

There are generally two kinds of immunity, "use immunity" and "transactional immunity." Transactional immunity provides a better incentive for the person offered immunity. Use immunity means that whatever you testify to in court cannot be used against you; transactional immunity means you can never be prosecuted for that crime even if the prosecutor obtains evidence from some other person about your guilt. If you accept immunity, you are legally bound to testify. Immunity sounds appealing; discuss it carefully with your attorney first because there could be a downside to it, too. For example, a practical downside is that you obviously will make enemies of the former friends and colleagues you help convict with your testimony.

CHAPTER 27

PROTECTION AGAINST GOLD-DIGGERS AND SCAM ARTISTS

"Scamming" is an old trick that has been brought to new levels of sophistication with the development of computers and electronic technology. Still there are a few very old tricks that scam artists still use successfully. One is the bank examiner trick. A man or woman may contact you and represent that they are from the FBI and are on the trail of a person suspected of bank robbery. They ask you to go to your bank, withdraw money from a certain teller, and give it to them "temporarily" to use as evidence. Predictably, if you do this, you will never see the "FBI agent" or your money again. This ploy sounds so ludicrous, it is amazing it still works, but it does.

More sophisticated ways of bilking people out of their money have occurred with the advent of electronics, credit cards, and computers. For example, a common scam today is what is called "ID Fraud" or "Identity Fraud." The first step involves the unscrupulous person obtaining your Social Security number and then applying for credit cards in your name using your Social Security number and address. Obtaining your Social Security number is much easier than you may think. Often people give their numbers freely to anyone who asks. For example, when you order something charged to your credit card, some venders want your Social Security number; some people foolishly have them printed on their checks; others give their number to phone solicitors. In some states, your Social Security number and your driver's license number are the same; every time you show your driver's license to cash a check, the clerk takes your Social Security number.

In ID Fraud, the crook obtains new credit cards in your name with your Social Security number, runs up substantial debts, then disposes of the cards to move on to another gullible person. In a classic case in Los Angeles and San Antonio, Lesley Wenger, found a $15,000 debt on phony credit cards issued in her name before she found out about it. Then, she had to fight with the credit reporting agencies and retailers to clear her record. This was in spite of the fact that the crook using the phony cards often misspelled her name, changed addresses five times in three months, and was the wrong sex. In the end, the innocent Ms. Wenger was awarded $200,000 in damages after she had spent months being harassed by creditors, collection agencies, retailers, and her credit was ruined.

Some of the things you can do to protect yourself from ID Fraud include:

■ Never give any credit card number or your Social Security number to anyone on the telephone unless you are the one who initiated the call.

■ Don't print your Social Security number on your checks.

■ Never give your Social Security number to anyone unless you are sure he/she has a legitimate right to the information and you know what it is to be used for by them. If you have any doubt, don't do it and insist on checking it out with a supervisor or some other authority in charge.

■ If anyone calls you about a credit card in your name that you know nothing about, call the credit card issuer immediately. Notify the appropriate authorities, and send a written notification to the three largest credit reporting agencies.

■ Have a list of all the current credit cards and accounts you have with their telephone numbers so you can notify every one of your creditors immediately if you suspect you are the victim of ID Fraud.

■ If you are the victim of a credit card fraud, notify the bunko or fraud unit of your local police. They may be able to help you. You may find that others have met with the same fate by the same crook or crooks operating in your community. Keep a record of whom you notified at the police department, time, date, and what was said. Follow up with a written notification. You may need proof that you notified the police in later legal action against retailers or credit card companies who may sue you for the bills the scam artist ran up in your name.

■ Check your own credit report at least once a year to make sure it is accurate and immediately demand corrections of any errors. Do all of this in writing. TRW Information Systems & Services will give you a free copy of your credit report once a year if you ask for it (800-392-1122). Equifax will usually charge $8, but it's worth it (800-685-1111).

Often the telephone will be the medium used to perpetrate a fraud. There are so-called "boiler room" operations where groups of smooth-talking, outwardly pleasant thieves gather together in a room and make telephone calls all over the country for the purpose of cheating people. The elderly are among the frequent targets, but telephone scams are not limited to the senior set. The caller usually identifies himself as calling for a recognized charity such as the March of Dimes, the Special

Olympics, or the Red Cross, and he/she wants to sell you a product that will benefit these causes. Another gimmick is to represent to you that the caller is collecting for the annual directory or some program of the local police such as buying bulletproof vests and implying the police will be offended if you don't support them. This is not to say that there aren't legitimate charities who solicit on the phone, but those that are legitimate can be verified.

Protect yourself by:

- Asking how much of what you send actually goes to the charity.

- Refuse to be pressured into making an immediate decision.

- If you're interested, say you will think it over and call back. If the caller refuses the delay or threatens, it's a scam.

- Never give your credit card number, Social Security number, bank account number, or other personal information to the caller.

- If the caller says you have won a "free" prize (another common gimmick) and asks that you pay only the "taxes" on your prize, hang up immediately.

- Remember from the first example in this section (the bank examiner scam) that no honest police authority or the FBI would ever ask you to withdraw money from your bank account.

- Don't be embarrassed to report it to the police if you are taken by a scam artist. Because of reluctance to report the incident, some of these people are able to continue plying their "trade" for much longer than they would have if the victim had immediately reported the scam. People are often too embarrassed to admit they acted foolishly.

- If you have an question about a solicitation, check with the local police bunko or fraud unit, the state consumer protection agency in your community, or other consumer fraud hot line that might be available.

TOLL-FREE TELEPHONE SCAMS

An up-to-date telephone scam makes use of the omnipresent and popular 800 or 888 telephone service used by many legitimate business. The scam operator advertises a toll-free 800 number and when you call, he/she secretly switches your call to an expensive 900 telephone line which charges your telephone account what is often an exorbitant fee. The advertisements of the switch-to-900 number operators frequently deal with personal advice, astrology, psychics, or pornography. Ironically, some "legitimate" sex-oriented phone lines actually do use a 800 number and carefully inform you of the per-minute charges. However, scam artists are very clever and always capable of inventing a new scheme to entice you to call their 800 number so they can switch you to a 900 number. Remember, too, that there may be other people with access to your telephone who could inadvertently run up your bill: friends, children, relatives.

Some telephone companies offer blocking devices that can keep your phone from being connected to a 900 number. However, it has always been true that, whatever one human mind can do, some other human mind can undo. Some scam artists have discovered how to overcome that block by advertising the 800 number and then switching the call to a 900. Most people don't want to block 800 or 888 numbers because it is convenient to use the toll-free numbers. These 800-to-900 switch scams first appeared in 1993 when the Federal government decided to allow some 800 number holders to charge for calls if they worked out a "presubscription agreement" with the person calling into the 800 number. In this agreement, the 800 number hold is to tell callers what the call will cost, allow the caller to hang up before starting charges, and limit the calls to people 18 years old or older. Originally, this was for legitimate callers such as those calling a computer company for help in solving a problem. To make this work, the caller is given an "identification code." The instant that you use that identification code, it can be assumed by the recipient of the call that you have agreed to be charged for the call.

Sometimes call switching is legal, but may be done in an illegal or misleading way. David Torok, a Federal Trade Commissioner has condemned activities that mislead the customer and says, "It's blatantly illegal to switch customers to a toll call without their permission." But the Federal Trade Commission has difficulty tracing these types of scams because of the transitory nature of the business.

Another variation of this scam is to convince the caller to dial an 011 number. In the U.S. 011 is the international telephone access code number, and when you dial an 011 number, you are connected with a number in another country. There, someone else who is part of the scam routes your call back to the American scam artist on an expensive 900 number with charges of $5 a minute and higher.

Children sitting around your house with nothing to do are likely targets for these kinds of telephone scams. One example occurred when two 9-year-old girls in Seattle, who had seen the Tim Allen movie *The Santa Clause* in which Allen laughingly refers to the number "1-800-SPANK-ME," called that number and, surprise, it was the working number of a scam artist. Five hundred dollars later, the scam was discovered by the parents and reported to authorities.

Getting your money back is not easy because the phone company often takes the position that the calls were legitimate, and it is not their job to police who uses your phone. Typically, when the victim calls the service that ran up their bill, there will be no answer, or the phone will be answered and then immediately hung up or you may be kept on hold for an extended times. Your call of complaint may be greeted with curses and demeaning language. Of course, your money will not be refunded. In many documented cases, these services—which may be technically in compliance with the law—remain in business year after year.

So, what should you do?

1. **Write Your Local Phone Company.** Do this immediately when you discover what has happened. From the minute you know something is wrong, put everything in writing and keep a careful log of what you do, who you contact and when, and what was said. By law, if you notify the phone company in writing within 60 days, the company must correct the problem or begin an investigation within 90 days. It is important to know that the phone company cannot legally disconnect your phone on the basis of such disputed charges,

2. **Next Step.** If you don't get satisfaction, your next step is to file a written complaint with your local consumer protection agency. You may want to bring a lawyer into the case at this point.

3. **More Steps.** If your local consumer protection agency does not give you satisfaction, you may want to file a compliant with the state consumer protection agency, the Federal Communications Commission in Washington, D.C., which licenses telephone companies, or the Federal Trade Commission. You may also want to bring the matter to the attention of the local media—newspapers, radio and TV—to present your side of the case. Often media ombudsmen will take over your situation and do an effective job of cleaning up the mess.

What it comes to is that, if you don't get satisfaction from step #1, make a nuisance of yourself. Most telephone companies don't want the grief, bad publicity, and expense of dealing with a vocal victim. It is cheaper for them to credit your account and move on.

INVESTMENT SCAMS

Just as we were talking about how holders of 900 numbers can sometimes be scam artists, we should note that one of the successful investment scams around currently has as its goal convincing you to purchase your own 900-number service.

The best way to deal with scam investments is to avoid them, and the best way to avoid them is to carefully investigate any offer you receive before you make the investment. The experts will tell you that, anytime the investments sounds too good to be true, it probably is.

You may be convinced to invest several thousand dollars in a 900-number company where your money is pooled with other investors. The 900-number company obtains its money when people (victims) call in paying from $5 to $25 a call. You are assured that investors in such services often double their investment in a year. What the hustler fails to mention is that the promotion costs are very high, and, as we have seen earlier, the vast majority of the charges earned are contested by the callers and ultimately have to be repaid. In these schemes, the only one making the big money from the 900-number company is the person selling the ownership shares.

In this time of corporate downsizing and high bankruptcies, the scam artist's mind is on overload attempting to find new ways of making money out of other people's misfortune. Thus, has been created one of the most imaginative scams currently going around, that of selling your good credit. If you have a good history—we discussed the matter of credit in the section on personal credit—there is a scam artist out there willing to make money on ruining it for you.

Basically, the scam artist convinces you to apply for credit—a loan, a mortgage, a charge account—usually of at least $25,000 or more. Once you secure the money from that loan, the scam artist turns it over to someone with bad credit for an immediate fee to you of several hundred or thousand dollars and a promissory note agreeing to pay off the loan that is in your name. The scam artist also skims off a hefty portion of the proceeds of your loan. Why anybody would make this kind of a deal that depends on a bad credit risk paying off a loan in your name is hard to understand, but it is done.

Of course, whether you realize it or not, you are still on the hook for paying off that loan if the person with the bad credit defaults on the loan. You will have to pay off the loan and go after the credit risk to collect. That person may be long gone and out of the state by that time. You are still on the hook for the money, and generally you can forget about recovering your loss from the scam artist or the bad credit risk.

Another scam relies on the name of the federal government to give it the sound of solidity and safety. You are advised to invest in a Federal Communications Commission (the scam artist emphasizes that phrase) license to own and run a paging, cellular phone, or wireless cable service. All you have to do, you are told, is put up a few thousand dollars for the application fee. The sales spiel runs something like this, "You can make a fortune leasing your FCC license to major paging companies because the FCC allows each company to obtain only one license in any market." It sounds wonderful, and it would be except it is a gross misrepresentation. Generally, there is no limit to the number of licenses that can be issued for a particular community for such communications systems. Too many people have in their mind it is like the telephone or cable television systems where there is a legal monopoly with only one licensee to a community. This is not true of these types of FCC licenses.

Before you consider any such type of investment, be sure to check with local or state consumer protection agencies. These agencies are listed in the telephone directory under the local or state listings or, for federal agencies, under United States Government. In the Appendix of this book you will find the numbers of one of the 10 regional offices of the Federal Trade Commission that serves your state. For the computer literate, you can reach some federal agencies on the Internet. For example, the Federal Trade Commission is at http://www.ftc.gov. There is also the NATIONAL FRAUD INFORMATION CENTER: (800) 876-7060. This number provides consumers with answers to questions about telephone or mail solicitations and about how and where to report fraud; it will provide you with referral services and help you in filing complaints.

The FTC also gives out free brochures on various kinds of investments and scams. Contact the FTC Public Reference Branch, Room 130, 6th and Pennsylvania Avenue, N.W. Washington, D.C. 20580 or call (202) 326-2222 or, for the hearing impaired, call the TTY number, (202) 326-2502. There is also the FTC NewsPhone at (202) 326-2710, on which a recording gives the latest FTC news of scams and frauds.

To give you some concept of what kind of consumer frauds and scams are out there lurking to take advantage of you, here is a small sampling of the actual cases the Federal Trade Commission has recently handled involving thousands and thousands of people just like you.

PHONY WORK-AT-HOME MARKETER— FTC RECOVERS $16 MILLION

A federal district court in Chicago, Illinois, ordered a firm that used deceptive ads to lure thousands of consumers to invest in home employment opportunity programs and other scams to pay back $16 million and has barred its president from deceptive practices in the future. The FTC had charged that Pase Corporation and its president, Robert J. Febre, falsely represented that consumers investing in the Pase "work-at-home" programs could reasonably expect to earn specified sums of money by performing certain tasks. The FTC alleged the defendants used deceptive advertisements and mailings in connection with five of their work-at-home business opportunities and with three programs that purported to offer grants, loans, and credit cards to consumers.

According to the complaint, Pase ads made claims such as:

"We'll pay you to type names and addresses from home. $500 per 1,000."

"Getting paid up to $1800 per day or more is easy with our amazing photo system that can mean to you a whopping $9,000 per week or more!"

"We will pay you for calls received by our 900 number. We will supply you with a system which tells you how to receive $3.50 per 900 call."

Basically, Pase was getting people to act as salespersons for other Pase financial products or services. These people paid an entry fee to get into the business of selling Pase products and services. Some other Pase programs were misrepresented as offers of grants and grant agents as loan services or as credit card offers. The ads that touted them claimed:

> "We have determined that you have met preliminary free grant guidelines and as a result could receive a free grant of up to $37,890 immediately."

Notice the weasel words "preliminary" and "could" that mean you're not entitled to anything at all. When you made an inquiry, you would have to pay money before they could proceed with your possible grant. Other ads said,

> "INTRODUCING SELF-LIQUIDATING LOANS. NOW BORROW THOUSANDS OF DOLLARS WITHOUT EVER REPAYING A PENNY!"

> "Account approval notice $30,000 credit limit. This account is reserved for you without obligation."

Again, the account is "reserved," but that doesn't mean it definitely is yours. So what was the Pase deal? In fact, according to the FTC, after you paid between $7 and $189.90, you learned that Pase was actually selling books containing general information about jobs, money-making schemes, entities that offered grants or tax havens, and soliciting you to selling products for Pase.

Sound silly? Probably, but **thousands** of people just like you were sucked up into the scam.

THE ULTIMATE SCAM ARTIST

Russell Mann may be the ultimate scam artist because he came up with a scheme to defraud victims of other scam artists. On a similar level with Mann were his colleagues in Meridian Capital Management of Las Vegas, Jeffrey A. Jordan, Richard and Susan Randall, Markos Mendoza, and Angelo Delon. According to the FTC, Meridian Capital was a telemarketing company making unsolicited calls around the country. They would tell people they were calling from Washington, D.C., and that they specialized in recovering money lost by consumers to fraudulent investment-promotion telemarketing firms! They said that for an advance fee of 10%—from $1,000 to $5,000—of the original "bad" investment, plus another 10% when they recovered it all, they would recover the entire amount the consumer had lost plus interest and punitive damages. To prove these claims, they told the consumers that they would recover the money from the people who were behind the original scam telemarketing scheme and that they would also recover money from bonds or insurance policies required by the states in which these scam companies were headquartered. Sometimes the Meridian people would embellish their pitch by saying that they planned to file a class action suit on behalf of all the people who had lost money to those crooks. Of course, if the consumer wanted to be part of the class action lawsuit and get back everything they lost plus punitive damages in the millions, the consumer would have to send Meridian Capital a filing fee or participant's fee.

SCAM FOR THE GENIUSES AND COMPUTER LITERATE

Just so you don't think that it is only the uneducated and gullible who get taken in by scams, consider the Fortuna Alliance scam. Started in November 1995 in the state of Washington, the Fortuna operation was marketed using home pages on the World Wide Web of the Internet and by telephone, mail, and fax using promotional materials of all kinds including audio and video tapes. It was one of the most comprehensive pyramid schemes appearing on the Internet that the law enforcement arm of the Federal Trade Commission had overtaken. The FTC obtained a federal court order temporarily halting the scheme, which by that point had already taken in some $6 million. The assets of the operator, Fortuna Alliance, were frozen while the FTC sought "a permanent injunction that will provide redress for the consumers who were victims of the scam," according to the FTC. The number of people taken in by the Fortuna Alliance was so large that the FTC had to set up a special hot line number, (206) 220-6358, just to handle complaints, evidence, and the consumers involved.

Jodie Bernstein, Director of FTC's Bureau of Consumer Protection said, "The brand new, high-tech scam is as old as Methuselah. Behind all the techno-jargon and the mathematical mumbo jumbo, this is just an elaborate version of a chain letter. People are told that if they sign up and send money, they'll eventually end up at the top of the pyramid, collecting from those at the bottom. But most people never make it to the top. Early entrants may make some money, but eventually, the pyramids collapse and most of the 'members' are left holding the bag."

The FTC charges that Fortuna Alliance and five officers marketed the pyramid scheme through a home page on the World Wide Web, using claims such as "What if you paid $250 a month which produced a minimum of $5,250 income each month for you, while you simply watched?" and also, "Would you want to continue this arrangement while you kept earning $5,000 a month?" With these ads they enticed thousands of consumers to pay between $250 and $1,750 to join their pyramid scheme by claiming that members would receive over $5,000 per month in profits as others were enticed to enroll. In addition, Fortuna and its officers provided advice and promotional materials for members to set up their own Web sites to recruit others to join the pyramid.

In fact, according to the FTC, most participants in any pyramid scheme lose money, so the claims that consumers who pay Fortuna $250 will receive high income or profits of over $5,000 a month were false and misleading. The only thing that wasn't false apparently was that Fortuna and its officers transferred the money they received to a bank in Antigua in the West Indies.

Investors in this scheme complained to various consumer protection agencies—just as we urge you to do in the case you are the victim of a fraud—and these government agencies joined together to close down Fortuna. They included the FTC's regional office in Seattle, the Washington State and Florida consumer protection agencies, and the Bellingham Washington state police.

CAR SCAMS

One of the unpleasant parts of buying and operating a car is that you are often the target of scam artists throughout the experience. A recent survey by the National Association of Consumer Agency Administrators revealed that car sales complaints are the most frequent consumer complaint in America. False promises, hidden charges, lies, and fraud in car sales makes it number one in scams perpetrated on the consumer according to this survey. And what is the second industry receiving the most complaints from consumers? You guessed it—car repairs. Just a year or two ago, for example, the apparently reputable Sears chain was punished throughout the state of California for ongoing car repair scams, and the state Attorney General was talking of closing down the entire Sears car repair operation for a time.

We cannot urge you enough to enlist knowledgeable help in buying a car and whenever you need to have a car repaired. In fact, one of your best protections against car repair scams would be to educate yourself about some of the basics of car repair. Interestingly, there is a growing women's movement in some parts of the country where women are provided with classes about car repair and what to look for when a mechanic tells you what your car's problem is. Some women enter the car repair business not only to establish a legitimate business but to assist other women in understanding the operation of their cars and how to protect against car repair scams. Some women who offer short seminars for women on car operation and repair basics. Since your car is often a critical part of your life and your ability to work, to shop, and to tend to family business, such a female owned repair shop might be worth checking out. But, of course, men do not have a lock on perpetrating fraud. Your best bet to protect yourself is thorough advance investigation, particularly by talking with other customers or checking with the Better Business Bureau.

CHAPTER 28

SURVIVING THE LETHAL STALKER

"We never tell a victim, It's okay. Nothing is going to happen to you. We realize anything can happen in these cases. Just when we think we've seen the most abnormal and bizarre, something else comes along to beat it."—Los Angeles Police Detective Supervisor Greg Boles.

There are thousands of people, mostly women, who have been beaten, harassed, tortured, and murdered by stalkers. The families of Kristin Lardner, Teresa Bender, Dawn Wilson, Lena Dioria, Shirley Lowery, Sharon Wiggs, Kathleen Gallagher Baty, and Regina Batkowski all know that stalkers can come into anyone's life to harass, threaten, and even murder loved ones. At the time we are writing this, Hollywood has released two movies in which the lead character is a stalker, *The Fan* and *The Cable Guy*. *USA TODAY* reported in September of 1996 that there are an estimated 200,000 stalkers in America after former loved ones, strangers, celebrities, and people they don't even know. Stalkers come from all walks of life and all classes of people. One stalker who threatened to kidnap and sexually assault his victim's young daughter was arrested in his car on the Long Island Expressway by the FBI. He was the highest ranking judge in the state of New York. He confessed and was sent to prison and is now back on the streets of New York. More recently, Denise Brown, the sister of murdered Nicole Brown Simpson, had to get a court order to thwart someone who was stalking her and her boyfriend. It was the boyfriend's ex-wife. No one is immune. Here are a few vignettes:

Kathleen Gallagher Baty is one of America's thousands of stalking victims. She was a carefree California coed and cheerleader until 1982 when she got a call from Lawrence Stagner, a classmate she barely knew. He began to stalk her everywhere, calling, following her, and circling her home. Restraining orders and jail meant nothing, and he came back again and again until he kidnapped her in 1990. She barely escaped with her life, but the experience is etched in her life forever.

In Virginia, Sharon Wiggs had been stalked for eight years by a man who slashed her tires, spray-painted her car, and repeatedly threatened her. On February 15, 1992, he burst into the home she shared with her husband and two young daughters. He shot and wounded the husband and gunned down Sharon.

Regina Butkowsky met Pernell Jefferson at a Virginia Beach health club. She didn't like him; he began harassing her. He stalked her insisting that she was his and that, if he couldn't have her, nobody else would either. Regina moved in with other young women, had co-workers accompany her home, and carefully screened her calls. The police said they couldn't do anything until Pernell actually did something illegal. In February of 1989, Pernell finally did something illegal: He smashed his way into her apartment, seized the terrified Regina, and dragged her away to a nearby creek where he shot her and then set fire to her corpse.

A classic example of a male stalker is Richard Wade Farley who was desperately in love with Laura Black, a co-worker at ESL, a defense plant in Sunnyvale, California where they both worked.

Farley constantly stalked Laura, leaving love notes and gifts of blueberry bread, sliced, buttered, and carefully wrapped in foil on her desk every Monday night for almost two months; he wrote her 200 love letters; threatened her friends; took pictures of her bending over in leotards at aerobics workouts; and, was absolutely certain that she would become his wife even though she refused to date him or even talk with him.

Finally, after four years of this unrequited erotomania, he assaulted the ESL premises loaded with 98 pounds of weapons and ammunition shooting everyone in sight during a 5½ hour siege. In the tragic outcome, he had slaughtered seven co-workers and wounded Laura critically before the police SWAT team stormed the place and seized him.

> "Too many times, law enforcement officials have been forced to stand by, legally helpless, as stalkers threaten, follow, and harass their targets."
>
> —Governor Jim Edgar, Illinois

> "My mother, Beth Blackburn, was stalked for eight months by a man who sent her death threats, harassed her at work by phone, and followed her all around town. He knew her every move. She was told by the police that there was nothing they could do to protect her. On April 22, 1993, my mother was murdered in her apartment in Baton Rouge. The man who stalked my mom for eight months and finally murdered her before committing suicide himself was my father."
>
> —Lisa Gallant Norris

The *Christian Science Monitor* reports that over 200,000 people, mostly women, are being stalked today by ex-lovers, sociopaths, and others suffering from types of borderline psychosis. We examine here this major danger you may have to face to assist you in protecting yourself from deadly harm. Stalkers may often send you blood, body parts, hair samples, bodily fluids, mutilated photographs; some may follow you, lurking nearby every time you go out; they may telephone you 50 to 100 times a day with strange and threatening messages or simply breathing in the phone. They are like a viral organism that punctures your protective skin, invades your inner-most life, and soon possesses your entire existence.

Police and court records demonstrate that stalking is a serious and dangerous phenomenon that threatens your peace of mind, your privacy, your lifestyle, and your life. Records also establish that a stalker can be ANYONE, a friend, an ex-lover or spouse, a cop, a bum, a business executive, a judge, a woman, an old man, or the pizza man. The same is true of the victim. The victim can be a woman, a man, a young adult and, even, a young child.

Stalking case histories emphasize two of the most significant messages about stalking. First, stalking is very serious and life threatening, and, second, **in the real world the victim is pretty much on her own.** Authorities generally are not equipped to help you when you need help. By the time the police are knocking on your door to help you it is usually too late. You have to protect yourself from stalkers—nobody else can do it in time for it to help unless, like Madonna, the Jackson family, and other celebrities, you have bodyguards to spot and arrest a stalker. Part of the problem is that there are troubling constitutional questions surrounding existing and proposed anti-stalker laws. Part of the problem is getting the attention of law enforcement.

The stalker is extremely persistent and sanguine. He—usually a male but not always—focuses on you, learns all about you, tracks your every move, knows who your friends, family, and acquaintances are, and is constantly in your shadow. He is obsessive-compulsive and is, unlike the common mugger, willing to take any chance and make any sacrifice including his own life to get at his victim. In fact, it is common that the stalker has murder-suicide fantasies—"If I can't have you, nobody will"—that drive him to extreme measures.

"One could reasonably infer that stalking is probably increasing," says San Diego forensic psychologist, Dr. Reid Meloy, "because America is experiencing problems with attachment and bonding." Sometimes stalkers are erotomaniacs pursuing a person they have deluded themselves into thinking loves them. Then, when it finally dawns on the stalker that he or she is not loved, the stalker is swept under by the rip tide of "abandonment rage" of a spurned lover whose sense of loss escalates into revenge fantasies that the stalker believes must be carried out.

PORTRAIT OF A STALKER

Susan Howley with the National Victims Center says stalking is a major problem nationally. Dr. Reid Meloy believes there are three types of typical stalkers:

1. **Won't-Let-Go Lovers.** Those who refuse to give up real relationships that have gone awry. Dr. Meloy says this class of stalker often is a spurned lover who can't properly mourn his loss and whose depression escalates into fantasies of revenge. Such fantasies can affect anyone: One of the first men charged with violating Florida's new antistalking law was a 66-year-old Fort Lauderdale man who stalked his former 75-year-old girlfriend.

2. **Wannabe Lovers.** Those who become obsessed with a superficial relationship established through work or leisure.

3. **Obsessed Strangers.** Those who invent a completely artificial relationship with someone, usually a woman, whom they may have never met. This is the toughest one to track and protect against because **you usually don't know he exists until a time when it could be nearly too late to protect yourself!**

Noel Koch, national security expert on stalkers, warns that categorization of stalkers is not easy. The truth is that the motivation and psychological makeup of the stalker is fuzzy and refuses to adhere to restrictive boundaries. The Obsessed Stranger could also be the won't-let-go lover—the lover who has been spurned. He could just as easily be the wannabe lover.

A key problem for women in protecting themselves is that the stalker is not immediately recognized. Sometimes, for example, the stalker's initial contact is lost on his stalking victim because she is oblivious to it. For example, he might pass you as he is riding the down escalator in a store while you are riding the up escalator. Even if no eye contact is made, he often fantasizes that the two of you have made such contact and you have discreetly acknowledged him with a look or a gesture.

The first rule of self protection is to be aware of what is going on around you. Watch for strangers who keep popping up in your space without any reason. Watch for the same car, the same outfit, the same man repeatedly showing up where you work, play, and live. Aside from the mailman and the newspaper boy this is a possible danger signal.

The greatest dangers to the stalking victim are the illusions she carries in her own mind. For example, there is the illusion that the system, the police, the courts, the law, will protect her. In an ideal world that might be true, but in the reality of the streets the system is too ponderous, too out-of-date, too timid to do much in time to save the stalking victim.

Dawn Wilson knows. The system failed her.

Dawn married Christopher Wilson, and they had a child, Christi. Dawn knew that Christopher had been abusive before, but after the marriage, he became violent and never let up on her. When she became pregnant three months after the wedding, he started sleeping around with other women and punching Dawn when he was home. He particularly enjoyed slamming his fists into her stomach. Once while Dawn was baby-sitting someone else's children, Christopher broke into the house, punching his fist through the window and beating her up while the terrified children looked on. She filed for divorce, but he contested it. She moved to hide from him, but the judge gave Christopher visitation rights and told him where Dawn lived. She obtained a court order of protection that Christopher violated nine times without any action from the police or the court. Just before Halloween of 1990, Dawn took Christi to the store and found Christopher waiting for her when they exited the store. He beat her up as six construction workers looked on and did nothing. He stole her keys and, while she was calling the police, went to her apartment and destroyed everything in it.

The police came; he threatened to commit suicide and was taken to a mental hospital from which he was released one month later. Immediately, he returned to Dawn's apartment and lay in wait for her. When she came out, she said, "He punched me and knocked me down, jerked me up, took my purse and keys, and pulled me down the crosswalk. I was screaming for help. He punched me in the nose. He kicked me and he kicked me and he kicked me—it seemed like 20 hours. I was choking, gagging on my own blood. I thought I would die." The building security guard appeared, but Christopher told him to leave and he did. Dawn was finally saved by some neighbors who ran to her rescue.

Finally, Christopher was arrested, tried for aggravated battery, and sentenced to three years in jail. In the weird arithmetic of our legal system, of course, three years actually means 15 months. Christopher was released to the street in April, 1993 and is once again hunting Dawn.

The lessons to keep in mind are several:

- Keep your home address private. Know how to thwart people from finding out where you live. Examples: Do not receive your mail at home. Get a post office box. Have all your mail sent there. Be careful when you pick up your mail that you are not followed home. Do not have your actual home address printed on your checks. Use a commercial mail drop. Otherwise, a stalker standing next to you at the checkout counter as you pay with a check can read the address.

- Also, do not open your door to strangers. TV actress Rebecca Schaeffer came down the stairs leading to her front door to see who rang her apartment bell in the Fairfax District of Los Angeles because the intercom was broken. Robert Bardo, a janitor in a fast food restaurant whose love for her had turned into frustrated hatred, gunned her down at the door. Interestingly, Robert

Bardo was arrested and sent to prison, and the assistant district attorney trying the case was Marcia Clark. Do not be suckered by a uniform. Be careful even when somebody shows up at your door in a jumpsuit saying he's with the water company and has to read your meter (most meters for utilities are outside anyhow). Demand that they show identification to you at the door peephole, and then telephone the company to verify they are who they say they are before opening the door.

Here's another case that started innocuously because people were too trusting. One New York tennis coach was a man highly regarded among New York City tennis coaches and a much sought-after mentor. Unbeknownst to the world at large, he was secretly a tormented man, torn between sexual fantasies and yearning for a family. He had previously stalked several children and rising young tennis stars going back eight years before this event. Finally, after he began stalking an 11-year-old boy on Manhattan's east side, he was arrested and released on the promise to seek psychiatric treatment. He never showed up for treatment and soon became fixated on Jennifer Rhodes, age 17. At this point, he leased a remote mountain cabin, paying a year's rent in advance in cash and stocking it with advanced security devices and sexual bondage instruments including whips, chains, handcuffs, and nipple clamps.

Then, as Jennifer and her mother were returning from dinner on April 23, 1993, he accosted them in the parking lot of their hotel in Colonie, New York and began beating Jennifer with a cattle prod to subdue and kidnap her. Jennifer's mother jumped on him and screamed at Jennifer to run for help as she struggled with the disguised assailant. Help came, but too late, and the coach escaped. Later, police spotted his white sedan and cornered him in a parking lot a few hours later. That's when he calmly pushed the muzzle of a rifle into his mouth and pulled the trigger.

There are several lessons here. For example, this tennis coach was stalking young girls for several years before he focused on Jennifer. The authorities knew about it, but didn't or couldn't do anything of significant impact to prevent continued stalking. Jennifer's mother had wisely suspected there was a problem with him and stopped Jennifer's tennis lessons. Having done that, she assumed that was the end of it not realizing the desperate determination of the typical stalker. The result was one tragedy averted and another tragedy literally triggered.

Jennifer's case is a perfect illustration of how helpless the law and the authorities are when you are the target of an obstinate stalker, even if he is demonstrably demented. Court orders, jail time, police—all are meaningless. You must accept your life either as it is decided by other people or as decided by you. Whatever your choice, you must make trade-offs: You give up something to get something else. If the stalker takes possession of a portion of your life and you seriously want to be rid of him, you have to be prepared to change your life so that it will freeze him out whether it means relocating or altering your identity.

Stalkers are not always crazy low-life types. Sometimes they are among the most respected in our society. Picture this:

> *"You're going to get a letter from me. You better listen to every word of it and do what it tells you to do, or you're gonna be in serious deep trouble and you're not gonna see your daughter again, you hear me? I'm a sick and desperate man, and you'll be hearing from me."*

It may sound like the dialog out of a bad movie, but it was the voice and threat of the highest judge in the state of New York, Chief Justice Sol Wachtler, threatening the woman he had been stalking for months, Joy Silverman. After his arrest for extortion and kidnapping threats, Wachtler plea-bargained the best deal he could: 15-months in the medium-security federal prison at Butner, North Carolina. He is now out, but he has been stripped of his judicial position and his reputation as a result of his illegal and demented activities.

The lesson we learn from this strange story is that stalkers come from all socio-economic classes. They are not just guys who would like to pick you up in a bar or at a health club. They can be judges, doctors, sports stars, professors, entertainers, or anybody. So, here again, it is important that you always be alert and not be deceived by social status or superficial appearances. ANYONE CAN BECOME A VICIOUS STALKER. This incidentally includes same gender stalkers as movie star Sharon Gless found out when heavily armed Joni Leigh Penn invaded her Studio City home with the objective of a night of lesbian love followed by murder-suicide. Fortunately, Ms. Gless wasn't home, and the police were summoned by neighbors who arrested Ms. Penn.

And, it can happen anywhere—not just in the big, bad city. Independence, Oregon is the personification of the bucolic small town where everybody knows everybody, and all is right with the world for its 3,500 citizens. Still, one day in 1988, Crystal Peterson became the focus of a stalker even though she didn't know it. Starting that summer, the stalker stood hour after hour at the window of the house across the road from the Peterson's home and watched Crystal. That's all he did: stood and stared.

This went on for almost three years until the man slipped over to the Peterson's house in the dark of the night and left an unsigned note for Crystal,

> *"I really like you. I think you're cute."*

The next day there was a longer letter saying that when he looked at her his, "heart felt funny, like it was melting and I have trouble breathing." The first reaction of the Peterson household was that sweet Crystal had a secret admirer. It couldn't be anything serious because, after all, Crystal was only 10. They assumed the letter writer was a classmate of Crystal's. Then the letters started coming every day accompanied by little gifts. A month into the mystery, the tone of the notes changed,

"I saw you down the street with that boy. You are just like the other girls. Sorry, don't like sluts."

From then on the letters kept coming, filled with hate and jealous rage mixed in with dreams of marrying Crystal and enjoying masturbatory fantasies with her. The Peterson's home became a prison with drawn shades, and doors, and windows locked with parents and four children kept inside. Mrs. Peterson canvassed mothers in the neighborhood to see if another classmate could give them a clue on who was writing the letters. They watched the front of their house at nights, but never spotted the stalker during those terrifying months. The police came repeatedly and shrugged that they couldn't do anything. No crime had been committed.

The family became obsessed with the stalker's obsession and yet, neither the police nor the Peterson's were able to stop him.

Then, one weekend the Petersons went away and returned home to find that the stalker had been in the house and called one of their friends, Mary Sellers, from a number listed by their telephone. Mary remembers the conversation,

"I heard a voice that sounded drunk or drugged. He told me he was in Crystal's house and I recognized his description of objects in the living room. He told me that if he couldn't have Crystal, no one would have her. He said they would be in heaven together."

In little Independence, Oregon, this stalker, a man of almost 30, was finally apprehended and sent to jail. He was a tenant in the house across the street and had learned how to break into the Peterson's house. Today, he has served his time and is out on the streets of Independence again.

The growing horror stories about stalking has prompted some state legislatures to pass laws against stalking, but there may be constitutional challenges to these. Voices are being raised against these laws because they violate everyone's right of free speech, free association, and other specific rights. Criminal defense attorney Jack Rimland says that anti-stalker laws create a punishment before the crime or before the ultimate decision as to whether or not a crime was committed.

Defense attorney William Murphy echoes that concern, "All you have to do is have the allegation, and there's no requirement that witnesses be brought in. So, the accused is robbed of his constitutional right to confront witnesses against him." Beyond that, Murphy says the injustice of throwing the alleged stalker in jail on such a flimsy basis will only aggravate the problem and make him vengeful.

Public Defender Linda Wickenkamp warns that bad-blood cases may be under anti-stalking laws, "They're highly subjective, and there will be some vindictiveness expressed. Somebody can be charged with a felony because of bad feelings from the past."

A former Washington, D.C. lawyer, Karen Van Susteren, who is now a correspondent for the Cable News Network (CNN) was the victim of a stalker for years. She understood the legal system and had extensive connections, but still got little help.

> *"It started in 1980 when I tried a number of celebrated homicide cases in Washington, D.C. and was all over the newspapers. Suddenly, this 6'5" man became obsessed with me and began following me all the time. He followed me to the courthouse and sat in the courtroom and stared at me. He asked people all about me, got my Wisconsin driving record, called my parents to talk about me—he wouldn't leave me alone. It went on and on and on for seven years, and I utilized all the resources available to me.*
>
> *"I was lucky in that I knew the court system and had the cooperation of the U.S. Attorney's office and the judges as well because they thought he could be dangerous. I got a Stay Away Order which he violated and was put into jail for a short time, but he got out and was unrelenting. He wouldn't give up, and, frankly, there was no law to protect me, so I just endured his obsessive phone calls and following me.*
>
> *"The irony of it all is that my stalker stopped stalking me because he found someone younger and prettier. So, I simply got dumped by a nut."*

Again, women can be stalkers too. Some of them can be deadly stalkers such as Carol Warmus, Elizabeth Broderick, Jennifer Reali, and Amy Fisher.

A triple zone defense is your best protection. Think of the neighborhood where you work, live, and move around as zone one; your residence, work, or car as zone two; and, your physical self as zone three. Your best defense is to keep the stalker out of all three zones. Ideally, but not always practical, the stalker should be kept away from zone three. Of course, you don't want him to know the world where you live, where you work, where you go to the store, where you go to the dry cleaners, health spa, or gas station. But such information is very easy to obtain. If he breaks through to zone three, the best solution is to move—to relocate zone three. The immediate reaction of most women is, I CAN'T do that.

When you refuse to remove yourself from danger, you display a fatal foolishness: (1) You do not take the threat of the stalker seriously. You regard it as an annoyance, but not anything really serious, and (2) You just DON'T WANT TO BE BOTHERED.

ZONE ONE SELF-DEFENSE

The best defense against a stalker is invisibility. If a potential stalker doesn't know who you are or that you exist, he will not invade your life. Obviously, this is difficult with the ex-boyfriend who knows all about you and is obsessed with getting you back or, more lethally, an ex who is determined that, if he can't have you, no one else will.

First, never give your name, address, or phone number to anybody you don't know and trust. Many people or companies that ask for private information about you don't have the right to that information. Don't let a merchant write your credit card numbers on the check or sales slip. Twenty-one states forbid that practice anyhow. Point out that it is useless because the law forbids charging anything to your credit card if your check bounces.

It may be useful to practice a quick response to questions with a phony name. When someone asks you suddenly what your name is while you're shopping or at the gym or in the park or elsewhere, learn to quickly answer with a phony name. You can correct it later, but if it turns out you don't want to know the person, it's harder for him to track you if he doesn't know your name.

Be particularly alert in the seven PRIME STALKER ATTACK SITUATIONS:

1. Walking at night

   ■ Walk with assurance. Walk briskly, with erect posture, and looking straight ahead. Avoid eye contact.

   ■ Be careful what you wear. Wear clothing and shoes that allow you to run or fight.

   ■ Walk away from doorways, bushes, shadows near buildings, and be wary of parked vans where the door can be slid open instantly and a stalker can snatch you off the street and be out of sight in a second or two.

   ■ Where traffic permits, walk down the middle of the street. Stick to streets that are well lit and have many pedestrians on them.

   ■ Know where there are 24-hour stores and gas stations along the route of your walk. Be aware of the location of telephones, and police and fire stations. Have a quarter in your hand so you can dial a friend to pick you up if you get nervous. Memorize the number of the local cab company, and always carry enough money on your person—not in a wallet—for cab fare. Stick a $5 or $10 bill in the lining of your jacket or in your shoe.

   ■ It is best never to walk alone.

   ■ Pay attention to people walking toward you. You may not know what your stalker looks like, and one stalker trick is to walk toward the victim, pass them, turn, and attack from the rear.

   ■ Let somebody know you're out walking, the route you're planning to take, when you plan to be back, and call that person before leaving and when you get back. It isn't childish. Very brave mountain climbers do the same thing.

   ■ Carry some easy-to-get-at weapon: spray, alarm, stun gun, or whatever you prefer.

2. Arriving home

   Often when you arrive home, you are vulnerable. For example, you may arrive home at night and have to get out of the car and open a garage door or your arms may be full. These are times when it's easy for a stalker to attack you. Get a garage door opener so you can open the garage, drive in, and close the door without getting out of the car. Keep access to your garage locked securely so you don't end up inside with the stalker. Try doing your shopping early in the day so you can come home with groceries in the daylight and when people are around. In any case, always be alert to your surroundings and suspicious of anything that seems abnormal or out of place. Always have your key out and ready so you can get your door open and get inside as quickly as possible. If you see signs of a break-in, as we warned you elsewhere, **DO NOT GO INTO THE HOUSE.** The intruder could still be inside waiting for you. Immediately go to a pay phone or a neighbor's house, and call 911.

3. In a bus, subway, or mall

   These are usually places where there are a lot of people and one tends to feel safer. However, a good upbringing can be your enemy in these otherwise relatively safe circumstances. The natural tendancy of not wanting to cause embarrassment or "a scene" may keep you from protesting when a stalker grabs you and tries to steer you to a car or secluded spot away from the crowd. Contrary to your nice upbringing, you should scream, fight, scratch, claw, yell, and generally raise hell at the very first suspicion of trouble. Don't wait until it gets serious—ACT IMMEDIATELY. Otherwise, it may be too late. When he has you isolated in a car or a corner or a dark spot, your chances of escape are sharply reduced.

4. Garages and parking lots

   These areas are often sprawling and dark, and many parts are isolated from most pedestrians and other people. Upon arrival, park your car close to the entrance, to the cashier booth, or to another attended location where people can see it and you. Don't make the mistake of parking in some far, dark corner just because you can't find a better spot. If you can't find a safe spot, don't park; come back later. Don't be afraid to say you're afraid. For example, a good idea is to tell the parking cashier or attendant that these big parking garages make you nervous and that you're going in to get your car that is in such-a-such place. Then, ask the attendant to send help if you are not back in a few minutes. Walk quickly and purposefully with your keys out and ready to use when you get to your car. Be alert to everyone and everything around you. Don't be so loaded down with packages that you can't defend yourself.

If you have a weapon or a whistle, have it ready to use. Of course, where it is possible to have valet parking, always do it. It costs a few dollars, but what's it worth to you not to be raped or murdered?

5. Jogging

In some ways, when you are jogging, you should follow the same rules we outlined for walking at night. However, most joggers tend to dress as lightly as the weather permits and don't have bags or purses to carry weapons, whistles, and so on. Ideally, never jog alone. Don't jog on isolated trails in parks and nature areas where you are out of the sight of people. Don't jog in the dark. Carry change for the telephone and a few dollars or, if you have one, a cell phone. Memorize where there are public phones and places of refuge to which you can run in a moment of danger. In short, don't make it easy for an attacker or stalker, and don't make it hard to get help.

6. On a date

As you already know, dates sometimes turn out to be far different than you thought they would be. One of the difficulties is that your mood on a date is often relaxed and off-guard. You have already been lectured about and learned from personal experience about problem dates. However, fundamentally, we caution you that your protection under the law against date rape or other problems may be greatly affected by how the events appear to a reasonable person. For example, if you drink or take drugs, behave or dress provocatively, and put yourself in a situation that invites an aggressive response from your date, your claim of rape or assault could be seriously weakened.

7. On a trip

Even in your own state or country, when you travel you are surrounded by strangers, and you have to be especially alert. Try to be as inconspicuous as possible. Do not dress or behave in a flashy way so as to call attention to yourself as a possible target. Spread around the money you have with you in different locations. Don't put all your money in your purse—put some in your purse, some in pockets, some in luggage, etc. Have a small amount of working cash where you can get to it easily to pay for things as you go, but do not flash large amounts of money in public. Avoid being in situations where it is deserted, you are alone, it is dark, or you are screened from people seeing you. Ideally, you should carefully rehearse where you are going and how to get there before you leave. Consult your travel agent or other guides to find out where the airport or train station is when you arrive and how you get from there to your hotel or other destination. Have numbers of people you can call for help if you get in trouble. And, remember, many people in other places make their living preying on, cheating, and misleading strangers in their town.

If some of these things sound humiliating and you refuse to do them just because you are in a modern and dangerous city, you are probably right, they are. If you reject such advice because you recoil from being intimidated by a stalker, know that such bravado has seen many a young life end up in the emergency ward or in the cemetery where nobody cares about your bravado.

Your greatest safety is to be able to keep moving. If threatened, you can drive to a safe place such as a police or fire station. If you are immobilized, you become a sitting duck and you have to fall back on your final zone one defense, which you want to avoid if possible.

If the stalker knows where you live or work, or the car you have, keep him from getting into any of these places where he can get to you. For example,

- Always fill your gas tank when you get down to half-full. The last thing you want to do is run out of gas at night with a stalker trying to trap you.

- Have a sign that says in large letters, "HELP, CALL THE POLICE, 911" that you can hold up while honking your horn and blinking your lights repeatedly to call for help.

- Have a large flashlight that you can shine and also use as a weapon.

- Have a list of emergency phone numbers in the car including police, ambulance, fire, and auto club. Belong to an auto club so you can get emergency road service if you get stranded. Often the fire department or an ambulance will respond quicker than the police.

- Have a map of your neighborhood with fire, police, hospitals, and all-night stores clearly marked.

- Have a loud, portable screamer alarm with you. This will help frighten a stalker away.

- Have some kind of defensive weapon with you. For example, a long-range, narrow-stream spray that you can use on a stalker with your window only down slightly and when he is still 10 or 15 feet away from the car. Use it carefully so it doesn't kick back in your face.

- Be careful of the phony undercover policeman trick where a stalker tries to pull you over under the ruse that he is a cop. The best thing to do if you are stopped by anyone claiming to be a cop is to acknowledge you are going to stop and drive to a well-lighted location such as a service station or restaurant or some place where lots of other people will witness the pull-over. A real cop doesn't care, and, in fact, many police departments train their officers to stop drivers in well-lit places so there cannot be later charges of police brutality or impropriety.

If all else fails and you are confronted with the stalker, here are tips on self-defense:

- In unarmed self-defense, the experts say that your number one asset is your instinct. When you feel that certain feeling of danger, of being followed, of being watched, pay attention! The human being is geared toward survival, and you, just like other animals, will often sense when something is wrong. Obey that sense, and take action to get out of danger.

- Your poise and manner of carrying yourself is important. Look as if you are prepared for trouble. Always have your keys out and ready to use. If you have to get into your house or your car, you don't want to be caught groping in your purse for your keys. Also, keys sticking out between the fingers of your fist can be an effective weapon for scratching the face of a stalker.

- Be noisy and act crazy and unpredictable if confronted by a stalker. Spit, yell, scream, bark like a dog—it will disorient many stalkers, and they will retreat. There are many other unarmed defense tricks that even the unskilled woman can use, such as jabbing the heel of the hand up into the stalker's nose, biting, using the knees and elbows, using a rolled-up newspaper or a magazine, umbrellas, hat pins, high heels, purse, books, pens, and many other tricks one doesn't normally think about using. Running may be your natural instinct, but most men will outrun you and drag you down, particularly if you are wearing restrictive clothing and heels.

- To adequately prepare yourself you may consider arming yourself with chemical sprays, pepper sprays, stun guns, firearms, knives, tasers, and other formal weapons. An improvised or homemade weapon such as a household squeeze bottle filled with ammonia will do, so long as it works.

SELF DEFENSE CLASSES: A GUIDE

You can benefit from taking a self-defense class if you take the one that's right for you. It is not necessary to be in top physical shape. There are classes that will help anybody, but you have to know what you're doing when you pick one. First it is a myth that martial arts classes—karate, tae kwon do, judo—are the best. These are techniques that take years to master, and they are very expensive. For the average woman, the best self-defense classes are those focusing on basic, easy-to-use moves that can be learned in six weeks or less. Many private and nonprofit organizations offer these classes for prices varying from nothing to several hundred dollars. Since most of these aren't regulated or licensed, it is up to you to check them out. Ask yourself these questions when picking out a self-defense class:

- Does it teach prevention and awareness?
- Are techniques simple and realistic?
- Is the environment supportive?
- Does it build self-confidence?

GUIDE TO SELF-DEFENSE EQUIPMENT

CHEMICAL SPRAYS

These are sprays of mace, pepper-based solutions, and tear gas. They produce burning of the eyes, choking, and painful lung irritation. You have to spray them into the unprotected face of your attacker up close—not more than 10 feet away. It will normally put him out of action for about 15 to 20 minutes.

The good part of such sprays is that they do not do any permanent harm to the attacker, and they usually work.

The bad part is that they will rarely stop a drugged, drunken, or mentally disturbed attacker. They also don't deter many attack dogs. You also have to get close to the attacker and spray him in the face.

STUN GUNS AND TASERS

These have become very popular. They deliver a high-voltage jolt that disables the stalker for at least five minutes. Just brandishing a stun gun, moreover, with its dangerous looking spark sputtering forth is often enough to make the stalker back down unless he has a gun and fires at you at the sight of your laser. The principal disadvantage is that you have to be close enough to touch the stalker, but for contact defense it is very effective.

ALARMS

These can give off a terrible shriek to attract attention and help, as well as scare and disorient the stalker. Most are small enough to put on a key chain or pin to your purse or coat. The disadvantage is that the proliferation of car alarms has gotten so widespread in some communities that no one pays attention anymore. Also, these are of little use in secluded areas or subterranean garages.

FIREARMS AND OTHER LETHAL WEAPONS

Today, 15 million women own guns. The firearm issue is controversial, but more and more people feel so threatened that they resort to them. Gun manufacturers are focusing on women customers, and more women are buying them. A good gun is expensive, but for many women worth the peace of mind it gives them. It is important, however, that if you decide to buy a gun, that you learn how to properly use it and take care of it.

THE PAINFUL AFTERMATH

The most common question that stalker victims ask themselves is the wrong question: "What did I do wrong?"

Stalker victims tend to blame themselves and that is made worse by confusion over what it was that they did to cause the stalking. In the majority of cases, the stalking victim DID NOTHING TO DESERVE WHAT HAPPENED TO HER.

The experience of being a stalking victim has devastating psychological consequences. Yet, this doesn't mean the victim is a weak or unstable person because she suffers from the invisible wounds of her victimization. The cure of stalking, the law of stalking, and the recovery of victims of stalking all seem to be advancing as this vicious conduct becomes more recognized in our society.

APPENDIX A

Here are lists of organizations to contact for specific problems.

9 to 5: National Association of Working Women
614 Superior Avenue NW
Cleveland, Ohio 44113-1387
Toll-free job-problem hotline
800-522-0925
For Cleveland residents: 621-9449

Business and Professional Women/USA
2012 Massachusetts Avenue NW
Washington, D.C. 20036
202-293-1100
Advocacy workshops, scholarships.

UNITE
1126 16th NW
Washington, DC 20036
202-466-4610
Deals with union issues.

9 to 5
1313 L Street NW
Washington, D.C. 20005
202-898-3200
Negotiates on behalf of women workers, pay equity.

Equal Employment Opportunity Commission (EEOC)
800-669-EEOC
202-634-7057 (For hearing-impaired callers)
Protects employees from discrimination.

DISTRICT OFFICES (EEOC)

Albuquerque, New Mexico
505-248-5201 (8:30-5)

Atlanta, Georgia
404-331-6093 (8:30-5)

Baltimore, Maryland
410-962-3932 (8:30-5)

Birmingham, Alabama
205-731-0082 (8:30-5)

Boston, Massachusetts
617-565-3200 (8:30-5)

Buffalo, New York
716-551-4441 (8:30-5)

Charlotte, North Carolina
704-344-6682 (8:30-5)

Chicago, Illinois
312-353-2713 (8:30-5)

Cincinnati, Ohio
513-684-2851 (8:15-5)

Cleveland, Ohio
216-522-2001 (8:15-5)

Dallas, Texas
214-767-7015 (8:30-5)

Denver, Colorado
303-866-1300 (8:30-5)

Detroit, Michigan
313-226-7636 (8:30-5)

El Paso, Texas
915-534-6550 (8:30-4:30)

Fresno, California
209-487-5793 (8:30-4:30)

Greensboro, North Carolina
919-333-5174 (8-4:30)

Greenville, South Carolina
864-241-4400 (8-4:30)

Honolulu, Hawaii
808-541-3120 (8-4)

Houston, Texas
713-209-3320 (8-5)

Indianapolis, Indiana
317-226-7212 (8-4:30)

Jackson, Mississippi
601-965-4537 (8-4:30)

Kansas City, Missouri
913-551-5655 (8-4:30)

Little Rock, Arkansas
501-324-5060 (8-4:30)
510-637-3230 (8-4:30)

Oklahoma City, Oklahoma
405-231-4911 (8-4:30)

Philadelphia, Pennsylvania
215-451-5800 (8-4)

Phoenix, Arizona
602-640-5000 (8-4:30)

Pittsburgh, Pennsylvania
412-644-3444 (8-4:30)

Raleigh, North Carolina
919-856-4064 (8-4:30)

Richmond, Virginia
804-278-4651 (8-4:30)

San Antonio, Texas
210-229-4810 (8:30-5)

San Diego, California
619-557-7235 (8:30-3)

San Francisco, California
415-554-2595 (8-4:30)

San Jose, California
408-291-7352 (8-4:30)

Savannah, Georgia
912-652-4234 (8-4:30)

Seattle, Washington
206-220-6883 (8-4:30)

St. Louis, Missouri
314-539-7800 (8-4:30)

Tampa, Florida
813-228-2310 (8-4:30)

Washington, D.C.
202-275-7377 (8-4:30)

Equal Rights Advocates
1663 Mission Street Suite 550
San Francisco, California 94103
415-621-0505
Legal counseling in Spanish & English.

Families and Work Institute
330 Seventh Avenue
New York, New York 10001
212-465-2044
Conducts research about balancing
family and work life. Has a national clearinghouse of information of both
and provides information to business,
government, and community groups plus
training programs on family and work
problems. Good source of information,
but doesn't help individuals as such. Has
various publications and studies on families and work. Also ranks companies on
their "family friendliness."

Federally Employed Women
1400 Eye Street NW
Washington, D.C. 20005
202-898-0994

**National Council on Research
for Women**
Sara Delano Roosevelt
Memorial House
47-49 East 65th Street
New York, New York 10021
212-570-5001

**National Assn. of Commissions
for Women**
2000—14th Street NW
Washington, D.C. 20009
800-338-9267 or 202-628-5030
This is a national coordinating organization for local and state commissions for
women. Doesn't give individual assistance but will refer you to the closest
commission.

**NOW Legal Defense &
Education Fund**
99 Hudson Street
New York, New York 10013
Detailed model policy & legal
resource kit.

**Wellesley College Center for
Research on Women**
Wellesley College
Wellesley, Massachusetts 02181-8259
617-283-2500
Conducts research and seminars on
women in a variety of roles and settings.
Membership organization charging dues
for which one is invited to programs and
gets publications at a discount.

Wider Opportunities for Women, Inc.
1325 G Street NW (LL)
Washington, D.C. 20005
202-638-3143
Network of local advocacy centers.

Women's Bureau
U.S. Department of Labor
200 Constitution Avenue NW
Washington, D.C. 20210
202-219-6652 (This is the publications
order number.)

Catalyst
250 Park Avenue South
New York, New York 10003
212-777-8900
Works with corporate managers to help
promote professional and management
women. Publishes directory of career
information counseling centers and publications about promoting managerial
women inside companies.

Center for Policy Alternatives
1875 Connecticut Avenue NW
Washington, D.C. 20009
202-387-6030
Lobbying organization working at the
state level to promote women's issues.

Center for Women Policy Studies
2000 P Street NW # 508
Washington, D.C. 20036
202-872-1770
A research, education, and lobbying
organization focusing on race and
women's policies.

Institute for Women's Policy Research
1400—20th Street NW
Washington, D.C. 20036
202-785-5100
Does research primarily on poor
women and children for women's
lobbying groups.

Women's Legal Defense Fund
1875 Connecticut Avenue NW
Washington, D.C. 20009—Suite 710
202-986-2600
Lobbying group dedicated to making
women's role on the job better.

APPENDIX B

AMERICAN BAR ASSOCIATION
750 Lake Shore Drive
Chicago, IL 60611
312-988-5000
Provides local attorney referral service.

ALABAMA
P.O. Drawer Box 2005
Mobile, 36652
334-269-1515
Women Lawyers Section
Contact: Karen Turner
334-433-9790

ALASKA
P.O. Box 104971
Anchorage, 99510
907-272-7469
Anchorage Assn. of Women Lawyers
Contact: Stephanie Galbraith
907-343-4545

ARIZONA
1940 E. Thunderbird Road #103
Phoenix, 85022
602-252-4804
Arizona Women Lawyers Association
Contact: Helen Grimwood
602-640-9321

ARKANSAS
State Bar: 501-375-4606
Arkansas Assn. of Women Lawyers
Contact: 501-682-7975

CALIFORNIA
San Francisco: 415-561-8200
Los Angeles: 213-765-1000
Sacramento: 916-444-2762
California Women Lawyers Assn.
916-441-3703
California Women's Law Center
Contact: Abby Leibman
213-935-4101

COLORADO
1900 Grant Street 9th Floor
Denver, 80203
303-860-1115
Colorado Women's Bar Assn.:
Contact: Julie Wells
303-298-1313

CONNECTICUT
101 Corporate Place
Rocky Hill, 06067-1894
860-721-0025

239

DELAWARE
1201 Orange Street
Suite 1100
Wilmington, 19801
302-658-5279
Women and the Law
Contact: Patti Schwartz
302-594-4500

DISTRICT OF COLUMBIA
1250 H Street NW
D.C., 20005-5937
202-737-4700
Women's Lawyer Association
Contact: Lora Pollari
202-785-1540

FLORIDA
650 Apalachee Parkway
Tallahassee, 32399-2300
904-561-5600
Tallahassee Women Lawyers Association
Contact: C. J. Weinman
904-922-6998

GEORGIA
800 The Hurt Building
50 Hurt Plaza
Atlanta, 30303
404-527-8700
Georgia Association of Women Lawyers
Contact: Romaine White
404-330-6400

HAWAII
1136 Union Wall
Penthouse 1
Honolulu, 96813

IDAHO
525 W. Jefferson Street
P.O. Box 895
Boise, 83701
208-334-4500
Women Lawyer Association
Contact: Judith Holcombe
208-342-6571

ILLINOIS
Bar Center
424 S. Second Street
Springfield, 62701-1779
800-252-8908 (In-state)
First National Plaza S. 900
20 S. Clark Street
Chicago, 60603-1802
312-726-8775
Women's Bar Association of Illinois
Contact: Sandra Opyt
312-341-8530

INDIANA
Indiana Bar Center
230 E. Ohio Street
Indianapolis, 46204-2199
317-639-5465
Women in the Law Section
Contact: Nellie Simbol
812-238-2109

KANSAS
1200 SW Harrison
P.O. Box 1037
Topeka, 66601-1037
913-234-5696
Women Attorney Association
Contact: Merrill Vefort
913-296-4902

KENTUCKY
514 W. Main Street
Frankfort, 40601-1883
502-564-3795
Kentucky Bar Association for Women
Contact: Marie Alagia-Cull
502-227-2001

LOUISIANA
601 St. Charles Avenue
New Orleans, 70130-3427
504-566-1600
Louisiana Bar Association for Women
504-525-8832

MAINE
P.O. Box 788
Augusta, 04332-0788
207-622-7523
Women's' Law
Contact: Catherine A. Lee
207-774-1200

MARYLAND
The Maryland Bar Center
520 W. Fayette Street
Baltimore, 21201
410-685-7878
Women's Bar Association
410-528-9681

MASSACHUSETTS
20 West Street
Boston, 02111
617-542-3602
Women Lawyers Association
617-423-1091

MICHIGAN
Michael Franck Building
306 Townsend Street
Lansing, 48933-2083
517-372-9030
Women Lawyers Association
517-487-3332

MINNESOTA
514 Nicollett Mall
Suite 300
Minneapolis, 55402
612-333-1183
Women Lawyers Association
612-338-3205

MISSISSIPPI
643 N. State Street
P.O. Box 2168,
Jackson, 39225-2168
601-948-4471

MISSOURI
The Missouri Bar Center
326 Monroe Street
P.O. Box #119
Jefferson City, 65102-0119
573-635-4128
Women Lawyers Association
of Kansas City
Contact: Honorable Christine Sill-Rogers
816-881-3524

MONTANA
46 N. Last Chance Gulch #2A
Helena, 59601
406-442-7660
Women's Law Section
Contact: Leslie Halligan
406-721-5700

NEBRASKA
Roman L. Hruska Law Center
635 S. 14th Street
Lincoln, 68508
402-475-7091

NEVADA
Reno
702-329-4100

NEW HAMPSHIRE
112 Pleasant St.
Concord, 03301-2947
603-224-6942

NEW JERSEY
One Constitution Square
New Brunswick, 08901-1500
908-249-5000
New Jersey Women Lawyers
201-343-7770

NEW MEXICO
Spring Square
121 Tijeras Avenue NE
P.O. Box 25883
Albuquerque, 87125
505-797-6000
New Mexico Women Lawyers
505-345-7182

NEW YORK
One Elk Street
Albany, 12207
518-463-3200
New York Women's Bar Association
Contact: Kathline VanDeLoo
518-434-9061

NORTH CAROLINA
208 Fayetteville Street Mall
Raleigh, 27601
919-828-4620
919-676-0561
Women Lawyers Association
919-479-2032

OHIO
1700 Lake Shore Drive
Columbus, 43216-6562
614-487-2050
Ohio Women's Bar
Contact: Kimberly Mahaney
216-446-9077

OKLAHOMA
P.O. Box 53036
1901 N. Lincoln
Oklahoma City, 73152
405-524-2365

OREGON
5200 S.W. Meadows Road
P.O. Box 1689
Lake Oswego, 97035-0889
503-620-0222
Women's Bar Association
503- 621-2135

NORTH DAKOTA
Suite 101
515 1/2 E. Broadway
P.O. Box 2136
Bismarck, 58502
701-255-1404
Women's Lawyers Section
Contact: Sonya Anderson
701-667-1200

PENNSYLVANIA
100 South Street
P.O. Box 186
Harrisburg, 17108-0186
717-238-6715

RHODE ISLAND
115 Cedar Street
Providence, 02903
401-421-5740
Women's Bar Association
Contact: Elizabeth McDonough Noonan
401-274-7200

SOUTH CAROLINA
950 Taylor Street
Columbia, 29201
803-799-6653
South Caroline Women Lawyers
Association
Contact: Darra Cothran
803-779-3080

SOUTH DAKOTA
222 E. Capitol
Pierre, 57501
605-224-7554

TENNESSEE
3622 W. End Avenue
Nashville, 37205-7421
615-383-7421
Lawyers Association for Women
Contact: Marianna Williams
901-285-5074

TEXAS
P.O. Box 12487
Austin, 78711
512-463-1463
Texas Women Lawyers
Contact: Nancy Bethurem
214-690-8005

UTAH
645 S. 200 E
Salt Lake City, 84111
801-531-9077
Utah Women Lawyers
Contact: Lisa Michelle Church
801-524-2752

VERMONT
35-37 Court Street
P.O. Box 100
Montpelier, 05601
802-223-2020
Vermont Women Lawyers
Contact: Julie Brill
802-828-3171

VIRGINIA
701 E. Franklin Street
Suite 1120
Richmond, 23219
804-644-0041
Virginia Women Attorneys
804-649-9251

WASHINGTON STATE
500 Westin Building
2001 Sixth Avenue
Seattle, 98121-2599
206-727-8200
Women Lawyers
206-622-5585

WEST VIRGINIA
P.O. Box 3956
Charleston, 25339
304-895-3663
304-558-2456

WISCONSIN
402 W. Wilson Street
Madison, 53707-7158
608-257-3838

WYOMING
500 Randell Avenue
Cheyenne, 82001
307-632-9061

APPENDIX C

FEDERAL TRADE COMMISSION (FTC)

The Federal Trade Commission is the major consumer protection agency of the federal government and is concerned about almost every good and service sold to the public. Besides publishing helpful pamphlets on a variety of consumer subjects, it also enforces federal consumer protection laws and conducts educational programs to protect the consumer.

NATIONAL FRAUD INFORMATION CENTER:
800-876-7060

This number provides consumers with answers to questions about telephone or mail solicitations, information about how and where to report fraud, referral services, and help in filing complaints.

The FTC also gives out free brochures on various kinds of investments and scams. Contact the FTC Public Reference Branch, Room 130, 6th and Pennsylvania Avenue N.W., Washington, D.C. 20580 or call 202-326-2222 or, for the hearing impaired, call the TTY number, 202-326-2502. There is also 202-326-2710, the FTC NewsPhone, on which a recording gives the latest FTC news of scams and frauds.

The FTC has 10 regional offices around the nation and these are listed below with the territories each office serves.

San Francisco Office
901 Market Street, Suite 570
San Francisco, California 94103
Consumer Complaint and Business
Calls: 415-356-5270
Fax: 415-356-5284
THIS OFFICE SERVES: Northern
California, Hawaii, and Nevada.

Dallas Office
100 N. Central Expressway, Suite 500
Dallas, Texas 75201
Consumer Complaint Calls: 214-767-5501
Business Calls: 214-767-5503
Fax: 214-767-5519
THIS OFFICE SERVES: Arizona,
Louisiana, New Mexico, Oklahoma, and
Texas.

Atlanta Office
1718 Peachtree Street, N.W.
Atlanta, Georgia 30367
Consumer Complaint Calls: 404-347-4836
Business Calls: 404-347-4837
Fax: 404-347-4725
THIS OFFICE SERVES: Alabama,
Florida, Georgia, Mississippi, North
Carolina, South Carolina, Tennessee,
and Virginia.

Cleveland Office
658 Euclid Avenue, Suite 520-A
Cleveland, Ohio 44114-3006
Consumer Complaint Calls: 216-522-4207
Business Calls: 216-522-7239
Fax: 216-522-7239
Speaker Telephone: 216-522-8312
THIS OFFICE SERVES: Delaware,
District of Columbia, Maryland, Michigan,
Ohio, Pennsylvania, and West Virginia.

New York Office
150 William Street, Suite 1300
New York, New York 10038
Consumer Complaint Calls: 212-264-1207
Business Calls: 212-264-1207
Fax: 212-264-0459
THIS OFFICE SERVES: New Jersey,
and New York.

Boston Office
101 Merrimac Street, Suite 810
Boston, Massachusetts 02114-4719
Consumer Complaint Calls: 617-424-5960
Business Calls: 617-424-5960
Fax: 617-424-5998
THIS OFFICE SERVES: Connecticut,
Maine, Massachusetts, New Hampshire,
Rhode Island, and Vermont.

Chicago Office
55 E. Monrow Street, Suite 1860
Chicago, Illinois 60604-1073
Consumer Complaint Calls: 312-353-4423
Business Calls: 312-353-8156
Fax: 312-353-4438
THIS OFFICE SERVES: Illinois, Indiana,
Iowa, Minnesota, Missouri, Wisconsin,
and Kentucky.

Denver Office
1961 Stout Street, Suite 1523
Denver, Colorado 80294-0101
Consumer Complaint Calls: 303-844-2271
Business Calls: 303-844-2272
Fax: 303-844-3599
THIS OFFICE SERVES: Colorado,
Kansas, Montana, Nebraska, North
Dakota, South Dakota, Utah, and
Wyoming.

Seattle Office
2806 Federal Building
915 Second Avenue
Seattle, Washington 98174
Consumer Complaint Calls: 206-220-6363
Business Calls: 206-220-6350
Fax: 206-220-6366
THIS OFFICE SERVES: Alaska, Idaho,
Oregon, and Washington.

Los Angeles Office
11000 Wilshire Boulevard, Suite 13209
Los Angeles, California 90024
Consumer Complaint Calls:
310-235-7575
Business Calls: 310-235-7890
Fax: 310-235-7976
THIS OFFICE SERVES: Arizona
and Southern California.

NATIONAL

America Federation of Teachers Women's Rights Committee
555 New Jersey Ave., N.W.
Washington, CA 20001
202-897-4400
Publishes an extensive sexual harassment resource guide.

American Arbitration Association
Center for Mediation
1660 Lincoln Street, Suite 2150
Denver, CO 80264-0210
800-678-0823
303-831-0823
Offers a sexual harassment claim resolution process.

Business and Professional Women's Foundation
2012 Massachusetts Avenue, N.W.
Washington DC 20036
202-293-1200
Offers pamphlet, "Crime of Power, Not Passion."

Coalition of Labor Union Women
15 Union Square
New York, NY 10003
212-242-0700
Provides information regarding the use of union representatives as mediators in sexual harassment cases.

Equal Employment Opportunity Commission
1801 L Street, N.W.
Washington DC 20507
202-663-4264
800-USA-EEOC
800-872-3362 - Spanish or English
Answers questions regarding employment discrimination.

IMPACT International, Inc.
301-589-1349
800-345-KICK
Referrals to local programs for teaching self defense.

Mother's Against Drunk Driving
P.O. Box 541688
Dallas 75354-1688
800-GET-MADD

National Council of Child Abuse and Family Violence
1050 Connecticut Avenue, N.W., Suite 300
Washington, DC 20036
202-429-6695
800-222-2000
Provides information and referrals regarding family violence and abuse.

NAACP Legal Defense and Educational Fund
99 Hudson Street
New York, NY 10013
Litigates some sexual harassment cases.

9 to 5, National Association of Working Women
Superior Avenue N.W.
Cleveland, OH 44115
216-566-9308
800-522-0925
Advises women on sexual harassment and other job problems.

National Organization for Women (NOW)
1000 16th Street N.W., Suite 700
Washington, DC 20036
202-331-0066
Offers information, support, and other resources.

Parents Anonymous
6733 S. Sepulveda, Suite 270
Los Angeles, CA 90045
800-352-0386 (Inside California)
800-421-0353 (Nationwide)
Provides weekly meetings of support to parents who are under stress and feel they are unable to communicate with their children.

RAINN (Rape, Abuse, Incest National Network)
800-656-4673 (Hotline 24 hours)

Women's Bureau
U.S. Department of Labor
200 Constitution Avenue, N.W.
Washington, DC 20210
800-827-5335
Has information on rights of working women.

The Webb Report
800-767-3062
Monthly newsletter on sexual harassment.

ALABAMA
Mobile Rape Crisis Center
501 N. Bishop Lane
Mobile, 36608
344-450-2244 (Office)
344-473-7273 (Hotline)

ALASKA
State agency: Alaska State Commission for Human Rights
800 A Street, Suite 204
Anchorage, 99501-3669
907-274-4692
800-478-4692

Women In Crisis
717 9th Avenue
Fairbanks, 99701
907-452-2293

Network on Domestic Violence & Sexual Assault
907-586-3650

Alaska Women's Resource Center
111 W. 9th Street
Anchorage, 99501
907-276-0528

Women's Resource Center Aiding Women from Abuse and Rape Emergencies (AWARE)
P.O. Box 020809
Juneau, 99802
907-586-2977 (Office)
907-586-1090 (Hotline)

ARIZONA
State Agency: Arizona Civil Rights Division
1275 W. Washington Street
Phoenix, 85007
602-542-5263

Center Against Sexual Abuse
5227 N. 7th Street, Suite 100
Phoenix, 85014
602-241-9443 (Office)
603-941-9010 (Hotline)

ARKANSAS

Rape Crisis, Inc.
7509 Cantrell, Suite 211
Little Rock, 72207
501-663-3334

River Valley Shelter
P.O. Box 2066
Russellville, 72801
501-968-3110

CALIFORNIA

State agency: California Department of Fair Employment and Housing
2014 T Street, Suite 210
Sacramento, 95814
800-884-1684
916-227-2873

About-Face: Domestic Violence Project
213-384-7084 (Bilingual)

Asian Immigrant Women Advocates
310 8th Street
Oakland, 94610
510-268-0192

Assistant League Family Service Agency:
213-469-5893
Counseling for parenting—charged on sliding scale.

Battered Service Center
134 E. First Street
Los Angeles, 90012
213-268-7564

Bilingual Shelter for Victims of Domestic Violence
213-268-7564
800-548-2722

Center for the Pacific Asian Family
213-653-4042
800-339-3940
24-hour hotline for domestic violence, confidential shelter, referral.

Equal Rights Advocates
1663 Mission Street, Suite 550
San Francisco, 94103
415-621-0505

Good Shepherd Shelter for Battered Women
213-737-6111

**Hastings Law School
Legal Aid Society, Employment Law Center, Workers' Rights Hotline**
1663 Mission Street, Suite 400
San Francisco, 94103
415-864-8848 (Office)
415-864-8208 (Workers' rights hotline)
Free legal advice to unemployed, low income persons; referrals.

L.A. Rape and Battering Hotline
213-626-3393
310-392-8381
213-462-8410 (Hearing impaired)

Parents United
P.O. Box 952
San Jose, 95108
408-280-5055
Provide assistance to individuals or families who have experienced any kind of sexual child abuse.

California Coalition/Battered Women
415-457-2464 (9 a.m. to 5 p.m.
Weekdays)

COLORADO
State agency: Colorado Civil Rights Division
1560 Broadway, Suite 1050
Denver, 80202

Discrimination and Sexual Harassment Support Group Boulder National Organization for Women
P.O. Box 7972
Boulder, 80306
303-444-7217
Support groups, legal advice, and attorney therapist referrals.

Domestic Violence Institut
50 South Steele Street, Suite 850
Denver, 80209
303-322-1831
Offers training, consultation and expert witness resources.

Rape Assistance and Awareness Program
640 Broadway, Suite 112
Denver, 80203
303-329-9922 (Office)
303-322-7273 (Hotline)
303-329-0031 (Spanish)

VOA-Brandon Center
1865 Larimer Street
Denver, 80204
303-620-9190

CONNECTICUT
State agency: Connecticut Commission on Human Rights and Opportunities
90 Washington Street
Hartford, 06106
203-566-3350

Connecticut Women's Education and Legal Fund
135 Broad Street
Hartford, 06105
203-865-0188 (Office)
203-524-0601 (Information)
Counseling for sex discrimination, legal referrals, education, and training.

Rape Crisis Center Connecticut Sexual Assault Crisis Services
203-282-9881 (Hotline)

Stamford Domestic Violence Service
141 Franklin
Stamford, 06901
203-357-8162

Coalition Against Domestic Violence
203-524-5890
Call collect 8:30 a.m. to 4:30 p.m.
Weekdays

DELAWARE
State agency: Delaware Department of Labor
State Office Building
820 N. French Street, 6th Floor
Wilmington, 19801
203-577-2882

Family Violence Program/Child, Inc.
507 Philadelphia
Pike, 19809
302-762-6110

DISTRICT OF COLUMBIA

District agency: D.C. Commission of Human Rights
2000 14th Street N.W., 3rd Floor
Washington, DC, 20009
202-939-8740

Federally Employed Women
1400 Eye Street N.W.
Washington, DC, 20009
202-898-0994
Provides legal referrals.

House of Ruth
#5 Thomas Suckle N.W.
Washington, DC, 20009
202-347-2777
Domestic violence.

FLORIDA

State Agency: Florida Commissions of Human Relations
325 John Knox Road, Building F
Suite 240
Tallahassee, 32303-4149
904-488-7082
800-342-8170

Family Service Center
2960 Roosevelt Boulevard
Clearwater, 34620
813-530-7233
Counseling and pamphlets on
sexual harassment.

Gulf Coast Legal Services
641 1st Street S.
St. Petersburg, 33701
813-821-0726
Offers legal advice.

Help Line
813-893-1141 (Office)
813-344-5555 (24 hours)

Lawyers Referral Service
407-422-4536
Referrals to sexual harassment
attorneys.

The South Florida Sexual Abuse and Assault Victims Program
5900 S.W. 73rd Street
Suite 301
Miami, 33143
305-663-6540 (24 hours)

Sunrise of Pasco County
P.O. Box 928
Dade City, 34297
352-521-3120

Coalition Against Domestic Violence
407-628-3885
Call collect 9 a.m. to 5 p.m. After hours,
answering machine gives toll-free hotline
number.

GEORGIA

State agency: Georgia Commission on Equal Opportunity
710 Cain Tower, Peachtree Center
229 Peachtree Street N.E.
Atlanta, 30303
404-656-7708

Advocates for Battered Women & Children
404-524-3847 (9 a.m. to 5 p.m.)

DeKalb Rape Crisis Center
403 Ponce De Leon Avenue
DeKalb, 30030
404-377-1428 (24 hours)

9 to 5 National Association of Working Women
404-616-4861
800-669-0769
Counseling, legal referrals.

Rape Crisis Center
P.O. Box 8492
Savannah, 31412
912-354-6742
912-233-7273

HAWAII

State agency: Hawaii Civil Rights Commission
888 Mililani Street, 2nd Floor
Honolulu, 96813
808-586-8636
800-468-4644 ext. 6-8636 (Neighbor islands)

Maluhia O'Wahine Program
Waikiki Community Center
808-923-1802

Office of the Sexual Harassment Counselor
University of Hawaii at Manoa
2600 Campus Road, Room 210
Honolulu, 96822
808-956-9499

Shelter for Abused Spouses & Children
808-841-0822

Military Shelter
808-533-7125

YWCA Family Violence Shelter
3094 Elua Street
Lihue, 96746
808-245-6362

IDAHO

State agency: Idaho Human Rights Commission
450 W. State Street, 1st Floor
Boise, 83720
203-344-2873

Council on Domestic Violence
208-334-5580 (Collect calls accepted)

Idaho Women's Network
P.O. Box 1385
Boise, 83701
208-344-5738

Women's and Children Crisis Center
720 W. Washington
Boise, 83702
208-343-3688 (Office)
208-343-7025 (Hotline)

Women Against Domestic Violence
P.O. Box 323
545 Shoup Avenue
Idaho Falls, 83401
208-525-1820

ILLINOIS

State agency: Department of Human Rights
100 W. Randolph Street
Suite 10-100
Chicago, 60601
312-814-6200

Apna Ghar
4753 N. Broadway, Suite 502
Chicago, 60604
312-334-0173 (Office)
312-334-4663 (Hotline)
Counseling, support groups, and legal referrals, especially for Asian women.

Coalition Against Domestic Violence
217-789-2830 (9 a.m. to 5 p.m.)

Pro Bono Advocates
CL88
50 W. Washington
Chicago, 60602
312-629-6945
Offers legal referrals.

Women Employed
22 W. Monroe, Suite 1400
Chicago, 60603
312-782-3902
Phone counseling and advice.

YWCA—Women's Services
180 N. Wabash
Chicago, 60601
312-372-6600
Counseling, support groups, and legal referrals.

INDIANA

State agency: Indiana Civil Rights Commission
100 N. Senate Avenue, Room N103
Indianapolis, 46204
317-232-2600
800-628-2909

Breaking Free
317-923-4260
Offers counseling and legal referrals.

The Caring Place Safe house
219-464-2128

Coalition Against Domestic Violence
812-882-7900
800-332-7385 (State hotline, 24 hours)

IOWA

State agency: Iowa Civil Rights Commission
Grimes State Office Building
211 E. Maple Street, 2nd Floor
Des Moines, 50309
515-281-4121

Rape Victim Advocacy Center
17 W. Prentice
Iowa City, 52240
319-335-6001
319-335-600 (24 hours)

University of Iowa Women's Resource and Action Center
130 N. Madison Street
Iowa City, 52242
319-335-1486
Provides legal counseling, referrals.

YWCA Battered Women Program
2013 Central Avenue
Dubuque, 52001
319-588-4016

KANSAS

State agency: Kansas Commission on Civil Rights
Landon State Office Building, 8th Floor
900 S.W. Jackson Street, Suite 851 S.
Topeka, 66612-1258
913-926-3206

The Crisis Center
P.O. Box 1526
Manhattan, 66502
913-539-2785

Reno County Rape Survivors Group
1 E. 9th
Hutchinson, 67501
316-665-3620 (Office)
316-663-2522 (24 hours)
Counseling, legal referrals, education.

KENTUCKY

State agency: Kentucky Commission on Human Rights
The Heyburn Building, Suite 700
332 W. Broadway
Louisville, 40202
502-595-4024
800-292-5566

Center for Women Safe House
606-255-9808

Center for Women and Families Rape Relief Center
226 W. Breckinridge Street
P.O. Box 2048
Louisville, 40201-2048
502-581-7273
Offers counseling, crisis intervention, legal referrals.

Lexington-Fayette Urban County Human Rights Commission
162 E. Main Street, Suite 226
Lexington, 40507
606-252-0071
Investigates complaints in Fayette County.

Lincoln Trail Domestic Violence Program
800-767-5838 (Elizabethtown)

YWCA Spouse Abuse Center (Lexington)
800-544-3755

LOUISIANA

Intervention Center
P.O. Box 2133
Baton Rouge, 70821
504-389-3001

Louisiana Foundation Against Sexual Assault
P.O. Box 1450
Independence, 70433
504-878-3949

Project S.A.V.E.
504-523-3755 (9 a.m. to 5 p.m.)

MAINE

State agency: Maine Human Rights Commission
Statehouse Station 51
Augusta, 04333
207-624-6050

Augusta Area Rape Crisis Center
3 Mulliken Court
Augusta, 04330
207-626-4325 (Office)
207-626-0660 (Hotline)
Support groups, legal referrals for sexual harassment prevention.

Caring Unlimited—Domestic Violence Center
P.O. Box 590
Sanford, 04073
207-324-1957 (Call collect, 24-hour hotline)

Rape Response Service
P.O. Box 2516
Bangor, 04401
207-941-2980
207-989-5678 (Office)
800-989-5678 (Hotline)

MARYLAND

State agency: Maryland Commission on Human Relations
20 E. Franklin Street
Baltimore, 21202
410-767-8600

Heartly House
P.O. Box 857
Frederick, 21705
301-662-8800

Sexual Assault and Domestic Center
6229 N. Charles Street
Baltimore, 21212
410-377-8111 (Office)
410-828-6390 (Hotline)

MASSACHUSETTS

State agency: Maryland Commission on Human Relations
20 E. Franklin Street
Baltimore, 21202
410-767-8600

Cambridge Women's Center
46 Pleasant Street
Cambridge, 02139
617-354-8807
Support groups, legal referrals.

Sexual Assault and Domestic Violence Center
6229 N. Charles Street
Baltimore, 21212
410-377-8111 (Office)
410-828-6390 (Hotline)

Transition House
P.O. Box 530
Cambridge, 02139
617-661-7203

Women's Crisis Center
24 Pleasant Street
Newburyport, 01950
508-465-2155
Telephone counseling, legal advice, support groups.

MICHIGAN

State agency: Michigan Department of Civil Rights
333 S. Capitol
Lansing, 48913
517-373-3590 (Lansing)
313-876-5544 (Detroit)
517-373-2884 (Women's Commission)

Women Involved in Giving Support
810-437-8091
Legal referrals, support groups.

YWCA Domestic Crisis Center
25 Sheldon S.E.
Grand Rapids, 49503

MINNESOTA

State agency: Minnesota Department of Human Rights
Bremer Tower
Seventh Place and Minnesota Street
St. Paul, 55101
612-296-5663

Carver and Scott County Sexual Violence Center
510 Chestnut Street N., Suite 204
Chaska, 55318
612-448-5425 (Hotline)
Offers support groups, counseling, legal referrals.

Washington County Sexual Assault Services
8200 Hadley
Cottage Grove, 55016
612-458-4116 (Office)
612-777-1117 (Hotline)

MISSISSIPPI

Rape Crisis Line
P.O. Box 2248
Jackson, 39225
601-366-3880 (Office)
601-982-7273 (Hotline)

Gulf Coast Women's Center
P.O. Box 333
Biloxi, 39533
601-435-1968 (Hotline)

MISSOURI

State agency: Missouri Commission on Human Rights
P.O. Box 1129
Jefferson City, 65102
314-751-3325
800-877-6247

Women's Self Help Center
2838 Olive Street
St. Louis, 63103
314-531-9100 (Office)
314-531-2003 (Hotline)

YWCA Women's Resource Center
140 N. Brentwood Avenue
Clayton, 63105
314-726-6665
Counseling, legal referrals.

MONTANA

State agency: Montana Human Rights Commission
616 Helena Avenue, Suite 302
P.O. Box 1728
Helena, 59624-1728
406-444-2884
800-542-0807

**Butte Christian Community Center
Safe House**
406-782-8511

Women's Place
501 W. Alder
Missoula, 59802
406-543-3320 (Office)
405-543-7606 (24 hours)
Counseling and legal referrals.

NEBRASKA

**University of Nebraska Women's
Center**
117 Nebraska Union
Lincoln, 68588-0446
402-472-2597

Women Against Violence
402-345-7273

NEVADA

**State agency: Nevada Equal Rights
Commission**
1515 Tropicana Avenue, Suite 590
Las Vegas, 89158
702-486-7161 (Las Vegas)
702-688-1288 (Reno)

Crisis Call Center
P.O. Box 8016
Reno, 89507
702-323-4533
Legal referrals.

**Temporary Assistance for Domestic
Crisis**
P.O. Box 43264
Las Vegas, 89116
702-646-4981

NEW HAMPSHIRE

**State agency: New Hampshire
Commission for Human Rights**
163 Loudon Road
Concord, 03301-6053
603-271-2767

Rape & Domestic Violence Center
P.O. Box 1344
Concord, 03301
603-225-9000

Sexual Assault Support Services
7 Junkins Avenue
Portsmouth, 03801
603-436-4107 (24 hours)

**University of New Hampshire
Sexual Harassment and Rape
Prevention**
Huddleston Hall
Durham, 03824
603-862-3494 (Hotline 8 a.m.-4:30 p.m.)
603-862-1212 (Hotline after 4:30 p.m.)
Counseling, crisis intervention, legal
assistance.

NEW JERSEY

**State agency: New Jersey Division on
Civil Rights**
383 W. State Street
Trenton, 08618
609-292-4605

**New Jersey Coalition Against Sexual
Assault**
908-418-1354

Rutgers Law School
Women's Rights Litigation Clinic
15 Washington Street
Newark, 07102
201-648-5637
Offers information on legal issues
regarding sexual harassment.

The Safe House
P.O. Box 1887
Bloomfield, 07003
201-759-2154

YWCA
140 E. Hanover Street
Trenton, 08608
609-989-9592
609-989-9332 (Hotline)
Counseling, referrals.

NEW MEXICO
**State Agency: New Mexico Human
Rights Commission**
Aspen Plaza
1596 Pacheco Street
Sante Fe, 87501
505-827-6838

Albuquerque Shelter for Victims
P.O. Box 25363
Albuquerque, 87125
505-247-4219

Rape Crisis Center
1025 Hermosa S.E.
Albuquerque, 87108
505-266-7711 (Hotline)

NEW YORK
**State agency: New York State Division
of Human Rights**
Office of Sexual Harassment Issues
55 Hanson Place, Suite 346
Brooklyn, 11217
718-722-2060
800-427-2773

**Ad Hoc Sexual Harassment Coalition
c/o Lauren Wechsler
Ms. Foundation for Women**
141 Fifth Avenue
New York, 10010
212-353-8580
A coalition of women's and civil rights
groups.

Jefferson County Women's Center
120 Arcade Street
Watertown, 13601
315-782-1855
Counseling, support groups, education
on sexual harassment.

New York Asian Women's Center
39 Bowery, Box 375
New York, 10002
212-732-5230
Counseling, legal advice, referrals.

NOW Hotline
15 W. 18th Street
New York, 10011
212-989-7230

NORTH CAROLINA
**State agency: North Caroline State
Office of Administrative Hearings**
424 N. Blount Street
Raleigh, 27601

North Carolina Equity
505 Oberlin Road
Raleigh, 27605
919-833-4055 (Office)
800-451-8065 (Hotline)

OHIO
State agency: Ohio Civil Rights Commission
220 Parsons Avenue
Columbus, 43215
614-466-5928

Committee Against Sexual Harassment (CASH) c/o YWCA
65 S. 4th Street
Columbus, 43215
614-224-9121

Lorain County Rape Crisis Center
W. G. Nord Community Health Center
6140 S. Broadway
Lorain, 44053
216-233-7273 (Office)
800-888-6161 (24 hours)

Victims Advocacy Program, The Link
315 Thurston Avenue
Bowling Green, 43402
419-352-5387
800-472-9411 (Hotline)
Support and legal referrals.

OKLAHOMA
State agency: Oklahoma Human Rights Commission
2101 N. Lincoln Boulevard
Room 480
Oklahoma City, 73105
405-521-3441

Call Rape
2121 S. Columbia, Room LL6
Tulsa, 74114
918-744-7273 (24-hour hotline)

OREGON
State agency: Oregon Bureau of Labor and Industry—Civil Rights Division
800 N.E. Oregon St.reet no.32
Suite 1070
Portland, 97232
503-731-4075 ext. 421

Portland Women's Crisis Line
P.O. Box 42610
Portland, 97242
503-232-9751 (Office)
503-235-5333 (24-hour hotline)

Sexual Assault Support Services
630 Lincoln Street
Eugene, 97401
503-484-9791 (Office)
800-788-4247 (Hotline)

PENNSYLVANIA
State agency: Pennsylvania Human Relations Commission
101 S. 2nd Street, Suite 300
Harrisburg, 17105-3145
717-787-9784
215-560-2496
412-565-5395

Women's Alliance for Job Equity
1422 Chestnut Street, Suite 1100
Philadelphia, 19102
215-561-1873
Support groups, training.

RHODE ISLAND

State agency: Rhode Island Commission for Human Rights
10 Abbott Park Place
Providence, 02903
401-277-2661

Rape Crisis Center
300 Richmond Street, Suite 205
Providence, 02903
401-421-4100 (Hotline)

SOUTH CAROLINA

State agency: South Carolina Human Affairs Commission
2611 Forest Drive
P.O. Box 4490
Columbia, 29240
803-253-6339
800-521-0725

Crisisline
803-271-8888

My Sister's House
P.O. Box 5341
North Charleston, 29406
803-747-4069
800-273-4673 (24-hour hotline)

SOUTH DAKOTA

State agency: South Dakota Division of Human Rights
222 E. Capitol, Suite 11
Pierre, 57501-5070
605-773-4493

Citizens Against Rape and Domestic Violence
300 North Dakota Avenue, Suite 220
Sioux Falls, 57102
605-339-0116

TENNESSEE

State agency: Tennessee Human Rights Commission
530 Church Street, Suite 400
Nashville, 37243
615-741-5825

Family Services of Memphis
2400 Poplar Avenue, Suite 500
Memphis, 38112
901-324-3637 (Office)
901-274-7477 (Hotline)

TEXAS

State agency: Texas Commission on Human Rights
8100 Cameron Road, Building B
Suite 525
Austin, 78754

The Dallas Rainbow Now Sexual Harassment Support Group
608 Whistler
Arlington, 76006
817-792-3736

Mothers Against Drunk Driving
P.O. Box 541688
Dallas, 75354-1688
800-GET-MADD

Texas Bar Referral, Legal Aid
205 W. 9th Street, Suite 200
Austin, 78701
800-252-9690 ext. 2146 (Texas bar)
512-476-7244 (Legal aid)

University YWCA
Women's Counseling and Resource
Center
55 North IH35, Suite 230
Austin, 78702
Counseling, referrals.

UTAH

State agency: Utah Industrial
Commission Anti-Discrimination
Division
160 E. 300 S.
Salt Lake City, 84114
801-530-6801

Utah Women's Lobby
P.O. Box 1586
Salt Lake City, 84110-1586

VERMONT

State agency: Vermont Attorney
General's Office
Civil rights Division
109 State Street
Montpelier, 05609
802-828-3657

Those Who Mourn
P.O. Box 937
Wilder, 05088
802-296-7109

VIRGINIA

State agency: Council on
Human Rights
1100 Bank Street
Washington Building, 12th Floor
Richmond, 23219
804-225-2292

Feminist Majority Sexual
Harassment Hotline
1600 Wilson Boulevard, Suite 704
Arlington, 22209
703-522-2501
Helps women learn to protect themselves against sexual harassment and expose violators.

Sexual Assault Resource Agency
P.O. Box 6705
Charlottesville, 22906
804-295-7273 (Office)
804-977-7273 (Hotline)

WASHINGTON STATE

State Agency: Washington State
Human Rights Commission
711 S. Capitol Way, Suite 402
Olympia, 98504
360-753-6770

Northwest Women's Law Center
119 S. Main Street
Suite 330
Seattle, 98104
206-621-7691
Offers attorney referrals.

WEST VIRGINIA

State agency: West Virginia Human Rights Commission
1321 Plaza East, Room 106
Charleston, 25301-1400
304-348-2616

Rape and domestic Violence Information Center
104 E. High Street
Kingwood, 26537
304-329-1687

WISCONSIN

State agency: Wisconsin Department of Industry Labor and Human Equal Rights Division
P.O. Box 8928
201 E. Washington Avenue
Madison, 53708
608-266-7552

Counseling Center of Milwaukee
414-271-2565

WYOMING

State agency: Wyoming Fair Employment Commission
6101 Yellowstone, Room 259C
Cheyenne, 82002
307-777-7261

Women's Center Collective
P.O. Box 581
Sheridan, 82801
307-672-7471 (Office)
307-672-3222 (Hotline)